The 2 to Shopping NYC

The Locavore Guide
434 6th Ave, NY, NY 10011

Copyright ©2025 Caroline Weaver
All rights reserved
Printed in New York, NY
First edition paperback, 2025

This book was made possible with the help of many great New Yorkers, including:

Maddy Bruster, Designer
Max Hoerner, Copy Editor
Clara Kirkpatrick, Illustrator
Camille Jorgensen, Data Manager
Xéla Perryman, Fact Checker

Printed by: Thomas Group Printing,
131 Varick Street, Manhattan

In support of the mission of this book, it was imperative that we print it locally. Thomas Group Printing is a fourth generation family-owned printer in Lower Manhattan.

ISBN: 979-8-218-78912-1

Table of Contents

Introduction	12
Letter from the Editor	14
Trend Report	17
How Did We Choose?	18
Why Shop Small?	19
Regular Rotation	20
Later List	21
Hot New Shops	22
In Memoriam	24
Amy Sedaris's Favorite Shops	27
Shop Astrology	29
Guide to the Greenmarket	33
Fruit Sticker Collection Page	45
The New Rules	46

The Shops   49

Arts & Crafts   50

Art Supplies	50
Beads	51
Craft Supplies	52
Dollhouse Miniatures	54
Dyes and Pigments	54
Fabrics	55
Knitting, Weaving, Crocheting	58
Needlepoint	60
Plastic	61
Rubber Stamps	61
Sculpting Supplies	62
Sewing Machines	63
Spray Paint	63
Trimmings and Notions	64

Bookshelf   68

Art Books	68
Bookstores with Bars	69

Children's Books	71
Comics and Graphic Novels	71
Cookbooks	73
Intersectional Books	73
Magazines	76
Rare Books	76
Secondhand Books	78
Single-genre Books	79
Building	**82**
Architectural Salvage	82
Deadstock Hardware	82
Decorative Hardware	83
Glass & Mirror	83
Locksmith	84
Lumber	84
Paint	84
Rubber & Foam	85
Salvaged Wood	85
The Oldest	85
The One With a Café	86
The Everything Store	86
Woodworking Tools	86
Clothing	**88**
Costumes	88
Clothes for Everybody	89
Screenprinting & Embroidery	92
Specialty Mending	94
Streetwear	94
Workwear	95
Menswear	98
Cool Menswear	98
Local Menswear Designers	100
Old-School Menswear	103
Suiting	106
Womenswear	107
Lingerie & Loungewear	107
Local Womenswear Designers	110

Maternity Clothing	115
Mature Womenswear	116
Multi-brand Womenswear	117
Special Occasions	120
Secondhand Clothes	122
Designer Consignment	122
Thrift	124
Vintage T-Shirts	125
Well-curated Vintage	126

Desk — 131
Contemporary Stationery	131
Custom Stationery	133
Fancy Pens	134
Greeting Cards	135
Office & School	136
Paper	137
Typewriters	137

Electronics & Appliances — 138
Audio/Visual	138
Gadgets & TV	139
Large Appliances	140
Photography	141
Vacuum Specialists	142

Entertainment — 144
Collectibles	144
Hobby Shops	145
Magic	146
Movies	147
Table Games	147
Trading Cards	149
Video Games	150

Food & Beverage — 151
Alcohol	151
Beer	151
Especially Good Wine & Liquor	153

Natural Wine	155
Specialty Spirits	156
Beverages	157
Coffee	157
Non-Alcoholic	158
Tea	159
Animal Products	160
Meat	160
Seafood	162
Kosher Grocery	164
Diet-Specific	166
Gluten-Free	166
Vegan	166
Most Food	167
Bulk Foods Refillery	167
Cheese	168
Fancy Pantry	170
Great General Grocers	172
Health Foods	174
Produce	175
Co-op Grocery Stores	176
Spices	178
Tofu	179
Regional Specialty	182
Asian	182
Caribbean & African	187
European	189
Latin American	194
Middle Eastern	195
Sweets	196
Candy	196
Chocolate	198
Footwear & Accessories	201
Shoes	202
Children's Shoes	202
Classic Brands	203
Cowboy Boots	204
Great Women's Shoes	204

Men's Dress Shoes	206
Sneakers	208
Vegan Shoes	209
Accessories	209
Bags	209
Eyewear	210
Hats	212
Leather Gloves	213
Neckwear	214
Hosiery & Socks	215
Jewelry	215
Contemporary Fine Jewelry	215
Fashion Jewelry	217
Traditional Jewelry	219
Watches	220

Gifting — 221
Culturally Specific Gifts	221
Locally Made Gifts	223
NYC Souvenirs	225
Pop Culture Gifts	229

Home — 231
Clocks	231
Decor	231
Framing	234
Lighting	235
Linens	237
Mattresses	238
Organization	239
Prints & Wall Art	239
Rugs	241
Furniture	242
Vintage Furniture	242
New Furniture	244
Custom Furniture	245
Secondhand Furniture	246

Health & Beauty   248
Fragrance   248
Herbal Medicine   250
Sex   251
Skincare & Cosmetics   252
Tatoo Supply   257
Vitamins & Supplements   257

Kids   258
Baby Stuff   258
Children's Clothing   259
Education and School Supplies   262
Toys   262

Kitchen & Dining   265
Baking Supplies   265
Chopsticks   266
Kitchen Supplies   266
Knife Specialist   268
Tableware   268

Music   274
CDs & Records   274
Guitars   277
Instruments   278

Pets   281
Aquarium   281
Dog Stuff   282
Exotics & Birds   283
Pet Supplies   284

Plants   286
Florists   286
Florist Supply   288
Garden Center   289
Houseplants   291
Specialty Plants   293

Recreation
All Sports	294
Bike Shops	295
Boating	296
Dance	296
Fishing	297
Golf	298
Horseback Riding	299
Martial Arts	299
Outdoors	300
Racquet Sports	301
Running	301
Snow Sports	302
Soccer	302
Skating	303
Surf	304

Everything Else
Esoteric and Mystical	305
Motorcycles	307
Luggage	307
Party Supplies	308
Trophies & Engraving	309

Index (Alphabetized) 311

Index (By Location) 318

Coupons 327

The Locavore Guide to Shopping NYC

By my estimate, there are over 17,000 independently owned small biz retail shops in New York City. These are shops that sell tangible retail goods, owned by actual people and not corporations. How do I know this? I've seen most of them with my own two eyes. By spending over three years walking New York City to catalog its independent retail shops, I've created an unbiased database to keep track of them. I'm not done yet, but for now, the data lives on a website, **thelocavore.com**, and is fully searchable and completely free for all to use. Anyone can go online to search by neighborhood or borough, category or subcategory, and generate a list of up-to-date options for actual local, small biz retail shops.

What you'll find in this book is a collection of organized listings for 789 of the 14,000+ businesses in The Locavore Guide database. They're organized by category and subcategory for easy searching, and are designed to give you just enough information — because what's the fun in knowing everything?

As algorithms and sponsored posts push pages for small busi-

By the numbers

Accurate as of: August 1, 2025

Number of shops: **14,120**
Neighborhoods covered: **260**
Approx. miles: **1,926**
Number of blocks: **12,159**

Explore more on **thelocavore.com**

nesses lower and lower on your Google search, and the same viral spots keep showing up on your social media channels, we aim to be the antidote: a resource made by actual people for those who value discovery, being part of a community, and cultivating a unique point of view.

When I first set out to do this project, the objective was always a physical guidebook. I was inspired by the content of guides I'd seen from the '70s–'90s, the functionality of the annually published *Zagat Guide*, and the quaintness, specificity, and organization of *The Old Farmer's Almanac*. In the style of these iconic information resources, this book will be revised and edited annually, because this fine city of ours is constantly changing. As we continue to move faster and faster through our everyday lives, as the ever-shifting zeitgeist continues to give us whiplash, isn't it nice to pause and give some permanence to the information of now?

What's here today might be gone tomorrow, but in its place comes something bright and new. Let's celebrate the places that add value to our city and our lives, accept that a good thing sometimes doesn't last forever, and do our very best to appreciate what's in front of us right now at this very moment. I hope this wacky little book will help you do that. Maybe something you find in these pages will be the catalyst for a great day out. Perhaps you'll learn something new. Most important of all — you'll leave your apartment and engage with the immense community that surrounds us. You'll talk to your neighbors, find the fun in shopping for boring things, and define your personal style with things that no one else has. You'll be better for it, New York City will be better for it.

**Follow us on IG and TikTok
@thelocavorenyc**

Letter from the Editor

Dear Reader,

Welcome to the second annual edition of *The Locavore Guide to Shopping New York City*! Because our fine city is always changing, I've updated our listings for accuracy, added new features, and tagged in a few of my fabulous friends to contribute their expertise. If you're new here: Hi! I've been a shop owner for the better part of the past 10 years and am the founder of The Locavore Guide. Our unique local communities and culture depend on vibrant, active, engaged storefront businesses, and I'm here to demonstrate how we can all do better by them, while enhancing our own everyday lives in the process.

Last year, this humble little guidebook took me all over the city, with appearances on local TV, a few radio spots, and visits to more shops than I can count. You can spot yellow "Locavore Guide Approved" decals in more windows than ever, and find this publication for sale in more than 60 independently owned shops. To self-publish a book is a tremendously difficult feat, and to do it annually makes me wonder if I'm a glutton for punishment. The truth, though, is that this small biz landscape is ever-evolving, and what makes books like this obsolete in this digital age is their inability to keep up. Physical media is making a comeback, and I think there's something really nice about having a tangible record of a period of time — and a resource that's the antithesis of the ephemerality of the digital content we consume every day. I'm *just* old enough to have experienced NYC as a young person with no social media and no smartphone, just a comfortable pair of shoes and a map. I remember what it was like to go out for dinner with nothing but a piece of paper with a recommendation and an address written on it. There weren't block-long lines to get into anything, except maybe a late night party or a really great sample sale. Everyone understood that they had the agency to find things on their own — to go for a walk with their curiosity hat on in search of the thrill of discovery. It's easy to romanticize this period of time, but what holds true is the fact that while digital media is an invaluable tool for learning and discovery, nothing beats the feeling that you've found something special on your own, IRL, simply because you were out in the world, and you were paying attention. That's exactly how I found the majority of the shops in this book: by putting on my curiosity hat and exploring this incredible matrix of a city with eyes open and my phone in my pocket.

Since we sent our 2025 edition to print, I've been working on a BIG book about the current state of independent retail in America, why it's so important, and what can be done to ensure a better future for it. This work has taken me all over the country to interview shop owners and observe all sorts of towns and cities, and every time I return home I have a renewed gratitude for living here. So much of what we experience as New Yorkers isn't so different from people in other places, but one thing that's unique about this place is how truly walkable and accessible it is. Jane Jacobs' theories still apply, even decades later: places that are walkable have more connected communities, a healthier climate for small businesses, and more economic stability. Despite our sidewalks and bike lanes becoming more and more clogged with Amazon crates, we're still surrounded by walkable places, people with great recommendations, and everything we could possibly want or need — without having to wait 2-5 business days for delivery, and without having a dirty box to break down and deal with.

As you work your way through this book, I want you to consider it a resource for finding the things you're looking for (a random ingredient! a really nice sofa! a special dress for your sister's wedding!), but also a catalyst to help you put your phone away, explore a new neighborhood, and see what you can discover on your own. Consider me your shop-world fairy godmother, here to open the door, cast a spell, and get your started on your journey.

Caroline Weaver
Founder, The Locavore Guide

The Locavore VARIETY STORE

PURVEYORS OF LOCAL GOOD

**Located in Greenwich Village, Manhattan at 434 6th Avenue
Open Every Day**

POWERED BY: **The Locavore Guide**

An emporium of local goods, all grown / baked / fabricated / assembled / crafted / concocted / sewn / stuffed / pickled within 100* miles of NYC.

*mostly

Trend Report

EVERYTHING'S VINTAGE

Vintage & Thrift remains the fastest-growing category in our directory with at least 16 openings in the past 12 months, by our count. It significantly outpaces any other category of non-essential shop and has me wondering: when will the supply of good vintage dry up? Or is the cycle of buying and re-selling moving so fast that it won't? Will things just continue to get more expensive? The line between what's "vintage" and what's "thrift" becomes more blurred; only time will tell when this category will max out.

BACK TO BASICS

In 2025, an undeniable trend was a reversion back to analog forms of media. We saw the first opening of a video store in decades with **Night Owl Video** in Brooklyn, and CD sales are reportedly seeing an uptick for the first time since their peak in 2002. In the world of fashion, I've seen several new boutiques open without online stores — and no plans to add them. Notable womenswear retailer **Outline** even ditched theirs in favor of a beautifully photographed physical catalog. I see it all as an indicator that, collectively, we're craving the pleasure, experience, and intention that comes with shopping IRL — and that shop owners are fed up with the expectations and frustrations of online retail.

How Did We Choose?

I'm not here to tell you what's "cool" or "the best" because this is New York City! How can I possibly minimize the diversity and wonder of what's available to such absolute language? Instead, what I look for is a distinctive point of view. In a sea of shops, what makes them stand out? There are a couple of things I'm always looking for:

EXTREME SPECIALISTS

These are shops that focus exclusively on one type or category of thing and do it well. Specialty shops are staffed with experts who will guide your experience, answer your questions, and tell you the truth. Places like these are the roots of our retail ecosystem and remind us that you really can find *everything* in New York City. As much as they are shops, they're also learning resources and ad hoc museums.

STANDOUT STYLE

There's no shortage of clothing, interiors, gift shops, and other types of shops that could fall under "lifestyle," but what makes some of them stand out more than others is their one-of-a-kind style. I'm most interested in the ones that are focused on creating a world for their customers that's rooted enough to outlast trends. Great style comes from intuition and creativity, and these shops encourage their customers to cultivate their own.

WHAT'S ALSO INCLUDED

Legacy businesses with charm and staying power, places with particularly wonderful shopkeepers, wacky historic landmarks of retail, my personal favorites, places that fulfill an important need, shops recommended to me by friends and strangers, selections by experts in categories I'm unfamiliar with, and a few total wildcards, because my job is to explore NYC and I've found some incredible places that are so singular I couldn't not include them.

DID I MISS SOMETHING?

Email us at **general@thelocavore.com** to tell us about a shop you think deserves a spot in the next edition of our guide!

WHY SHOP SMALL?

1. Your money goes back into the community, not the pockets of corporate overlords
2. Storefronts full of mindful businesses = safer streets
3. Access to expert help from folks who know better than you do
4. A more unique, culturally diverse cityscape for everyone to enjoy

Regular Rotation

At the core of any New Yorker's shopping habits is a solid arsenal of regular spots. For those who have yet to discover theirs, or practiced locavores who love a worksheet, here's a fill-in list for keeping track of your tried-and-trues.

Hardware Store

Pharmacy

Favorite Bodega

Beverages

Home Goods

Grocery

Specialty Foods

Variety Store

Clothes

Accessories

Go-To For Gifts

Hobbies

Other

Later List

As you discover new shops in this book or elsewhere, keep track of them here. Great places for holiday gifts, that spot you think your visitors would love, a specialist so obscure you're sure you'll forget it — add it to the list!

TOTALLY STUMPED?

Become a Supporting Member of The Locavore Guide for access to our **SHOPPING HELP HOTLINE**!

Text us for a recommendation and we'll get back to you within 24 hours. Go to **thelocavore.com** to sign up!

Hot New Shops

It's our job to keep up with what's new so you don't have to! Here's a list of dazzling new spots, all of which have opened since our last edition went to print. Be sure to find their full listings organized throughout the book.

Art of Play (BK)
◎ *Brooklyn Heights*
Household curiosities and stylish games by this cult-favorite card brand. (pg. 148)

Collina Strada (MANH)
◎ *Lower East Side*
Edgy local womenswear brand known for utilizing lots of volume and texture. (pg. 110)

Flower Aggregate (BK)
◎ *East Williamsburg*
Floral wholesaler specializing in blooms sourced from regional farms. (pg. 287)

Gem Home (MANH)
◎ *Nolita*
By Chef Flynn McGarry, a café and shop full of handmade home goods and fancy food products. (pg. 269)

Irving Green (MANH)
◎ *East Village*
Lovely gifts and home goods sourced from small biz makers in Ireland. (pg. 221)

Kartik Research (MANH)
◎ *Lower East Side*
A fresh take on traditional embroidered, printed, and woven menswear from India. (pg. 99)

Linder Sport (MANH)
◎ *West Village*
Quality, preppy menswear classics at prices that are shockingly accessible. (pg. 102)

Merlette (MANH)
◎ *Tribeca*
Flirty, grown-up, and truly day-to-night styles for the downtown everywoman. (pg. 114)

Misha & Puff (BK)
◎ *Boerum Hill*
Kids clothes in wildly retro prints, bold colors, and funky silhouettes. (pg.260)

Modify (MANH)
◎ *Harlem*
NYC's first thrift store catering to folks following Islamic principles of modest dressing. (pg. 124)

Night Owl Video (BK)
◎ *Williamsburg*
DVDs, Blu-Ray, and VHS tapes are proof that physical media is back and more fun than ever. (pg. 147)

Old The Best (MANH)
◎ *West Village*
An unbelievable selection of vintage and secondhand designer handbags. (pg. 128)

Steven Alan (MANH)
◎ *Chelsea*
Utilitarian and classic American sportswear with a signature twist — a return to retail for an early aughts OG. (pg. 100)

Tamara Malas (MANH)
◎ *Lower East Side*
Size inclusive (0–36!) and wildly fun separates, swimwear, outerwear, and more. (pg. 113)

The Analog Stationer (BK)
◎ *Prospect Heights*
Friendly new stationery shop, stocked with hard-to-find imports. (pg. 132)

In Memoriam

Not all good things can last forever in the lifecycle of a city. In the past year, we've lost twenty of the shops included in our 2025 guidebook. Here are the places we won't soon forget:

Bedford Cheese Shop (MANH)
◎ *Gramercy*
Founded in 2003, this shop was a pillar in the specialty grocery community for its attention to detail and stellar globally sourced selection.

Beer Witch (BK)
◎ *Park Slope*
This woman-owned beer shop and bar was a breath of fresh air for its stylish design and friendly, inclusive attitude. It even hosted its own book club!

Casa Muza (BK)
◎ *Williamsburg*
Stocking Latin American brands and her own line of womenswear, designer Polet Guzmán's shop was a bright and tropical fashion destination.

FloraLuce (BK) **NOW ONLINE**
◎ *Greenpoint*
Collector and restorer Mike Karnell's incredible selection of mid-century designer fixtures might not be found IRL anymore, but you can still shop online!

Hey Kids Comics (BK) **NOW ONLINE**
◉ *Greenpoint*
With a specialty in comic books for kids ages 5–18, this bookstore grew from a 2020 father-son sidewalk operation and was truly one-of-a-kind.

Jane Cookshop (MANH)
◉ *East Village*
Small but mighty, this home and kitchen shop stocked lovely treasures from all corners of the world. Find owner Jen's superb taste on display at her family's shop East Village Postal.

Love Only (MANH) (BK)
◉ *East Village and Williamsburg*
These twin womenswear shops stocked colorful and quirky indie designers for trendy girls with a point of view.

Mikey's Hook Up (BK) **NOW IN LA**
◉ *Williamsburg*
Something of a musician's hardware store, this AV specialist was popular with DJs and vintage collecting audiophiles. Check out their new shop in LA!

Moonlab 42 (MANH)
◉ *Harlem*
Handmade treasures from the country of Georgia, including architectural candles, small press books, and objects for the home.

Orange Glou (MANH) **NOW ONLINE**
◉ *Lower East Side*
Starting as a subscription service for lovers of skin contact wine, this storefront specialized in only orange wine.

Roxelana Designer Jewelry (QNS)
◉ *Astoria*
This gift and jewelry shop is stocked with all sorts of dazzling goods from Turkey, and had a magical ceiling full of colorful lamps.

Starhawk Designs (BK)
◎ *Greenpoint*

An icon of Greenpoint, owner Thom is a true tie-dye master and filled his new age shop with racks and racks of garments for all ages.

STORM Books & Candy (BK)
◎ *Greenpoint*

With a focus on books about Southwest Asian and North African cultures, this minimalist bookstore also doubled as a community space and candy store.

The March Hare (MANH)
◎ *East Village*

Adamantly analog, The March Hare was a tiny toy shop with no electronics in sight. They took pride in sourcing nostalgic toys and unique gifts for kids by independent brands.

The Hunt (MANH) **NOW ONLINE**
◎ *Lower East Side*

Known for their chunky signet rings and silvery jewelry depicting skulls, swords, snakes, and their signature eye, this shop of curiosities was a carpet clad paradise for the coolest LES punks.

Village Tannery (MANH)
◎ *Greenwich Village*

For nearly 50 years, this old-school leather specialist sold bags and accessories in all shapes and sizes, and offered custom-made pieces.

West Side Kids (MANH)
◎ *Upper West Side*

A children's everything store, this beloved store supplied neighborhood families with everything from scooters to dress-up clothes.

An Alphabetized List of
Amy Sedaris's Favorite Shops

You might recognize Amy Sedaris as a superstar comedian and actress, a lover of rabbits, and an enthusiastic New Yorker, but I know her best as NYC's Most Prolific Local Shopper. Her distinctive sense of style is sourced from shops all over town, and she's shared a list of them with us.

- 180 The Store
- Aedes Perfumery
- Ansonia Pharmacy
- Big Night
- Bode Women's
- Bonberi Mart
- BonBon
- C.O. Bigelow Chemists
- C.O. Bigelow Surgical
- Cobblestones
- COMME des GARÇONS
- Cure Thrift
- Dave's New York
- Economy Candy
- Essex Market
- Fishs Eddy
- Garber Hardware
- Greenwich Letterpress
- Happier Grocery
- Hudson & Charles
- IF SOHO NEW YORK
- Janet West at Chelsea Flea
- John Derian Company
- Kalustyan's
- Le Fanion
- Li-Lac Chocolates
- Mannahatta NYC
- McNally Jackson Books
- November 19
- Old The Best
- Pearl River Mart
- Sandy Liang
- Stevdan Stationers
- Surreal Skincare
- The Locavore Variety Store
- Three Lives & Company
- Tiny Doll House
- Top Hat
- Village Party Store
- Whiskers Holistic Petcare
- Wigs and Plus
- Yamadaya
- ZITOMER

Shop Astrology

This book is an almanac of sorts, and no almanac is complete without a little insight into the planetary forces that surround us. We enlisted our resident astro buff Sara Quiroz to tell us about the shopping habits of each star sign.

"In New York, shopping is never just about buying things – it's a lifestyle, a love language and a full contact sport. Whether you're queuing for a buzzy Bushwick pop-up or meandering through Union Square Greenmarket, your sun sign might explain a lot about your shopping list. Here's a cosmic look at how each sign shops locally!" – Sara Quiroz

Aries

(March 21st - April 19th)
These impulsive trend setters max out for the thrill then forget what they bought within the week. They enter a shop saying "I'm just browsing," and end up with three tote bags and no regrets. They love pop-ups, flash sales, and anything limited-edition. Bonus points if there's a line to wait in! **Artists & Fleas** in Williamsburg and Chelsea will keep the ram spoiled for variety.

Taurus

(April 20th - May 20th)
The slow and intentional bull will splurge, but only on *the good stuff*. I'm talking strictly gourmet groceries, luxury health and beauty products, and opulent home goods for this sensual sign. Taurus must try everything prior to purchase by touching every textile and smelling every sample. **SOS Chefs** appeals to their love of the finer things for the kitchen and a sensory shopping experience. For the less culinary inclined, head to **Bios Apothecary** to develop a custom fragrance.

Gemini

(May 21st - June 21st)
Chaotically chic Gemini will buy six random things for every one that they actually need. A shopping trip isn't just to check off their list, but also to connect with their community and explore their latest curiosity. These eclectic shoppers are drawn to bookstores, art supply shops, and vintage markets they can name drop later. They curate the pieces for their eclectic style at **Amarcord** and scratch their intellectual itch at **McNally Jackson**.

Cancer

(June 22nd - July 22nd)
As the most nostalgic and cozy of all the signs, Cancer loves to invest in homey, heartfelt purchases. They have a different candle for every mood, and are sentimental shoppers who love to pick up items "for the apartment," which double as emotional security objects. The thoughtful sourcing at **November 19** will make a sensitive Cancer heart sing.

Leo

(July 23rd - August 22nd)
Luxe Leo likes a highly curated shopping experience with attention-grabbing shelf displays. They favor quality over quantity with statement pieces and will buy a $300 mug just to post about it. The lion is drawn to bold, aesthetics-forward spaces with great lighting and even better mirrors, like **Coming Soon**.

Sara Quiroz is a lifelong student of astrology, prolific tarot reader and all-around beverage witch. Find her on instagram at **@supernaturalsara**

Virgo

(August 23rd - September 22nd)
Thoughtful and minimalist, Virgos will research, price-compare, and eco-vet any and all purchases. They shop like they're on a mission, with a list, a tote, and a podcast queued. Virgos will come for three things and leave with exactly three things. **Earth & Me** and **Flower Power** both appeal well to their earthy ethos.

Libra

(September 23rd - October 23rd)
These romantic aesthetes buy with their heart — then return it after changing their mind several times. Libra is likely to ask everyone's opinion before choosing what to purchase, so a patient and well-informed shopkeeper is essential. Attracted to symmetry, clean lines and cafes that double as concept stores, they will love browsing **Sincerely, Tommy** and **dear friends books** next door.

Scorpio

(October 24th - November 21st)
Moody, intentional, and secretive, Scorpios love to invest in niche and deeply personal things. Their shopping is ritualistic: think incense, hand-bound journals, and one perfect black coat. The subterranean occult shop **Enchantments** is dark and mysterious enough for the scorpion while the more amorous Scorpios will love stocking up on latex and leather at **Purple Passion**.

Sagittarius

(November 22nd - December 21st)
Free-spirited splurgers, Sagittarians will drop cash like it's Monopoly money then vanish for a wild weekend trip. Joyfully

chaotic, their cart is full of passport covers, saffron from Morocco, and a new carry-on for their next adventure. The globe-trotting vibe of **Hatchet Supply Outdoor Supply Co.** will speak to the archer wanderlust and love of outdoor movement.

Capricorn

(December 22nd - January 19th)
Classic, pragmatic, and refined, Capricorn has a budget and respects it. They will absolutely calculate cost-per-use on any purchase and shop with purpose focusing on investment pieces and quiet luxury. **Ven Space** or **Kallmeyer** are must visits for the Capricorn seeking quality staples for a sophisticated wardrobe.

Aquarius

(January 20th - February 18th)
Experimental Aquarius is a cause-driven shopper, supporting stores with a mission statement. Unconcerned with trends, they always have reusable bags and conspiracy theories on hand. **Park Slope Food Coop** and **Bluestockings Cooperative Bookstore** allow them to feel good about doing good with a business that can stand up to their values.

Pisces

(February 19th - March 20th)
Dreamy Pisces will buy beautiful things then forget they exist. This fish follows vibes, not directions! Think pastel ceramics, lavender bundles and self published tomes of faraway places to stoke their wanderlust. At **Lockwood**, they can find the perfect gift for their favorite person (themselves.)

Guide to the Greenmarket

How much do you know about the diversity of produce that grows in this region of the country? Barring tropical fruit and citrus, just about *everything* has a season here in the mid-Atlantic, and you can find all of it at the farmers market. There are over 130 markets and farm stands in all five boroughs where anyone can shop fresh produce and locally made food products from all over the region, and it's more accessible than you might think!

GrowNYC hosts the largest network of farmer's markets in the city and has been pioneering environmental education initiatives since the 1970s. Learn more at **grownyc.com**.

DID YOU KNOW?

The majority of NYC farmers markets accept SNAP. You even get $2 back in market-redeemable "Health Bucks" for using your SNAP benefits at the market (up to $10/day)!

Does shopping at the market cost more?

It depends on what you're buying! Prices vary by vendor and, if you shop around, you'll likely find what you're looking for at a price comparable to the supermarket. One important thing to keep in mind is that farmers market produce is generally significantly fresher, which means it lasts longer! If you shop smart and create less food waste, you'll most certainly save money by shopping at the farmers market.

GREENMARKET TIP

Go early! Especially if you're shopping at the Union Square Greenmarket on Wednesday or Saturday, aim to be there around 8 or 9 to beat the crowds.

Greenmarkets by Borough

There are a few different market systems and independent operators hosting markets all over the city. Here's a chart detailing markets that can be found across the city.*

Bronx

Bissel Gardens Farmers Market — July–November
Baychester Ave & Camp St — Sat 8AM–4PM

Bronx Borough Hall Greenmarket — June–November
161st & Grand Concourse — Tues 8AM–4PM

Bronx Park East Farmers Market — June–November
2045 Bronx Park E — Sun 9AM–4PM

Harvest Home Jacobi Hospital Market — July–November
1400 Pelham Parkway — Fri 8AM–3PM

Harvest Home Mt. Eden Market — July–November
Mt. Eden & Morris Aves — Tues / Thurs 8AM–3PM

JBOLC Garden Community Market — June–October
100 W Mosholu Parkway S — Sat 10AM–3PM

La Familia Verde Farmers' Market — July–November
E Tremont & Arthur Ave — Tues 9AM–3PM

La Familia Verde Highbridge Market — July–November
1430 Plimpton Ave — Weds 10AM–2PM

La Familia Verde Southern Blvd — July–November
1070 Southern Blvd — Thurs 10AM–1PM

Lincoln Hospital Greenmarket — June–November
E 149th St (bet. Park & Morris Ave) — Tues / Fri 8AM–3PM

Morning Glory Market at NYBG — June–October
2900 Southern Blvd (at Mosholu Gate) — Weds 10AM–3PM

Parkchester Greenmarket　　　　　　　June–November
Westchester Ave & White Plains Rd　　　　Fri 8AM–3PM

Poe Park Greenmarket　　　　　　　　　June–November
E 192nd St bet.　　　　　　　　　　　　　Tues 8AM–3PM
Grand Concourse & Valentine

Riverdale Neighborhood House Market　May–September
5521 Mosholu Ave　　　　　　　　　　　Thurs 1PM–6PM

Riverdale Y Sunday Market　　　　　　May–December
4545 Independence Ave　　　　　　　　　Sun 9AM–2PM

Manhattan

175th Street Greenmarket　　　　　　　June–November
W 175th St bet. Broadway & Wadsworth　Thurs 8AM–4PM

57th Street Greenmarket　　　　　　　　June–November
57th St & 10th Ave　　　　　　　　　　　Sat 8AM–3PM

79th Street Greenmarket　　　　　　　　Year-Round
W 79th St & Columbus Ave　　　　　　　Sun 9AM–4PM

82nd Street Greenmarket　　　　　　　　Year-Round
408 E 82nd St　　　　　　　　　　　　　Sat 9AM–2:30PM

Ruppert Park Greenmarket　　　　　　　June–November
E 94th St & 1st Ave　　　　　　　　　　　Sun 9AM–3PM

97th Street Greenmarket　　　　　　　　Year-Round
120-122 W 97th St　　　　　　　　　　　Fri 8AM–2PM

Abingdon Square Park Greenmarket　　Year-Round
Hudson St & W 12th St　　　　　　　　　Sat 8AM–2PM

Bowling Green Greenmarket　　　　　　May–November
Broadway & Whitehall St　　　　　　　　Tues 8AM–3PM

Bro Sis Green Youth Market `NEW!` — Year-Round
Amsterdam Ave bet. W 143rd & 144th Sts — Weds 10:30AM–6PM

City Hall Greenmarket `NEW!` — May–November
Broadway bet. Chambers & Warren St — Tues 8AM–4PM

Columbia Greenmarket — Year-Round
Broadway & W 114th St — Thurs/Sun 8AM–4PM

Dag Hammarskjold Plaza Greenmarket — Year-Round
E 47th St & 2nd Ave — Weds 8AM–3PM

Down to Earth Battery Park City Market — Thru November
2–4 River Terrace — Sun 9AM–2PM

Down to Earth Chelsea Market — Thru December
355 W 23rd St — Sat 9AM–2PM

Down to Earth Morningside Park Market — Year-Round
237–331 Manhattan Ave — Sat 9AM–2PM

Fort Washington Greenmarket — June–December
W 168th St & Fort Washington Ave — Tues 8AM–4PM

Fulton Stall Market (Indoor) `NEW!` — Year-round
91 South St bet. Fulton & John St — Mon-Sat 11:30AM–5PM

Grass Roots Farmers Market — Year-Round
W 145th St bet. Edgecombe & Bradhurst Ave (Jackie Robinson Park) — Tues/Sat 9AM–4PM

Greenmarket at Rockefeller Center — August–October
Rockefeller Center Plaza at 50th St — 8AM–5PM

Harlem Unity Market `NEW!` — June–November
163 W 125th St — Sat 9AM–3PM

Harvest Home East Harlem Market — July–November
E 104th St & 3rd Ave — Thurs 8AM–3PM

Harvest Home Metropolitan Hospital — July–November
E 97th St & 2nd Ave — Fri 8AM–3PM

Inwood Greenmarket — Year-Round
Isham St bet. Seaman Ave & Cooper St — Sat 8AM–3PM

Mount Sinai Greenmarket `NEW!` — June–November
Madison Ave & 99th St — Weds 8AM–3PM

P.S. 11 Farm Market (No EBT) `NEW!` — Year-round
320 W 21st St — Weds 8AM–10AM

Stuyvesant Town Greenmarket — May–December
South end of Stuyvesant Town Oval, near 14th Street Loop bet. 1st Ave & Ave A — Sun 9:30AM–4PM

Tompkins Square Greenmarket — Year-round
E 7th St & Ave A — Sun 9AM–4PM

Tribeca Greenmarket — Year-round
Greenwich St bet. Duane and Chambers St — Sat 8AM–2PM

Tucker Square Greenmarket — Year-round
W 66th St & Broadway — Thurs / Sat 8AM–4PM

Two Bridges Youth Market `NEW!` — Year-round
50 Madison St — Sun 10:30AM–3PM

Union Square Greenmarket — Year-round
E 17th St & Union Square W — Mon / Weds / Fri / Sat 8AM–6PM

Uptown Good Food Farmers Market — June–November
St. Nicholas Ave & West 137th St (St.Nicholas Park) — Sat 9AM–3PM

Brooklyn

4th Ave. Sunset Park Greenmarket July–November
4th Ave bet. 59th & 60th St Sat 8AM–3PM

7th Ave. Sunset Park Greenmarket Year-Round
7th Ave & 44th St Sat 8AM–3PM

Bartel-Pritchard Square Greenmarket Year-Round
Prospect Park West at 15th St Weds 8AM–2PM
 Sun 9AM-2PM

Bay Ridge Greenmarket May–November
3rd Ave & 95th St Sat 8AM–3PM

Bensonhurst Greenmarket July–November
18th Ave bet. 81st & 82nd St Thurs 8AM–2PM

Boro Park Greenmarket **NEW!** June–November
14th Ave bet. 49th & 50th St Thurs 8AM–3PM

Brooklyn Borough Hall Greenmarket Year-Round
Court & Montague Sts Tues/Sat 8AM–3PM

Carroll Gardens Greenmarket Year-round
Carroll St bet. Smith & Court St Sun 8AM–2PM

Cortelyou Greenmarket Year-round
Cortelyou Rd bet. Rugby & Argyle Rd Sun 8AM–2PM

Domino Park Greenmarket June–November
River St bet. S 3rd & 4th St Sun 8AM–3PM

Down to Earth McGolrick Park Market Year-round
McGolrick Park Sun 9AM–2PM

Down to Earth Park Slope Market July–November
Washington Park Sun 9AM–2PM

East New York Farmers Market — June–November
Schenck Ave bet. New Lots & Livonia Aves — Sat 9AM–3PM

Fort Greene Greenmarket — Year-round
Washington Park & Dekalb Ave — Sat 8AM–3PM

Fresh Vibes Market at Brookdale Hospital — Year-round
1 Brookdale Plaza — Every 1st and 3rd Fri 11AM–2PM

Fresh Vibes Market at BBNH — Year-round
485 Throop Ave — Every 2nd and 4th Fri 11AM–2PM

Fresh Vibes Market Crown Heights — Year-round
546 Eastern Pkwy — Every 3rd Weds 11AM–3PM

Fresh Vibes Market East New York — Year-round
101 Pennsylvania Ave — Every 2nd Weds 11AM–3PM

Fresh Vibes Market LDC Crown Heights — Year-round
252 Kingston Ave — Every 1st Tues 11AM–2PM

Grand Army Plaza Greenmarket — Year-round
Grand Army Plaza — Sat 8AM–4PM

Harvest Home Coney Isl. Hospital Mkt. — June–November
Ocean Pkwy bet. Ave Z & Shore Pkwy — Fri 8AM–3PM

Isabahlia Market at ISO Student Farm `NEW!` — Year-round
514 Rockaway Ave — Fri/Sat 8AM–3PM

Isabahlia Market at Powell Street Garden — Year-round
410 Livonia Ave — Fri/Sat 8AM–3PM

McCarren Park Greenmarket — Year-round
N 12th St bet. Union & Driggs Ave — Sat 8AM–3PM

P.S. 178 Farmers Market `NEW!` — Year-round
2163 Dean St — Weds 12:30–3:30PM

Riseboro Farmer's Market
Hope Ballfield

May–November
Weds 9AM–3PM

Riseboro Farmer's Market
Irving Square Park

May–November
Sun 9AM–2PM

Riseboro Farmer's Market
Maria Hernandez Park

May–November
Sat 8AM–3PM

Queens

Astoria Farmers Market NEW!
31st Ave bet. 34 & 35th St

May–November
Every 2nd Sun 1PM–3PM

Corona Greenmarket
Roosevelt Ave & 103rd St

June–November
Fri 8AM–3PM

Down to Earth Cunningham Park Mkt.
19600 Union Turnpike

April–December
Sun 9AM–2PM

Elmhurst Greenmarket
41st Ave bet. 80th and 81st St

June–November
Tues 8AM–3PM

Flushing Greenmarket NEW!
140-49 Sanford Ave

July–November
Weds 8AM–3PM

Forest Hills Greenmarket
70th Ave & Queens Blvd

Year-round
Sun 8AM–2PM

Jackson Heights Greenmarket
34th Ave bet. 79th and 80th St

Year-round
Sun 8AM–2PM (Jan-May)
Sun 8AM–3PM (June-Dec)

Queens Farm at Jamaica Hospital
8900 Van Wyck Expy

May–October
Fri 10AM–3PM

Queens Farm at Queens Borough Hall
120-55 Queens Blvd

July–November
Thurs 10AM–3PM

Sunnyside Greenmarket Year-round Saturdays
Skillman Ave bet. 42nd and 43rd St 8AM-2PM (Jan-April)
8AM-3PM (May-Dec)

NEW IN 2024!

Astoria finally has a market! It's independently operated and is located at 31st Ave, bet. 34-35th St on the second Sunday of every month. Learn more at **astoriafarmersmarket.com.**

Staten Island

St. George Greenmarket Year-round
Hyatt St & St. Marks Pl Sat 8AM–1PM

Staten Island Mall Greenmarket June–November
Marsh Ave & Ring Rd Sat 8AM–2PM

*Accurate as of August 2025, subject to change annually

What's in season?

This is something you'll come to learn as you get used to shopping the market. Be sure to ask someone if you're curious about when something will be available or if you want to know what a farm is growing later in the season.

Especially at GrowNYC markets, the folks at the information tent can help you with this. They sometimes even have cooking demos and printouts for great recipes to use with what's currently available. Visit grownyc.org for a chart detailing what's in season and when.

Outstanding Market Vendors

Here are a few standout favorites of the TLG staff.
*Look up these vendors to see their current market schedules

Oak Grove Plantation
This family-owned New Jersey farm has a few specialties, the most notable of which is a stunning variety of herbs. Pineapple sage, lime thyme, chocolate mint, lemon verbena, and all sorts of basil — you won't find a larger selection of exotic herbs in the tri-state area. They're also great for finding the perfect BLT bacon, whole wheat flour, and always-ripe peaches.

Lani's Farm
Some of the most unique produce at the market comes from Lani's Farm, which specializes in vegetables for Asian cuisines. Find a tremendous variety of greens, tons of beans, fresh turmeric and ginger root, and house-made kimchi, gochujang, sambal, and pre-made foods like dumplings, soups, and juices.

Knead Love
Known for their dense, nutritious sourdough loaves and decadent pastries, Knead Love is a truly spectacular gluten-free bakery. Get cinnamon rolls, s'mores cookies, seasonal muffins, granola, and order fabulous GF Thanksgiving pies. This bakery has a sassy personality and makes a boring dietary restriction feel less uncool.

Buzzard Crest Vineyards
You've never tasted a grape until you've had these. This family-owned organic farm grows about a dozen varieties of both seeded and seedless grape varieties, each of which impart their own distinctive flavors. Find traditional grapes like Concord, punchy and sweet Canadice, or candy-like Mars. On any given day, you'll likely have at least six to choose from, in addition to the freshest grape juice you've ever had, and gorgeous wines from the farm's own Barrington Cellars brand.

Andrew's Honey

With hives on roofs across dozens of neighborhoods in all five boroughs, beekeeper Andrew Coté has stories to tell (literally! Read his book *Honey and Venom: Confessions of an Urban Beekeeper*), and something for any city dweller who believes in the benefits of local honey or is looking for adjacent products like bottles of bee pollen, honeycomb, and royal jelly. It doesn't get more local than this!

Tweefontein Herb Farm

For those who believe in the benefits of plant medicine, Tweefontein Herb Farm is an unparalleled resource for potent tinctures made from locally grown herbs. Shop the tea blends, balms, syrups, and fire cider, or find what you're looking for on the extensive list of medicinal herbs available.

The River Garden

In the summer, find affordable bunches of hot pink zinnias, exotic dahlias, and alien-like scabiosa, but come autumn, this stand turns into a heaven of dried floral arrangements and wreaths. We love picking up colorful little long-lasting bouquets to give to friends, and autumnal wreaths to adorn our doors.

Hudson Valley Fisheries

This fish farm grows only steelhead trout, with the highest level of sustainability practices in place. Using advanced technology Recirculating Aquaculture System, they can farm these salmon-like fish year round with significantly less environmental impact than wild-caught, or traditionally farm-raised alternatives. Get sushi-grade filets, whole fish, and pastrami-spiced trout lox and applewood-smoked filets.

FIND A MARKET!

Text "So Good" or "Muy Rico" to 55676 to get information on the three nearest markets to your zip code!

Unexpected Farmers Market Finds

Get more than produce, baked goods, and animal products!

Tofu

Great Joy Family Farm makes their own fresh-pressed tofu and also grows six heirloom varieties of rice!

Yarn

Catskill Merino is a sheep farm that spins luscious merino wool yarn in six weights and over a dozen colors.

Vodka

1857 Spirits makes a gorgeous, refined vodka from potatoes they grow on their own farm.

Ashwagandha

Furnace Creek Farm grows and grinds their own ashwagandha, a powerful and popular adaptogenic root.

GREENMARKET TIP

Don't quit the market in the winter! Several are open year-round, especially the big Union Square Greenmarket. You can still find things like: root veggies, hydroponic greens, a plethora of apple varieties, and non-seasonal things like meat, fish, dairy, condiments, and preserved fruits and vegetables.

Fruit Sticker Collection Page

For scavengers, urban explorers, produce freaks, and children: a fun and (sort of) free activity to do while out and about is fruit sticker hunting! Stick your favorites here for safekeeping and bring your filled page to The Locavore Variety Store for a special prize ☺

The New Rules

Essential etiquette for the 21st century shopper

It doesn't matter if you're just window shopping, on a hurried errand mission or planning to drop some serious cash — we're New Yorkers, not heathens, and there are few points of etiquette that we must always keep in mind.

PUT YOUR PHONE AWAY

While it's normal to make a quick call to ask a question or get a second opinion when shopping, it's downright rude to conduct a full-on conversation (or worse, a video call) in a shop. Put the person you're talking to on hold while you do what you need to do, or take it outside.

BEHAVE NICELY

In shopping and in life, you get the energy you give. Acknowledging the person working in a store, being polite, and exercising patience goes a long way. If you're asking for an exception or something out of the norm, remember that shopkeepers make their own rules, and they're way more likely to bend them for those who are nice.

ASK BEFORE YOU VIDEO

Most shops are cool with you filming or taking photos in their space, but asking first is always appreciated. Be sure to keep others — customers or staff — out of your shot unless you have their consent.

READ THE SIGNS

A good shop will have hours, rules, return policies, and useful information posted, and a good customer will make sure they read and follow it. Especially when it comes to door signage: if it's important enough to put ...

(cont'd.) on a door, you should probably pay attention to it.

BE MINDFUL OF TIME

Shopkeepers love sharing their knowledge, but please be mindful of their time, especially if it's a busy day at the shop or you have no intention of buying the thing you're inquiring about — or worse, you're gathering information to go buy it elsewhere. This is a cardinal consumer sin!

DON'T BE GROSS

Please don't ever consume food in a shop, and if beverages are permitted, do not put them on any surfaces where products are merchandised. This includes books, display cases, packaged goods, etc. Your sweaty iced coffee can cause serious damage to valuable inventory!

RESPECT THE INVENTORY

If a skincare or beauty product isn't clearly a tester, don't open or use it. If you're wearing a ton of makeup, don't try on clothes that need to go over your head. If your hands are greasy, don't flip through a pristine book. If you bring children into a store, it's your job to make sure they're careful.

DON'T ASK FOR A DISCOUNT

Unless there's an advertised sale happening, never ask an independent retailer for a discount on something, no matter what quantity you're buying. Small businesses simply operate on slimmer margins than big ones and don't have room (or time) to haggle with you.

The Shops

Arts & Crafts

Art Supplies

Soho Art Materials (MANH) (BK)
⊚ *3 Wooster St, Soho*
⊚ *36 Gardner Ave #2, East Williamsburg*
⊕ *sohoartmaterials.com*
Since 1999, Soho Art Materials has been serving artists of all kinds in their well-stocked stores. While they specialize in custom Tri-mar™ aluminum stretchers and painting materials, you'll also find a well-edited selection of pencils, lovely papers, and a small selection of other tools. Expect high quality, small-brand materials from independent supply companies that are hard to find elsewhere — and canvas stretching services! This is also the most reliable source in the city for a beloved household tool: the Tube-Wringer™!

Janoff's Stationery (MANH)
⊚ *2870 Broadway bet. W 112th and 111th St, Morningside Heights*
It's a family affair at the jam-packed art and office shop Janoff's Stationery. Insiders know that it's one of the best places in the city for fountain pen collectors, but the shop mostly caters to art and architecture students from nearby Columbia University. You'll find a little bit of everything here — from great journals to Italian terracotta modeling clay.

Art Retail Therapy (A.R.T.)
⊚ *84-26 37th Ave, Jackson Heights*
⊕ *artretailtherapy.com*
A true neighborhood hub for the creative kind, Art Retail Therapy is a Latinx, queer-owned shop selling all manners of art supply, with a big focus on education and community building. Pop by for supplies for your latest project, and stay for a workshop. Hot tip: Art Retail Therapy also stocks basic, affordable school supplies and stationery!

KC Arts (BK)
◎ *252 Court St, Cobble Hill*
⊕ *kcartsny.com*

Art supply shops like this one are a dying breed. From kid's craft kits and school supplies to popular art materials and painting tools — you'll find it all here. Better yet, you can return with your new masterpiece for framing at the custom framing counter in the back of the store. It's the only shop of its kind in this area of Brooklyn and is a true neighborhood staple for all things creative.

Tiny Arts Supply (QNS)
◎ *58-42a Catalpa Ave, Ridgewood*
⊕ *tinyartssupply.com*

In a neighborhood full of artists with nowhere nearby to buy materials, Tiny Arts Supply fills an important void. Owner Vanessa presides over a small shop that's full of inspiration and an assortment of supplies, but what's especially useful is that she's well-equipped to place special orders for her customers. Come by for a figure drawing class and be sure to ask for recommendations for things to fuel your creativity at home.

Beads

BeadKraft (MANH)
◎ *146 W 29th St 2nd Fl bet. 7th and 6th Ave, Chelsea*
⊕ *beadkraft.com*

With quite possibly the largest assortment of craft beads in the city, BeadKraft has it all: glass seed beads in all colors, plastic beads, crystal beads, metals beads, lots and lots of ever-popular alphabet beads, and inexpensive charms. This is the place you go if you want to have a little creative fun without breaking the bank.

Beads of Paradise (MANH)
◎ *16 E 17th St bet. 5th Ave and Union Sq W, Union Square*
⊕ *beadsofparadisenyc.com*

It's hard to tell exactly what Beads of Paradise actually sells from the sidewalk. The window is full of tribal artifacts, with cases containing hundreds of glass Christmas ornaments peeking out from behind. Enter the store and walk to the back, however, and you'll find a treasure trove of beads. Strands of semi-precious stones in a wide variety of shapes and sizes, rare antique beads for sale individually, and rainbows of glass beads from all over the world. As any good specialty shop should be, Beads of Paradise is staffed with friendly makers who are happy to assist you in planning your project and finding the tools you need to execute your vision.

Craft Supplies

Brooklyn Craft Company (BK)
◎ *165 Greenpoint Ave, Greenpoint*
⊕ *brooklyncraftcompany.com*

While this modern craft store specializes mostly in fiber arts and needlecrafts, stocking a terrific selection of yarns, notions, and fabrics, you'll also find craft store staples like beading kits, a rainbow of puffy paints, fabric dyes, and hot glue guns. For the uninitiated crafter, there's an awesome selection of kits for felting, punch needle, embroidery, weaving, and crochet, as well as a whole roster of classes and sewing workshops. Brooklyn Craft Company isn't your grandma's craft store, though — they've got a keen eye on brands making kits and supplies with a younger, cooler audience in mind.

Save-a-Thon (MANH) (BK) (BX)
◎ *1887 3rd Ave, East Harlem*
◎ *2452 Flatbush Ave, Marine Park*
◎ *2 W Fordham Rd, University Heights*

Best for discount fabrics and old-school things like faux flowers or cake- and candy-making tools and notions, this local chain of craft stores has been a mainstay in New York City for over 30 years. Need a really specific craft glue? Have a vision for a handmade Halloween costume and don't want to break the bank? This is the place.

Scribbles (BK)

⊚ *1308 40th St, Borough Park*
⊕ *scribblescrafts.com*

Boasting over 3000 in-stock items, Scribbles is a kid crafter's dream. Expect to find your usual tempera paint, Sculpey clay, and stacks of felt sheets, in addition to educational tools, kits of all kinds, and things for school projects. Because Scribbles is in a predominantly Jewish neighborhood, there's also a selection of specifically Jewish projects!

Cook's Arts and Crafts Shoppe (QNS)

⊚ *80-09 Myrtle Ave, Glendale*
⊕ *cookscrafts.com*

In a quaint residential area in central Queens lies Cook's Arts and Crafts Shoppe, which reminds me fondly of the type of craft stores my grandmother used to take me to. Don't be fooled by the size of the shop — the shelves that line the narrow aisles are packed full of supplies for knitting, decorating, painting, model-making, and sewing. There are games, kits for kids, and surprising old stock that'll make any supply hoarder's heart sing.

Honorable Mention

East Williamsburg is home to one of the greatest book-binding and conservation resources in America! **Talas** is a retailer that specializes in tools and materials for archival storage, book arts, and paper conservation, and while their showroom is no longer open to the public, their online store can be found at **talasonline.com.**

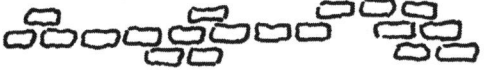

Dollhouse Miniatures

Tiny Doll House (MANH)
◎ *314 E 78th St bet. 2nd and 1st Ave, Upper East Side*
⊕ *tinydollhouse.com*

A shop deserving of its own subcategory, Tiny Dollhouse is the type of shop you happen upon and say to yourself, "Only in New York!" As described, it's a place that specializes in dollhouse miniatures, custom dollhouses, and dollhouse supplies. Carefully arranged in sections by category and maker, you'll find extraordinarily detailed (mostly 1/12 scale) objects made by miniature artists from all over the world. Even if you're not a dollhouse enthusiast, it's hard to leave without a bevy of hyper-specific tiny things.

Dyes & Pigments

Aljo Dyes (MANH)
◎ *72 Walker St 4th Fl, entrance on Cortlandt Alley bet. Walker and Canal, Tribeca*
⊕ *aljodye.com*

For professional-grade textile dyes, this is the place! For over 100 years, Aljo Dyes has been a garment industry and art community staple for their broad selection of dyes of all kinds: acid dyes, basic dyes, direct dyes, disperse dyes, fiber reactive dyes, and vat dyes. Under the same roof, W.D. Lockwood manufactures water, solvent, and oil soluble dyes for wood. But you don't need to be a dye expert to shop here! The knowledgeable staff can help you find just the right dye, whatever the project.

Kremer Pigments (MANH)
◎ *247 W 29th St bet. 8th and 7th Ave, Chelsea*
⊕ *kremerpigments.com*

For nearly 50 years, this family-owned pigment company has been working to revive interest in rare natural pigments, as well as producing high-quality modern synthetic ones. With outposts in Germany and here in New York, they serve a niche community of artists and conservation experts looking for specific hues, dyes, binders, and solvents. Don't miss their "30 Years of NY

Soil" watercolor set, featuring eight colors — five of which were sourced from locations in NY state.

Guerra Paint & Pigment (QNS)
◎ 57-55 58th Pl, Maspeth
⊕ guerrapaint.com
True masters in their craft, the folks at Guerra Paint & Pigment produce the largest selection of water-based single pigment concentrates in the world. These lightfast pigments can be combined with water-based or resin binders to create paint exactly to your liking, or for other color applications. Also available: pigments, fillers, and additives.

Fabrics

The Garment District is one of the geographically smallest neighborhoods in The Locavore Guide, but this area contained within the rough boundaries of 9th Ave–6th Ave and W 40th St–W 34th St is jam-packed with independently owned businesses serving garment makers from all over the region. Zig-zag your way through the neighborhood and you're sure to find a shop selling just what you're looking for, but if you're in need of a little guidance, here are a few stand-outs within the district and elsewhere.

B&J Fabrics (MANH)
◎ 525 7th Ave 2nd Fl bet. W 39th and 38th St, Garment District
⊕ bandjfabrics.com
Favored by designers of high-end fashion, B&J is a family-owned treasure trove that's organized in a way that minimizes the inevitably overwhelming nature of shopping for fabric. From delicious silk charmeuse to crisp shirting fabric and beaded tulle — B&J has it all. Hot tip: B&J is NYC's premier retailer for Liberty of London fabrics, including the seasonal prints.

Mood Fabrics (MANH)

◎ *225 W 37th St 3rd Fl bet. 8th and 7th Ave, Garment District*
⊕ *moodfabrics.com*

Certainly, you don't need anyone to tell you about Mood, but we'd be remiss if we didn't include it because there really isn't anything quite like this place. First brought to mainstream attention by early seasons of Bravo's Project Runway, Mood is hectic, jam-packed, and home to everything you could ever want, if only you can find it. Shopping here is like a fabric scavenger hunt and, for the casual shopper, it's a whole lot of fun to just go and see what you can find.

Spandex House (MANH)

◎ *263 W 38th St bet. 8th and 7th Ave, Garment District*
⊕ *spandexhouse.com*

It's true that there's a shop for every specialty, and Spandex House specializes in, you guessed it — spandex! Actually, they specialize in all manners of stretchy fabric and are well respected by designers of athletic outfits, costumes, and swimwear.

Keaton Quilts (MANH)

◎ *150 W 28th St Ste 804 bet. 7th and 6th Ave, Chelsea*
⊕ *keatonquilts.com*

Currently the only quilt fabric specialist in all of New York City, Keaton Quilts is tucked inside an unassuming building on the northern edge of Chelsea. Folks come here for the hundreds of different fabrics, patterns, Bernina and Bernette machines, threads, and even supplies for the visible mending art of Sashiko. New to the art of quilting? Keaton has a full schedule of workshops and sewing socials to attend.

Loom & Stars (MANH)

◎ *1133 Broadway #1401 nr. 26th St, Flatiron*
⊕ *loomandstars.com*

A slow fashion fabric store, Loom & Stars specializes in textiles that are either made by hand, or with extra attention paid to quality and process. In their sunny 14th-floor studio, you'll find a selection of tidy bolts in stripes, block prints, and even hard-to-find fabrics like woven Jamdani from the Bengal region of India. The selection of Japanese fabrics is a major draw for seasoned sewers, especially the delicate prints by cult-favorite Nani Iro. Come inspired, and leave with everything you need to make a new wardrobe heirloom.

Mendel Goldberg Fabrics (MANH)
⊚ *72 Hester St bet. Allen and Orchard St, Lower East Side*
⊕ *mendelgoldbergfabrics.com*

With humble beginnings as a sewing supply pushcart in the 1890s, and growing into the esteemed fourth generation family-owned fabric destination that it now is, Mendel Goldberg Fabrics is one of the last of its kind. The Goldbergs operate with a keen eye for couture-quality fabrics that's trusted by world-renowned costume designers and fashion folks. Visit for fabrics with so much personality they speak for themselves.

Zarin Fabrics (MANH)
⊚ *72 Allen St bet. Grand and Broome St, Lower East Side*
⊕ *zarinfabrics.com*

Whether you're refreshing your draperies or salvaging an old sofa with good bones, Zarin Fabrics is a terrific place to start when searching for *just right* home and upholstery textiles. They've got deep roots on the Lower East Side and have a

---

Tips for shopping the Garment District:

1 If you're new to a shop, be sure to ask about protocol regarding pulling boxes or rolls of fabrics and trims.

2 Have a question? Don't be afraid to ask! These people are true experts in their field.

3 Bring a little cash! Most shops take cards, but if you're just buying a few buttons or a couple yards of trim, it's typically preferred to pay with cash.

FABSCRAP (BK)

⊚ *140 58th Street Brooklyn Army Terminal,
Building B, Unit 5H-4, Sunset Park*
⊕ *fabscrap.org*

The folks at FABSCRAP are on a serious mission to save textile waste from landfills, and they do a damn good job of it. Visit their online shop or Brooklyn Army Terminal location and you're bound to be surprised by what you find, because it's ever-evolving. One day, there might be enormous bolts of fabric from a designer's studio, and the next you could find stacks of colored leather hides. Something that always seems to be plentiful is weaving yarn, so if that's your textile art of choice, FABSCRAP is a must-visit! For the savvy creative, it's a whole lot of fun to dig around for something inexpensive and inspiring.

Wanna put in some volunteer hours? Check out FABSCRAP for opportunities!

Tip Top Super Fine Fabrics (BK)

⊚ *232 Calyer St, Greenpoint*

A semi-secret spot for quality, European-milled silks, cashmeres, and suiting fabrics, Tip Top has a reputation for supplying well-priced fancy fabrics to New York City designers. It's rare to find a shop like this outside of the Garment District, and it's well worth a trip to Greenpoint for the vast selection of gorgeous fabrics for making clothes.

Knitting, Weaving, Crocheting

Downtown Yarns (MANH)

⊚ *45 Ave A bet. E 4th and 3rd St, Alphabet City*

Cozy and packed to the ceiling with skeins and skeins of wool, Downtown Yarns is what a 90's rom-com version of a yarn shop looks like. They sell all of the familiar brands you'd expect in a quality-focused yarn shop alongside niche, hand-dyed, small-batch beauties. The owner, Leti, is a delight to work with and can help you realize any project — the wackier and more creative, the better!

Loop of the Loom (MANH) (BK)
◉ *227 E 87th St bet. 3rd and 2nd Ave, Upper East Side*
◉ *197 Plymouth St, Dumbo*
⊕ *loopoftheloom.com*

Shop weaving yarns, supplies, and natural textile dyes in these twin studios. The real specialty here is Japanese Zen weaving, which you can sign up for in multi-week courses, project-based classes, or just drop in with a studio pass. It's the only studio of its kind in New York City, and is a nice departure for those looking to explore an alternative to needle-based fiber arts.

Cleo's Yarn Shop (BK)
◉ *222 Varet St, Bushwick*
⊕ *cleosyarnshop.com*

A queer-owned space for the next generation of knitters and crocheters, Cleo's is packed with small brands, exclusively natural fibers, embroidery supplies, a thorough selection of tools, and stellar community vibes. Order a beverage at the cafe counter, work on your project at one of the big tables, and maybe sign up for a class!

> GIVE BACK! Do you have yarn and tools you're not going to use? Donate it to the Little Free Library of Yarn at **Cleo's**, and a crafty local will put it to good use.

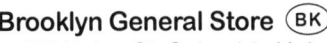

Brooklyn General Store (BK)
◉ *128 Union St, Columbia Heights*
⊕ *brooklyngeneral.com*

We couldn't include Brooklyn General Store in more than one category, but if we could: Fabric, Notions & Trimmings, Craft Supplies, and Sewing Machines would all be appropriate. Where they shine brightest, though, is in their yarn selection. This is the kind of place you can go to with a vague idea in mind, and leave with a bag full of delicious yarn, a pattern to work from, all the tools you need, and even a little extra confidence.

Argyle Yarn Shop (BK)
⊚ *288 Prospect Park W, Windsor Terrace*
⊕ *argyleyarnshop.com*

This quaint neighborhood yarn shop has something for every style of fiber artist, no matter the budget — but Argyle's most unique feature is their own line of hand-dyed yarns! Luminous Brooklyn is the house brand of luscious, all-natural yarns in a full spectrum of colors and weights, skillfully dyed by the Argyle staff in the back of the shop!

Needlepoint

Rita's Needlepoint (MANH)
⊚ *303 E 81st St bet. 2nd and 1st Ave, Upper East Side*
⊕ *ritasneedlepoint.com*

Since 1977, Rita's Needlepoint has been an NYC staple for this particular needlecraft and is very recently under new ownership. Find an immense catalog of hand-painted canvases, as well as all of the threads and tools you'll need. New to needlepoint? No problem! The experts are here to help. Be sure to bring your finished canvas back to the shop for Rita's finishing services so it can be turned into whatever your heart desires.

> CRAFT CLUB! **Rita's Needlepoint** hosts Stitch Nights on Tuesdays, which we're told are always packed with friendly stitchers.

West Village Knit & Needle (MANH)
⊚ *225 W 10th St bet. Hudson and Bleecker, West Village*
⊕ *wvknitandneedle.com*

For the contemporary crafter, West Village Knit & Needle sells needlepoint canvases with the modern New Yorker in mind, like an exclusive cocktail napkins motif featuring the logos of popular NYC speakeasies! With a selection of lovely yarns and knitting tools, it's a one-stop shop for all modalities of needlecraft.

Plastic

Canal Plastics Center (MANH)
⊚ *345 Canal St bet. Wooster and Greene, SoHo*
⊕ *canalplastic.com*

Since 1963, Canal Plastics has been dealing plastic in all its decorative forms for local artists and fabricators. The average person might wonder what they'd need a plastic shop for, but just one glimpse at the acrylic sheet rainbow and piles of luminous crystal clear rods, and you'll be dreaming up things to do with them. For most, it's an excellent resource for fabricating acrylic objects for art, shop or gallery display, small hobby projects, or practical things like use in windows. On offer: same-day cutting services.

Rubber Stamps

Casey Rubber Stamps (MANH)
⊚ *322 E 11th St bet. 2nd and 1st Ave, East Village*
⊕ *caseyrubberstamps.com*

A certifiable small biz legend, owner John Casey has been the city's premier rubber stamp dealer for decades. The compact shop is lined with hundreds of ready-to-buy stamps in antique encyclopedia-esque illustration style, but what most come here for is customization! Choose a pre-designed option from the stack of books, or send in your own design to be made in-house.

> New in 2025: an in-house line of colored ink pads!

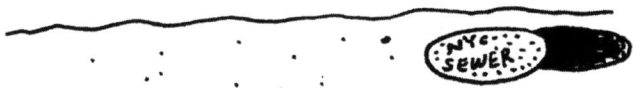

Sculpting Supplies

The Compleat Sculptor (MANH)
◎ *110 W 19th St bet. 7th and 6th Ave, Chelsea*
⊕ *sculpt.com*
With the motto "You Supply the Talent…We Supply the Rest," this place is a no-joke one-stop shop for artists who work in 3D mediums. Chunks of marble, resin materials, a range of chisels, vacuum chambers, sacks of plaster, encaustic mediums, foam sheets, pottery tools, and so much more. It's remarkable that a place selling such large, bulky materials can exist in the middle of Manhattan, but what a godsend it is for the art community.

All-in-One Suppliers (MANH)
◎ *344 W 38th St bet. 9th and 8th Ave, Hell's Kitchen*
⊕ *allinonesuppliers.com*

A retail shop for retail fixtures — a rare sight these days! All-in-One Suppliers sells everything you need for displaying, storing, or selling clothes. This isn't just for garment industry insiders, though. Here are some suggestions for three demographics of customers:

Fashion designers and studio managers shop here for dress forms, organizational tags, garment bags and trunks for safe transport, and heavy-duty racks for rolling around the studio.

Shop owners can find slat wall accessories, merchandising tools, display units, standing racks, jewelry displays, and even things like price sticker guns, tagging guns, dozens of types of mannequins in various poses (including tree pose), custom hang tags, and shopping bags.

Regular people should skip IKEA or the Container Store and come here for apartment-friendly garment racks and bulk hangers in more than 100 styles and materials.

Sewing Machines

Miju Sewing Corp. (MANH)
◎ *306 W 37th St #2 bet. 9th and 8th Ave, Garment District*
A staple of the Garment District, family-owned Miju Sewing Corp. specializes in selling and repairing industrial sewing machines, especially by popular Japanese manufacturer Juki. Aside from great customer service and efficient repairs, Miju also stocks a selection of thread, zippers, and other useful notions.

Sunset Sewing Machine Supplies (BK)
◎ *410 39th St, Sunset Park*
For sewing machine parts and repairs, Hector at Sunset Sewing Machine Supplies has a seriously flawless reputation. From industrial machines to home models, he can service just about anything. The shop is small, but it's also packed with basic notions and tools, and a selection of machines for sale, too.

Also see: **Brooklyn General Store** *(in Knitting, Weaving, Crocheting, pg. 59) for new Bernina machines, and* **Brooke's Appliances** *(in Gadgets & TV, pg. 139) for home sewing machines.*

Spray Paint

All City Legends (MANH)
◎ *2854 Frederick Douglass Blvd*
on the corner of 152nd St, Harlem
⊕ *allcitylegends.com*
A haven for street artists! All City Legends is a true specialist, and deals entirely in tools for graffiti and street art. Since opening in 2020, it's become a hub for uptown artists to buy supplies and share their work. You'll find an unreal selection of quality spray paints in addition to caps and adapters, markers, canvases, sticker blanks, and sprayers.

> **FUN FACT**
>
> **All City Legends** is the first woman-owned graffiti shop in NYC!

Outta Pocket (BK)
⊚ *930 Myrtle Ave, Bed-Stuy*
⊕ *outtapocket.nyc*

This community-focused paint shop specializes in supplies for street art, with a big focus on showing and supporting the work of local street artists. It's a small shop, but it's packed to the brim with a full spectrum of paint and markers, in addition to small press media about the global graffiti art scene.

Trimmings and Notions

M&S Schmalberg (MANH)
⊚ *242 W 36th St 7th Fl bet. 8th Ave and 7th Ave, Garment District*
⊕ *customfabricflowers.com*

The last remaining artificial flower specialist in America, this national treasure is currently on its fourth generation of family ownership. It's a working factory, operated by skilled artisans who use 100-year-old dies to form flowers before fashioning them into something special. Most of what they do here is custom orders and large-scale production, but regular retail customers can shop online or inquire about visiting to hunt the shelves for something specific.

Lauren Trimming (MANH)
⊚ *247 W 37th St bet. 8th Ave and 7th Ave, Garment District*

A favorite of Katie Sue, master glovemaker at Wing + Weft, Lauren Trimming is an especially fabulous go-to for all things dazzling. Find a whole wall filled with packets of sequins in every shape, size, and color. Or an aisle stacked with boxes containing intricate beaded fringes. How about hundreds of decorative patches? Maybe wacky novelty buttons? This tidy shop is full of surprises.

Steinlauf & Stoller (MANH)

◎ *221 W 37th St bet. 8th and 7th Ave, Garment District*
⊕ *steinlaufandstoller.com*

This no-frills shop has been at it since the 1940s and is the place you go when you need really specific needles or technical supplies like interfacing, adjustable strap sliders, eyelets, and boning. The folks running the shop are bonafide experts and are known for their hands-on service and excellent advice.

East Coast Trimming (MANH)

◎ *142 W 38th St bet. 7th and 6th Ave, Garment District*
⊕ *eastcoasttrimming.com*

Collectors rejoice! A first-time visit to East Coast Trimming might bring you to tears. The aisles here are stacked high with ribbons and trims, many of which are deadstock vintage — inherited from the 100+ year-old Hyman Hendler. For those unfamiliar with this New York trim giant: Hyman Hendler, which closed in 2014, was highly regarded as the finest stockist of ribbon in the city. Like so many garment industry suppliers, this Russian immigrant founded business started as a Lower East Side pushcart and grew into a jam-packed storefront. A visit to Hyman Hendler was always a thrill — you never knew what you'd find in the stacks, which were diverse in range: delicious cotton grosgrain, silk moiré ribbon, intricate jacquards, and printed velvets. I vividly remember the day I went to buy a few yards of goldenrod grosgrain and found the store to be closed. Lucky for us, the experts at East Coast Trimming have carried on the legacy by generously sharing this immense inventory with the public.

Pacific Trimming (MANH)

◎ *220 W 38th St bet. 8th and 7th Ave, Garment District*
⊕ *pacifictrimming.com*

Since 1982, Pacific Trimming has been a staple of the Garment District and is one of the less intimidating options for the timid shopper, especially considering the vast array of what's on offer: aisles and aisles of trims, drawers and drawers of buttons, and shelves of dyes, appliqués, and hand-sewing tools. What real industry folk know, however, is that Pacific is the place to go when you need a zipper cut to size on the spot.

Sil Thread (MANH)

◎ *257 W 38th St bet. 8th and 7th Ave, Garment District*
⊕ *silthreadinc.com*

Upon first glance, Sil Thread appears to be a regular well-stocked sewing shop just like all the others in the immediate area, but look closer and you'll discover that, as the name implies, they specialize in thread. Shelves upon shelves of open boxes house industrial-sized spools in every color and type. Just ask for what you're looking for and someone will magically materialize with just the right thing.

Daytona Trimming (MANH)

◎ *251 W 39th St bet. 8th and 7th Ave, Garment District*

A true specialist in decorative trim, I can't even begin to describe everything that's packed into this little shop. Go for the beaded tassels, rows of ricrac, delicious laces, rainbow cords, bags of beads, and strips of sequins. *Wanna know a little secret?* Daytona is known to have a selection of deadstock paper sewing patterns, too.

Trim Fabrics (BK)

◎ *758 Flatbush Ave, Flatbush*

This place first caught my eye because of its wall packed full of unique buttons. That, and rolls of colorful trims hanging from the ceiling, strands of gold cord, and dazzling appliquesdangling above shoppers looking at vibrant African fabrics. The prices are right, the owner is charismatic, and you might just feel like you walked through the Narnia wardrobe of sparkly trim.

Civics Lesson

The Garment District in Midtown has historically been zoned for light manufacturing, helping keep spaces affordable for the local fashion industry, operating in a circular ecosystem. But in 2025, the city threatened to re-zone this tiny pocket of Manhattan for mixed-use, meaning that housing would be allowed for the first time, potentially driving up rents for the existing commercial businesses. With the effective campaigning of a coalition of garment workers, led by glovemaker Katie Sue Nicklos, a negotiation was made, allowing for re-zoning with provisions to protect the existing garment industry businesses. It's a terrific example of civics leaders working together to find a solution that benefits everyone!

Bookshelf

There's no shortage of well-stocked general-interest bookstores in NYC. In fact, more bookstores have opened in the past 5 years than have closed! From the vast range of genres at **McNally Jackson's** five locations to the undeniable charm of **Three Lives Bookstore** and the community spirit of **Astoria Bookstore** — there are wonderful options peppered throughout the city for every type of reader. What's especially unique, however, is the sheer quantity of specialty bookstores in New York City. Here are a few to check out next time you need something out of the ordinary.

Art Books

Mast Books (MANH)
⊚ *72 Ave A nr. E 5th St, Alphabet City*
⊕ *mastbooks.com*
Some of the hardest-to-find, most beautiful art books can be found at this Alphabet City retail magnet, but the selection is wider than that. Covering all areas of creativity and material culture, Mast is where you go when you want to find something to be inspired by. Small press books, periodicals, rare editions — it's all here.

Printed Matter (MANH)
⊚ *231 11th Ave nr. W 26th St, Chelsea*
The world of art publication as we know it now would not exist without the tireless efforts of this nearly 50 year-old non-profit organization. In addition to selling, printing, and distributing the works of artists big and small, Printed Matter manages a bibliographic database of over 42,000 art books for public use, runs a robust roster on online programming, and hosts the popular East Village Zine Fair.

Dashwood Books

◎ *33 Bond St bet. Lafayette and Bowery, NoHo*
⊕ *dashwoodbooks.com*

Look no further for the most thorough and well-edited selection of photography books in New York City. Dashwood specializes in contemporary photography, and is the place for hard-to-find foreign and limited release editions, as well as rare and out-of-print titles. Outside of the city, Dashwood Books is revered as a publisher of contemporary photography books by artists such as Ari Marcopoulos, Jason Nocito, and Nick Sethi.

Secret Riso Club (BK) **NEW!**

◎ *122 Central Ave, Bushwick*
⊕ *secretrisoclub.com*

Dedicated to building a community around independent publishing, Secret Riso Club is a storefront that hosts workshops for Risograph printing (often described as digital screen-printing) in addition to keeping retail hours. From Thursday through Sunday, their sunny storefront is open for all to peruse works on paper by artists near and far. Pick up colorful prints, books, and paper ephemera, and learn more about this popular and decidedly analog form of printmaking.

Bookstores with Bars

Book Club Bar

◎ *197 E 3rd St bet. Ave A and Ave B, Alphabet City*
◎ *380 Troutman St, Bushwick*
⊕ *bookclubbar.com*

Since 2019, this social media darling has been a Manhattan hotspot for alternative nightlife and a place for bookish folks to socialize. With a bar at the front serving coffee, cocktails, and a fully-stocked bookstore in the back, Book Club Bar functions as much as a social club as it does a shop. There are places to sit, people to talk to, and an especially good New York City books selection to browse.

dear friend books (BK)
◎ *343a Tompkins Ave, Bed-Stuy*
⊕ *dearfriendbooks.com*

Beautiful vintage and used books sourced by leaves in Greenpoint, a thoughtful curation of contemporary magazines, a small selection of Japanese stationery, and hard-to-find treasures like artist Niki de Saint Phalle's tarot deck fill this airy space in Bed-Stuy. It's hard to pinpoint who the target audience is here, but I'd best describe it as curious and gentle city dwellers. Have a glass of natural wine while flipping through something inspiring, or sign up for one of the many events, which run the gamut from flower arranging to fishing.

Anaïs (BK)
◎ *196 Bergen St, Boerum Hill*
⊕ *anaisbk.com*

More of a wine bar than a bookstore, Anaïs (by neighborhood restaurateur Henry Rich) serves a gorgeous selection of natural wines surrounded by shelves full of books "inspired by the life and lifestyle of Anaïs Nin." Translation: early feminist erotica and literary fiction by mid-century female authors.

Liz's Book Bar (BK)
◎ *315 Smith St, Carroll Gardens*
⊕ *lizsbookbar.com*

Lovingly named after owner Maura's grandmother, Liz's stocks an impressive 4,000 titles and serves snacks, coffee, and wine at the bar. In a clever way to foster shop regulars, there's a program for monthly subscribers to come by, pick out a new hardcover (at a discount!), and stick around for a drink.

Topos Too (QNS)
◎ *5922 Myrtle Ave, Ridgewood*
⊕ *toposbookstore.com*

Known for its quirky yet reliable selection of mostly used books (and very good coffee), Ridgewood mainstay Topos opened this sister store a few blocks away in 2023 to specialize in the opposite: mostly new books (and very good beer and wine). The two together have created a healthy little bookish ecosystem for an already beloved neighborhood hub.

Children's Books

Books of Wonder (MANH)
◉ *42 W 17th St bet. 6th and 5th Ave, Union Square*
⊕ *booksofwonder.com*

For kids, Books of Wonder is a reading paradise with titles in all genres, ranging from board books to YA. And for adults and parents, it's packed full of nostalgia, with cases of stunning antique editions and a real-life Shop Around the Corner vibe. Each purchase awards the buyer "Books of Wonder Bucks," which are adorably printed and meant to be used by children towards future books.

Books Are Magic (BK)
◉ *225 Smith St, Boerum Hill*
◉ *122 Montague St, Brooklyn Heights*
⊕ *booksaremagic.com*

Originally opened in 2017 to fill a void in the neighborhood, Books Are Magic has quickly grown into a local institution in its quaint corner of Brooklyn. Though both locations are general-interest bookstores, they've become especially well-respected for their children's sections, which are stocked with the best new titles, with a focus on diversity and inclusivity.

Comics and Graphic Novels

Desert Island Comics (BK)
◉ *490 Metropolitan Ave, Williamsburg*
⊕ *desertislandbrooklyn.com*

For the offbeat and indie, there's no better place to shop for comics and zines in NYC than Desert Island. Sure, you can find an ample dose of newly published, classic, and vintage books here, but what regulars know is that the fun lies in the discovery within the enormous collection of underground and independent publications, many of which are by local artists. Desert Island even publishes their own comic tabloid, called Smoke Signal.

Everyone Comics & Collectibles (QNS)
41-26 27th St, Long Island City
⊕ *everyonecomics.com*

A haven for comic book readers, Everyone Comics is the sister shop of the popular Brooklyn shop Anyone Comics — both of which are revered in the community for their friendly service and diverse selection of mainstream comics, indie publications, and the work of local artists. While enthusiasts visit with specific titles in mind, Everyone Comics also offers a friendly entry point for those who are new to the genre. Be sure to check out the roster of events, too!

Anime Castle (QNS)
35-32 Union St, Flushing
⊕ *animecastle.com*

Jam-packed with manga, Anime Castle is a paradise for fans of Japanese graphic novels and the figures, merch, and accoutrements that go with them. Aficionados love Anime Castle for their selection, which includes classic, brand new, and even out-of-print titles. Located near the bustling epicenter of Flushing, Queens, it's a destination worthy of a culture-filled day out.

Silver Age Comics (QNS)
22-55 31st St #208, Ditmars-Steinway
⊕ *silveragecomics.com*

Silver Age Comics is far from your average comic book shop — beginning with the fact that it's attached to the elevated Astoria-Ditmars Blvd subway station. All it takes is a quick double take to realize that this place is something special. Sure, you'll find new titles at Silver Age Comics, but what collectors go for is the immense selection of rare and vintage books, dating all the way back to the 1930s.

Royal Collectibles (QNS)
96-01 Metropolitan Ave, Forest Hills
⊕ *royalcomicsnyc.com*

Royal Collectibles is something of a Forest Hills institution with two storefronts on Metropolitan Ave — one for sports memorabilia and one that's all about comics. While they stock comics from the Silver Age to the Modern Age, alongside figurines and collectible toys, what they're known for is their service. Visit Royal Collectibles to get pieces in your collection graded or for help tracking down something rare.

Cookbooks

Bonnie Slotnick Cookbooks (MANH)
28 E 2nd St bet. Bowery and 2nd Ave, East Village
bonnieslotnickcookbooks.com

Talk about a beloved shop! Since 1997, Bonnie Slotnick has been building and sharing her inventory of out-of-print and antiquarian cookbooks. Located in a cozy space on an East Village side street, it's as much a museum and history lesson as it is a shop, but you're certain to be absolutely charmed into leaving with a new treasure in hand.

Kitchen Arts & Letters (MANH)
1435 Lexington Ave bet. E 94th and 93rd St, Upper East Side
kitchenartsandletters.com

With out-of-print titles alongside the newest books in the genre, Kitchen Arts & Letters has possibly the most comprehensive selection of books on food and drink in the country. Home cooks and chefs alike make the pilgrimage uptown to scoop up a signed copy of the hottest new book, or search for something hard-to-find.

Intersectional Books

New York City is home to one of the most diverse populations in the world, so it's fitting that we've got some amazing bookstores celebrating that intersectionality here, too. From places to find seminal works on queer theory, to exceptional fiction by Black authors, these shops highlight demographics that are often marginalized.

Bluestockings (MANH)

◎ *116 Suffolk St nr. Rivington St, Lower East Side*
⊕ *bluestockings.com*

Employee-owned and run by activists, Bluestockings is a shop that's not afraid of ruffling feathers. It's long been the leader in feminist literature and functions as much as a community space as it does a bookstore. With sections for activism, politics, queer fiction, decolonization, disability justice, and more — this shop has deep roots and a deep understanding of how to provide the resources needed for understanding and fighting against the most oppressive aspects of our modern world.

Sister's Uptown Bookstore (MANH)

◎ *1942 Amsterdam Ave nr. W 156th St, Washington Heights*
⊕ *sistersuptownbookstore.com*

For over 20 years, this family-owned community hub has been sharing the very best of Black literature with their community. This is an inclusive space though, and while the focus is specific, you'll also find a terrific selection of children's books, works in Spanish, and thoughtful selections in other genres.

Yu & Me Books (MANH)

◎ *44 Mulberry St, Chinatown*
⊕ *yuandmebooks.com*

NYC's only bookstore specializing in immigrant stories and AAPI authors, Yu & Me Books is celebrated for shining a light on often overlooked cultural subgenres of fiction. It's been championed by high-profile Asian authors and plays host to great events and signings. There are places to sit, a cafe counter, and good vibes all around. Owner Lucy endeavored to create a bookish home for herself and others, and she's done just that.

Playground (BK)

◎ *1114 Bedford Ave, Bed-Stuy*
⊕ *playgroundcoffeeshop.com*

At the back of a beloved Bed-Stuy coffee shop is a cooler-than-cool book haven that prioritizes BIPOC and LGBTQIA+ voices. Fiction, art books, poetry, and small press delights fill the shelves here. Pick up something special from the tightly curated selection, and then settle in for a glass of wine or a coffee up front.

Cafe con Libros (BK)
◎ *724 Prospect Pl, Crown Heights*
⊕ *cafeconlibrosbk.com*

Walk into this pint-sized space and you'll feel like you're entering the home of someone familiar. It's a bookstore as a bookstore ought to be — cozy, friendly, and full of wonder. Cafe con Libros specializes in intersectional feminist literature and work by, for, and about women and girls around the globe, with particular attention to the African diaspora. Owner Kalima is from the neighborhood herself, and has set up a space that reflects the diversity of Brooklyn.

Mil Mundos Books (BK)
◎ *323 Linden St, Bushwick*
⊕ *milmundosbooks.com*

This volunteer-run co-op is one of the city's only bilingual bookstores! Created by Cuban-American and native New Yorker Maria Herron, the thorough selection of books in both English and Spanish especially celebrates works by Black, Latinx, and Indigenous authors with anti-gentrification values in mind. The space also operates as a community and education center with a full schedule of Spanish classes on offer.

The Lit. Bar (BX)
◎ *131 Alexander Ave, Mott Haven*
⊕ *thelitbar.com*

When Barnes & Noble — the only bookstore in the Bronx — closed in 2016, lifelong resident Noëlle Santos made it her mission to do something about it. So, she opened her very own bookstore, an independent one tailored to her very own community. The Lit. Bar is the bright star of Mott Haven and serves up books of all genres, with a focus on Black and Latinx authors and books by and about Bronx natives.

Magazines

Magazine Cafe (MANH)
◉ *15 W 37th St bet. 6th and 5th Ave, Garment District*
⊕ *magazinecafestore.com*

Right in the middle of the Garment District lies the preeminent resource for international fashion magazines in the city. Sure, they sell other types of periodicals (and lots of knick knacks, stationery, and gifts), but where Magazine Cafe shines is in their reliability when it comes to both niche fashion titles and all of the international Vogues.

Casa Magazines (MANH)
◉ *22 8th Ave on the corner of W 12th St, West Village*

When looking for a very specific magazine in New York City, your first stop should always be Casa Magazines. It recently changed ownership and added a space for art books and a cafe next door, but its original charm and immense selection remain. From today's issue of the New York Post to imports from far reaches of the world — it's all here. It only takes one visit to this place to be reminded of why print media must continue to exist.

Rare Books

Strand Books (MANH)
◉ *828 Broadway nr. E 12th St, Greenwich Village*
◉ *450 Columbus Ave, Upper West Side*
⊕ *strandbooks.com*

Strand Book Store is without question the largest and most well-known independent bookstore in the city, but have you seen the rare book room upstairs? It's the space where most events and talks take place, but it's also open for shopping on the weekend. This cross-genre collection includes 200 year-old tomes, as well as more contemporary first editions, and is a must-visit for collectors, curious book shoppers, and those looking for the perfect gift. While the rare books live at the flagship location, the Strand also has a beloved Central Park outdoor kiosk and additional shop on the Upper West Side.

Argosy Books (MANH)

⊚ *116 E 59th St bet. Park and Lexington Ave, Midtown*
⊕ *argosybooks.com*

Family-owned and occupying a charming 6-floor building in the middle of the shiniest part of Midtown, Argosy Book is the kind of bookstore that will make you feel like you've walked onto a movie set version of an antiquarian bookstore. The service, however, is friendly and inviting, as is the selection of books, which skews 100+ years old, and includes an incredible selection of prints, maps, letters, and documents. For readers of more contemporary works, the basement level is full of newer used books at excellent prices.

Left Bank Books (MANH)

⊚ *41 Perry St bet. W 4th St and Waverly Pl, West Village*
⊕ *leftbankbooksny.com*

The best way to describe Left Bank Books is as the library of the coolest person you know. The selection is eclectic but extraordinarily tight, and the level of trust it imbues in the shopper is a rare treat. From pristine issues of Warhol-era Interview, to niche out-of-print erotica, it's an only-in-New York kind of shop that warrants a visit from any contemporary book collector.

Black Spring Books (BK)

⊚ *672 Driggs Ave, Williamsburg*
⊕ *blackspringbookstore.com*

Located next to Henry Miller's childhood home, Black Spring Books might not have a front window to peer into, but dare to open the discreet metal door and you'll enter a paradise of literature. There's a garden and a cat, but most importantly, there's a wonder-filled selection of used books in a handful of specific genres like poetry, and Russian and French literature, though the owner's affinity for rare and first editions shines through.

Secondhand Books

Sweet Pickle Books (MANH)
◎ *47 Orchard St nr. Hester St, Lower East Side*
⊕ *sweetpicklebooks.com*
Name a used book shop with more personality than Sweet Pickle Books — I dare you. This place is packed to the gills with books that arrive at the shop by way of the private collections of thousands of New Yorkers who seek out owner Leigh, or who come by to swap their books for a jar of her famous pickles. The eclectic offerings include a reliable selection of literary fiction and every other possible genre, no matter how specific.

Aeon Bookstore (MANH)
◎ *151 E Broadway, Lower East Side*
⊕ *aeonbookstore.com*
If you're looking for something esoteric, ultra-specific, or something that'll make you say "I can't believe this exists," Aeon is the place. This discreet lower-level bookstore is merchandised like a too-cool art bookstore, but actually specializes in genres like occult, philosophy, film, poetry, and nature. There is, of course, a healthy selection of art books and high-brow fiction for the less adventurous shopper, too.

Burnt Books (BK)
◎ *It's nomadic! Currently inside* **For The Record**, *Greenpoint*
Back in 2022, Burnt Books got media coverage for the fact that it was hidden in the back of unassuming Greenpoint variety store Green Discount Corp. It's since moved on to set up camp inside For The Record, where the selection is difficult to describe apart from the fact that it's apparently curated by a creative person with delightfully offbeat taste. Find pulp fiction with great covers, guidebooks from the 60s, and outdated science books.

Troubled Sleep (BK)
◎ *129 6th Ave, Park Slope*
Walk into Troubled Sleep and you'll probably have the feeling that this is precisely what a used bookstore ought to be. It's organized, but full. It's tightly edited, but still full of surprises.

You're guaranteed to find something that's been hanging out on your To-Buy list here, but you'll also likely leave with something unexpected. And thankfully, the prices are such that you'll do so without batting an eye.

Unnameable Books (BK)
◉ *615 Vanderbilt Ave, Prospect Heights*
⊕ *unnameablebooks.square.site*
This is the type of used (and new) bookstore that you get lost in. Literally, because it's surprisingly large and full, and figuratively because there's just so much to look through that you'll lose track of time. What locals know, though, and what really makes Unnameable Books stand out is their outstanding poetry selection, which has a dedicated room.

Every Thing Goes Book Cafe (SI)
◉ *208 Bay St, North Shore*
⊕ *etgstores.com*
Not only is Every Thing Goes the only independent bookstore on Staten Island, it's also a staple of the community for its popular cafe and event schedule. Come by to browse the vast selection of used books in every genre and stay for a snack and a show. While you're in the neighborhood, don't miss the sister store (also listed later in this book), which is chock full of vintage clothes and furniture.

Single-genre Books

Pillow-Cat Books (MANH)
◉ *328 E 9th St bet. 2nd and 1st Ave, East Village*
⊕ *pillowcatbooks.com*
Decorated in a spectrum of greens and oozing with style and charm, this bookstore specializes in something unexpected: animal-themed books. From the tried-and-true children's classics to rare titles like Snoopy in Fashion and vintage copies of *The Muppets Take Manhattan*, this little jewel-box is home to hundreds of treasures, and an actual live cat aptly named Pillow.

Village Works (MANH)
◉ *12 St. Marks Pl bet. 3rd and 2nd Ave, East Village*
⊕ *villageworksnyc.com*

These days it's hard to find the punk rock energy that once embodied St. Marks Place, but what remains can be found in Village Works. This no-phones-zone houses hundreds of works about New York City culture, from niche books on subcultures in the art scene, to histories on social movements. It's relatively new still, but has become an essential bookstore for New Yorkers who just love New York. In true St. Marks style, it's open late and also plays host to a variety of events and performance nights.

The Drama Book Shop (MANH)
◉ *266 W 39th St bet. 8th and 7th Ave, Garment District*
⊕ *dramabookshop.com*

For over 100 years, the Drama Book Shop has been New York City's main source for plays, scripts, and any printed material relating to theater. It recently received a gorgeous makeover, with the help of part-owner Lin Manuel Miranda, and now features a lovely cafe with abundant seating.

The Mysterious Bookshop (MANH)
◉ *58 Warren St nr. W Broadway, Tribeca*
⊕ *mysteriousbookshop.com*

What a place this is! The Mysterious Bookshop is the oldest specialist in mystery books in America and sells just that: mystery books, in subgenres such as hardboiled, noir, espionage, crime, psychological suspense, thriller, etc. Overwhelmed by all of the options? The shop also offers eight different themed Crime Club subscriptions, which grants the receiver a signed copy of a special book selection each month.

The Ripped Bodice (BK)
◉ *218 5th Ave, Park Slope*
⊕ *therippedbodice.com*

Sparking a wave of interest in contemporary romance fiction, The Ripped Bodice's Brooklyn outpost of their popular LA shop made a big splash when it opened in 2023. It's owned by sisters with a penchant for destigmatizing the genre and making it accessible to readers of all demographics. It's a colorful, uplifting space that'll make any skeptic fall in love.

Quimby's Bookstore (BK)
◎ *536 Metropolitan Ave, Williamsburg*
⊕ *quimbysnyc.com*
Curiosities abound in this tiny shop! Most of the books for sale are of the esoteric or niche kind, but the immense selection of zines is what most come for. Well, zines and Gracie the cat, who is extremely popular with the locals. Made by artists and thinkers near and far, this home-made form of sharing art and information is celebrated at Quimby's in a rare and special way.

The Locavore Library

A Booklover's Guide to New York by Cleo Le-Tan
An illustrated guideby Cleo, the owner of Pillow-Cat Books.

Walking New York by Keith Taillon
Dive deep into the history of Manhattan by way of twelve different walking routes.

Crafted with Pride by Grown & Sewn
This incredible resource catalogs ever made-in-America clothing brand by state and category!

NYC Storefronts by Joel Holland
Charming drawings of cult-favorite and deep-cut shops alike; also available: Brooklyn Storefronts.

A Town Without Time: Gay Talese's New York
by Gay Talese
Essays on the small wonders of our city, by the famed reporter.

Building

There is no shortage of hardware and building supply stores in New York City because it's a category of goods that people still prefer to buy IRL. A lot of this stuff isn't easily shippable anyway, but I think we can also all agree that for the average Joe it's better to pick out paint swatches, drawer knobs, and countertop surfaces in person. The writer of this book can make no assertions about the "best" in any of these categories, as the truth is that all neighborhood hardware and building supply stores are useful and great. Instead, here are a few specialists that I've noted on my neighborhood walks for being unique or outstanding.

Architectural Salvage

Olde Good Things (MANH)
⊚ *333 West 52nd St, Midtown*
⊕ *ogtstore.com*

Many of us first learned about Olde Good Things by spotting their curious antique-laden flatbed advertising truck all over town. At present, they have two Manhattan shops full of furniture and decor, but mostly architectural salvage. You'll find antique hardware, enormous mirrors, features like old transoms and stained glass, and even pieces saved from some of NYC's most storied hotels. No restoration project is complete without a visit to this treasure trove for accent pieces to add a little old-world character.

Deadstock Hardware

M. Kessler Hardware (MANH)
⊚ *229 Grand St bet. Elizabeth St and Bowery, Chinatown*

What looks like a possibly closed relic from the outside is actually home to a tremendous collection of deadstock kitchen and bath hardware. Instead of shoppable shelves, visitors to M. Kessler Hardware arrive to find owner Allan ready to listen patiently and scale the ladder and find something special. When I visited and asked for lime green drawer pulls, he produced a ceramic option that was exactly as I imagined — and for only $6 each! Visit for quality in-stock hardware that's cheaper and more interesting than typical hardware store offerings; just be prepared to spend a little time while Allan works his magic.

Decorative Hardware

Simon's Hardware and Bath (MANH)
⊚ *421 3rd Ave bet. E 30th and 29th St, Kips Bay*
⊕ *shop.simonsny.com*

No shop in New York City has more options than Simon's Hardware and Bath. Want fish-shaped drawer pulls? You got it! 30 different types of round polished nickel knobs? No problem! What makes this shop great is that they don't cater to one style in particular, and stock brands both large and small. Find walls covered in hardware samples on one side, and a kitchen and bath showroom on the other, making it a one-stop shop.

Glass & Mirror

Bernie's Glass & Mirror (BK)
⊚ *1554 Fulton St, Bed-Stuy*
⊕ *berniesglass.com*

Bernie loves glass, and Brooklyn loves Bernie. This beloved glass and mirror shop does it all: custom-cut glass, mirror installation, window replacements, and even stained glass restoration. The thought of dealing with glass and mirrors seems intimidating and expensive to most folks (myself included), but this neighborhood shop makes replacing a coffee table top or installing a new shower door a breeze.

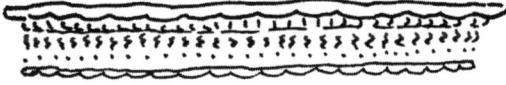

Locksmith

Greenwich Locksmiths (MANH)

◎ 56 7th Ave S, West Village
⊕ greenwichlocksmiths.com

Not your average locksmith! This tiny building wedged into a bustling stretch of 7th Ave S looks like a movie set of 'charming Village locksmith,' but go inside and you'll find an expert at work. You can repair a lock or have any kind of key made, but what's really special is their ability to make rare skeleton keys and, famously, keys attached to vintage NYC subway tokens!

FUN FACT: Greenwich Locksmiths is the smallest free-standing building in NYC at only 125 sq ft!

Lumber

Chinatown Lumber (MANH)

◎ 140 E Broadway bet. Pike and Rutgers St, Lower East Side
⊕ chinatownlumber.com

It's hard to imagine a lumber shop in the heart of one of the busiest downtown areas, especially one as labyrinth-like as Chinatown Lumber. Local builders come here for wood and drywall, but a brave consumer will find that if they follow the pathway to the back, there's a well-stocked hardware store where you can find the usual supplies, alongside harder-to-find things like Formica samples, molding/trim, and glass blocks.

Paint

Epstein's Paint Center (MANH)

◎ 562 W 52nd St bet. 11th and 10th Ave, Hell's Kitchen
⊕ epsteinspaint.com

Since 1895, this family-owned paint shop has been supplying home decorators with quality paint, wall coverings, flooring, and more, but what they're really known for is their selection of scenic design supplies. From faux brick to stenciling tools and extra matte Rosco Scenic Paint, Epstein's is a vital resource for Broadway and television set designers.

Rubber & Foam

Canal Rubber Supply Co. (MANH)
⊚ *329 Canal St nr. Greene St, SoHo*
⊕ *canalrubber.com*

Whether you need insulation foam, anti-fatigue mats, stair treads, new couch cushions, or colorful craft foam for DIY projects, Canal Rubber has you covered. You can even find rolls of colored latex by the yard for making latex clothing! Talk about a true specialist. If it's rubber and has a practical use, this place has it. And for those with no immediate need for creative rubber supplies, there's also especially good merch featuring their iconic yellow sign.

Salvaged Wood

M. Fine Lumber (BK)
⊚ *200 Morgan Ave, East Williamsburg*
⊕ *mfinelumber.com*

For over 85 years, M. Fine Lumber has been recycling lumber from demolition sites to repurpose as flooring and for furniture-making. Ready-to-install flooring and paneling comes in several wood and natural finish types, but this place isn't just for designers and builders. For those who are less inclined to take on a big renovation project, you can get custom shelves made here, too.

The Oldest

Garber Hardware (MANH)
⊚ *207a 9th Ave, Chelsea*
⊚ *710 Greenwich St, West Village*
⊕ *garberhardware.com*

Now in its fifth generation of family ownership, this friendly hardware store stocks everything needed to maintain the old apartments that surround their two locations in the West Village and Chelsea. While the selection is extensive and includes local brands and gardening supplies, most folks keep coming back for the boundless knowledge and stellar customer service. It's

The One With a Café

Mushtari Hardware (MANH)
⊚ *31 W 125th St, Harlem*

This hardware store is keeping a secret. Amidst the usual hardware offerings and enormous selection of plants is a café, pouring great espresso drinks and slinging pastries. Sit down, take a break, soak up the DIY energy, and leave inspired to plant or build something. Mushtari is owned by the same folks who own Jamali Garden in the Flower District, and the beloved Saifee Hardware in the East Village.

The Everything Store

Liberty Panel and Home Center (BK)
⊚ *1009 Liberty Ave, Cypress Hills*
⊕ *libertypanel.com*

Who needs Home Depot when there's Liberty Panel and Home Center! When I first encountered this superstore, I couldn't believe the vastness of the selection, which is well-organized and approachable for all levels of DIY-er. Paint, power tools, lumber, cleaning supplies, plumbing supplies, ladders — you can find it all here, and have it delivered right to your door.

Woodworking Tools

Tools for Working Wood (BK)
⊚ *112 26th St, Sunset Park*
⊕ *toolsforworkingwood.com*

Hidden away on an industrial street in Brooklyn but well-known to woodworkers worldwide, Tools for Working Wood is not your ordinary specialty shop. Housed in a warehouse, the front of the space is set up for browsing while the back is a workshop for making many of the house-brand tools, which are designed with painstaking attention to detail and inspired by historic woodworking tools. Holdfasts, spoonmaker's drawknives, handmade rasps and American-made shellac brushes are for sale here alongside finishing products like traditional milk paint and specialty waxes and oils. It's not all analog here: you'll also find premium German-made power tools by Festool, too. Tools for Working Wood also serves as a clearinghouse for all kinds of technical information about woodworking tools, attracting tool nerds and DIYers in crisis from all over the country.

Glowing Endorsements For Hardware Stores

Frank Hardware (BK)
⊚ *485 Rogers Ave, Prospect Lefferts Gardens*
"Any time I've needed to do some work on my apartment, I've been able to find supplies at Frank, and the owner is so helpful. When I needed copper scrubbers, he ordered them. Twice, when I needed specific screws to fix a lock, he had them. When I discovered ants one hour before I was due to leave for an overseas trip for two months, he had ant bait, and when my father checked a few days later, the problem was gone. It's a small shop but the aisles are full of useful tools, parts, and machines. It was just there last week for a C-clamp. He had it! Why order online or go to the big box store when you can walk a few blocks and get back to your project right away?"
– **Adalena K** in Prospect Lefferts Gardens

Nuthouse Hardware (MANH)
⊚ *202 E 29th St, Nomad*
"You know that moment when you're making your own yarn from raw wool, and you need laundry bags, rubber gloves, and paracord to wash it and make a DIY rooftop clothesline? And then later when you're dyeing the yarn you need a 10-gallon enamel pot? And also it's 10pm because this project has taken over your life? Nuthouse has all of that, and they're open 24/7!"
– **Macy G** in Nomad

Clothing

Quiet the naysayers! New York City is still the fashion capital of America and is home to an incredible diversity of imaginative boutiques and local designers. While it's not quite like it was in the previous century, it's still possible to find garments made right here in the city — if you know where to find them! In this section, you'll find shops that are marked with a **Made in NYC** label if they make all or some of their garments locally.

Costumes

Gothic Renaissance (MANH)
◎ *110 4th Ave bet. E 12th and 11th St, East Village*
⊕ *gothren.com*
Since 1999, this wildly fun shop has been outfitting rave-goers, renfaire revelers, masquerade attendees, and hot goths. Corsets, spikes, latex, and fishnets abound in this one-stop shop for participants in fringe subcultures and niche party scenes.

Halloween Adventure Shop (MANH)
◎ *104 4th Ave bet. E 12th and 11th St, East Village*
⊕ *nychalloweenadventure.com*
The line snakes out the door every day of the week before Halloween at the Largest Halloween Shop in NYC, but this place is open year-round and is the place to go for easy costumes for all ages. While the options are mostly of your standard packaged variety, the accessory and prop selection is extensive and worth visiting for.

Abracadabra (MANH)
◎ *19 W 21st St bet. 6th and 5th Ave, Flatiron*
⊕ *abracadabranyc.com*
A visit to Abracadabra is sure to make you feel like you stumbled upon the costume department of an old theater. This is where

you go when you want something higher-end, which can be either rented or purchased. Pick out a costume and then be sure to check out the accessories, wigs, and makeup — all of which are nice enough to make you want to play dress-up every day. It doesn't stop there, though, because Abracadra's selection also extends to magic supplies, horror props, and professional prosthetics.

Screaming Mimi's (MANH)
◎ *240 W 14th St bet. 7th and 8th Ave, West Village*
⊕ *screamingmimis.com*

Screaming Mimi's isn't your average vintage shop. Racks are organized by decade and category and tend to skew more towards costuming than regular wear. In fact, the shop made headlines about 10 years ago for acquiring an enormous collection of costumes when the New York City Opera closed its doors. Especially for looks from the '60s–'80s, Screaming Mimi's is a sure bet for something wild and specific, but for the creative vintage shopper, it's also a paradise of accessories and statement pieces. Their full inventory covers the '20s through Y2K and includes curated '20s and '30s replica pieces.

Purim Megastore (BK)
◎ *1488 Coney Island Ave, Midwood*

Along busy Coney Island Ave in an Orthodox area of Brooklyn lies the most specific costume shop in the city. Purim Megastore, as you might guess, specializes in costumes and accessories for the Jewish holiday of Purim, which happens in March. In addition to costumes specific to Jewish culture, you'll find wholesome and fun options for the whole family (no gore or horror here!).

Clothes for Everybody

These are shops that sell both menswear and womenswear equally, gender-neutral clothes, and maybe a few other categories. The point is, they can't be pigeonholed into a specific category — they're just shops that have something special to offer everyone.

Eckhaus Latta (MANH)

⊚ *75 E Broadway #206, under the Manh. Bridge, Chinatown*
⊕ *world.eckhauslatta.com*

A little over a decade old, this bi-coastal brand is the brainchild of two friends who've cultivated a distinctly wearable yet gender non-conforming, seasonless, trend-skewing brand that's beloved by the corner of the fashion set that oozes cool without the pretense of cool. It's art as clothes that you can actually wear in your everyday life. Does any of this make sense? Just go try on the clothes and you'll understand.

Trash & Vaudeville (MANH)

⊚ *96 E 7th St bet. 1st Ave and Ave A, East Village*
⊕ *trashandvaudeville.com*

Outfitting East Village punks since 1975, Trash & Vaudeville is a bonafide New York City cultural landmark. Studs, skulls, straps, leather, and stripes abound in this electric pink storefront. Don't miss the excellent footwear selection, which includes lug sole creepers, animal-print heels, and boots heavy with hardware.

Assembly New York (MANH)

⊚ *170 Ludlow St bet. Houston and Stanton St, Lower East Side*
⊕ *assemblynewyork.com*

More than any other multi-brand boutique, Assembly New York knows how to take the alternative and ultramodern and make it accessible for the fashion-curious. With both men's and women's sections, and a selection of accessories and jewelry, you can expect international brands like Roberto Collina and Miista, alongside local ones like Sandy Liang and Agme

Bungee Space (MANH)

⊚ *13 Stanton St bet. Bowery and Chrystie St, Lower East Side*
⊕ *3ssstudios.com*

This shop could easily fit into at least four categories, but we've put it here because, although this interdisciplinary space functions as an art space, indie art book specialist, and lifestyle store, their selection of small-brand clothing, and curated designer vintage is something to behold. Unisex, avant garde, and zero-waste brands hang alongside art scene favorites like Paloma

Wool and Henrik Vibskov.

Colorant (MANH)

⊚ *9 Spring Street, bet. Elizabeth St and Bowery, Nolita*
⊕ *thisiscolorant.com*

With shops in Nolita and upstate in Beacon, Colorant makes clothes for men and women that are dyed entirely with natural dyes. Sure, everything is natural fiber and botanically colored, but this brand isn't at all crunchy. Contemporary silhouettes and chic styling make this brand a rare treat for the sophisticated eco-shopper.

Schott (MANH)

⊚ *32 Howard St bet. Broadway and Crosby St, Nolita*
⊕ *schottnyc.com*

Since 2013, the Schott family has been a leader in distinctly American jacket styles. In fact, their leather and shearling G-1 bomber jacket and wool naval peacoats were both commissioned by the US military at the start of WWII, and are styles that are still made and sold today! These days, they're most known for their heavy, heirloom-quality Perfecto motorcycle jacket, but there's a classic style for everyone to be found here, and bonus: it's most likely manufactured in nearby Union, NJ!

180 the Store (MANH)

⊚ *180 Duane St bet. Greenwich & Hudson St, Tribeca*
⊕ *180thestore.com*

A shop well-suited for the clientele one might find in Tribeca (or Amagansett, where their second location is), this place sells fancy clothes for casual people. Nordic-style knits, French linen, and niche Japanese designers for men and women fill the racks at 180 the Store, which also regularly assembles beautiful displays of pottery and glassware from an international roster of artists.

VERS :: Clothing for People (BK)
◎ *1329 Willoughby Ave, Bushwick*
⊕ *versbk.nyc*

A must-visit for any Bushwick denizen or neighborhood tourist, VERS is home to a community of over 30 local designers with a focus on sustainability and inclusivity. Playing host to workshops, performances, drop parties, and clothing swaps, VERS is a perfect distillation of the subversive creativity that one expects to find in one of the city's wackiest and wildest neighborhoods. The vibe skews avant garde, delightfully queer, and undeniably youthful, but everyone is welcome in this paradise of play.

Screenprinting & Embroidery

Screenprinted t-shirts and custom embroidered goods are things you should never buy online because our city is full of shops that can make them faster, and probably with lower minimums. I'm no expert on this topic, though, so use the directory on thelocavore.com to find a great local print shop near you. Here's my local spot, and a couple of notable specialists

T-Shirt City (MANH)
◎ *68 Henry St, Under the Manhattan Bridge, Chinatown*
⊕ *tshirtcity.nyc*

Since 1989, T-Shirt City (formerly known as T-Shirt Express) has been supplying the businesses of the Lower East Side and Chinatown with all of their custom t-shirts, hats, and more. It's a family affair at this neighborhood print shop, which is also responsible for doing our merch for The Locavore Guide.

Abbode (MANH)
◎ *252 Elizabeth St nr. E Houston, Nolita*
⊕ *shopabbode.com*

Every generation has its own unique type of monogram girl. She's a little preppy, she's stylish and organized, and in this generation, she shops at Abbode for faux-croc makeup cases for her vacation to Europe, party favors for her bachelorette party, and personalized cocktail napkins for her best friend's housewarming. Using the latest technology in machine embroidery, you can choose from a menu of options in-store or order online.

General Wear Inc. (BK)
◎ *37 Greenpoint Ave #415, Greenpoint*
⊕ *generalwearinc.com*

I'd be remiss to not mention General Wear Inc as the city's premier custom embroidery specialist. Enlist these guys for extraordinarily precise machine embroidery, raised embroidery, and even appliqué. Their attention to detail and exceptional sourcing is what really sets them apart. Most of the garment vendors they work with are independent brands, themselves!

Stitches (QNS)
◎ *150-32 12th Rd, Whitestone*
⊕ *stitchesny.com*

Psst... did you know that this is where the Mets, Yankees, and Islanders all have their official team uniforms made?

YES, they're local! And you can buy jerseys here, too! New Yorkers send their jerseys to Stitches to have names embroidered on the back, or have professional-quality customs made for their own events and teams.

Parkview Sports Center (BX)
◎ *5973 Broadway, Kingsbridge*

For jerseys, team shirts, and sports merch, look no further than Parkview Sports Center. These guys are real experts in all things sports uniforms and also have a notable selection of retro styles on offer. In addition to screenprinting and embroidery services, they're also well-stocked with sporting equipment. A one-stop shop for team sports, I'd say!

Specialty Mending

Eva Joan (MANH)
⊚ *28 Jane St nr. 8th Ave, West Village*
⊕ *evajoanrepair.info*

Repair, repurpose, reinvent. Eva Joan isn't just a tailoring shop, it's a creative studio where any garment is worth reimagining. Visit Bjørn and Emma for imaginative alterations, to revive something forgotten, or for statement patches and mending. This is where you go to reclaim a garment as something entirely yours, and to celebrate the stories our clothes tell about us.

Streetwear

As a category of clothing that defines the inimitable aesthetic of New York City, streetwear probably occupies more space in our collective wardrobe than any other category. We could write a whole guidebook on the subject, but for now, here are four exceptional shops selling streetwear made by New Yorkers for New Yorkers.

BEDSTUYFLY (BK)
⊚ *287 Ralph Ave, Bed-Stuy*
⊕ *bedstuyfly.com*

Since 2009, BEDSTUYFLY has been serving up streetwear that's all about Brooklyn. Find creative designs by local artists, neighborhood-specific references, and even styles for children here! Spike Lee t-shirts, hats embroidered with "We Need More Black Billionaires," and creative branded merch line the shelves of this shop.

FYL NYC (BK)
⊚ *1612 Mermaid Ave, Coney Island*
⊕ *fyl.nyc*

Local rapper Gorilla Nems is affectionately referred to as The Mayor of Coney Island, but did you know that he also has a streetwear line? His brand FYL NYC occupies this Mermaid Ave storefront, which is clad with mural work by local artist Snoeman and also offers screenprinting services. The pieces for sale here feature a combination of Gorilla Nems iconography mashed up with Coney Island graphics and playful interventions with the logos for the Knicks and the Mets.

Alizé Clothing NY (QNS)
⊚ *1927 Mott Ave, Far Rockaway*

This shop first caught my eye because of its colorful A train shirts on the window mannequins. Alizé stocks a well-rounded assortment of men's and women's streetwear in this large storefront, but locals know that they also have their own neighborhood-specific line that includes A train references, Far Rockaway merch, and even Mott Ave-specific designs.

Bronx Native (BX)
⊚ *127 Lincoln Ave, Mott Haven*
⊕ *bronxnativeshop.com*

As much a nostalgic museum of Bronx culture as it is a shop, Bronx Native is jam-packed with ephemera and art alongside its ever-changing line of borough-specific clothing and accessories, with nods to bodega culture, the Dominican community, and the 6 train. Founder Amaurys Grullon puts a huge emphasis on social impact and community support by hosting events, participating in local politics, and shining a light on young local creatives.

Workwear

Dave's (MANH)
⊚ *581 6th Ave bet. W 17th and 16th St, Chelsea*
⊕ *davesnewyork.com*

Currently managed by its second and third generation of owners, Dave's is a bona fide Manhattan wardrobe staple, and possibly the most reliable place to shop for the largest selection of classics from Levi's, Carhartt, and Dickies. This type of shop can best be described as workwear, but it's also Americana — tried-and-true utilitarian brands for feeling comfortable and getting things done. But don't sleep on the collabs, like Dave's exclusive t-shirts designed by local tattoo artist Henbo Henning.

Left Field (MANH) (QNS) MADE IN NYC

◎ *280 Mott St, Nolita*
◎ *657 Woodward Ave, Ridgewood*
⊕ *leftfieldnyc.com*

Drawing inspiration from American workwear of the previous century, Left Field was born in Brooklyn in 1998 and has been cutting and sewing vintage Americana-inspired garments in the US ever since. Japanese selvedge denim that's made to last, slubby cotton Wakayama t-shirts, Western-style hand-loomed work shirts, and wool sweaters knit down the street in Ridgewood round out the full range of denim and workwear — oh, and don't sleep on the gorgeous tweed coats. They're sewn in our very own Garment District!

FUN FACT!

Did you know? Until the 1990s, Ridgewood, Queens, was known for its incredible density of knitting factories, which, at its peak, accounted for 25% of the sweaters sold in America!

Cato's Army & Navy (BK)

◎ *106a Nassau Ave, Greenpoint*
⊕ *catosarmynavy.blogspot.com*

Beloved by locals for quality, Cato's has been family-owned since 1975. This place is old-school and sells utilitarian workwear styles for men, women, and children. Alongside brands like Schott, Pendleton, and Carhartt, they also sell Converse sneakers, Manhattan Portage bags, and classic Stanley camping gear.

Frankel's (BK)

◎ *3924 3rd Ave, Sunset Park*
⊕ *frankelsny.com*

Established in 1890, Frankel's remains an incredible source for work boots by brands including but certainly not limited to Red Wing. Sure, you'll find classic workwear with a selection of safety gear and accessories, but what most loyal regulars come for is the stacks and stacks of boots, and the guarantee that the perfect pair can be found at Frankel's.

A Wardrobe Everything Shop

Manhattan Wardrobe Supply (MANH)
⊚ *245 W 29th St, 8th Fl bet. 8th and 7th Ave, Chelsea*
⊕ *wardrobesupplies.com*

I've said it on video many times, and I'll say it again: every New Yorker needs to know about Manhattan Wardrobe Supply. It's a vital resource for folks in the garment industry, professional makeup artists, costume designers, and stylists, but despite being hidden on the 8th floor of a midtown building, it's also accessible for us regular people. For anyone interested in getting more wear out of their beloved garments and footwear, especially, Manhattan Wardrobe Supply is your one-stop shop for over-dying something old, fixing up your loafers, or getting the underthings you need to actually wear that top you've been afraid of. Need advice? The people who work here are extraordinarily helpful.

Owners Tommy and Cheryl dreamed up this paradise of supplies in the back of a wardrobe truck while working on You've Got Mail, and officially opened in 1998. A list of everything one can find at Manhattan Wardrobe Supply would take up an entire book on its own, but here's an abbreviated list of things that might be especially useful to the audience of this guidebook:

- Seamless underwear
- Sticky undergarments
- Leather cleaner
- Fabric dye
- Fabric paint
- Fake facial hair
- Industrial steamers
- Fake blood
- Costume makeup
- Containers for organizing
- Clothing racks
- Shoe laces
- Colored hang tags
- Very specific fabric glues
- Sewing kits
- Mending supplies
- Wig supplies
- Pads and gels for shoes

Menswear

Disclaimer: this book is written by a woman who, despite not regularly shopping at men's stores, has consulted scores of dudes with superb sartorial opinions and scoped out shops all over town through the lens of her generally good sense of style and keen eye for quality. With these things in mind, here is a diverse range of menswear shops with particularly distinctive points of view.

Cool Menswear

Nepenthes New York (MANH)
◉ *307 W 38th St bet. 9th and 8th Ave, Hell's Kitchen*
⊕ *nepenthesny.com*

Where else can you find heritage British footwear alongside avant garde fishing vests and plastic-packaged American-made tube socks? Oh, and you can buy running shoes here, too. Much of what's for sale is the shop's own brands, including the popular Engineered Garments, which also makes slightly androgynous womenswear. This Japanese-founded shop has been pushing boundaries of subversive cool since 1988 and remains at the forefront of the Japanese Americana aesthetic. Nothing is quite like Nepenthes.

Colbo (MANH) MADE IN NYC
◉ *51 Orchard St bet. Grand and Hester St, Lower East Side*
⊕ *colbo.nyc*

Sidle up to this downtown menswear mainstay to enjoy a very good coffee, listen to whatever's spinning on the turntable, and shop a selection of mostly menswear in a gentle color palette and effortlessly cool styles, including the store's own made-in-NYC brand. Though it fits right in on fashion's favorite street, Colbo sells an international style that you'd find just as easily in Paris or Tokyo.

C'H'C'M (MANH)

⊚ *2 Bond St bet. Broadway and Lafayette, NoHo*
⊕ *chcmshop.com*

This is a shop for creative, worldly men who want those they encounter to wonder, "Where'd he get that?" but not actually ask because he seems too cool to share his secret. With perhaps the most diverse range of niche European and Japanese menswear designers in the city, C'H'C'M caters to an ageless crowd — look impossibly put-together at age 25, or 75.

Cueva (MANH) (BK)

⊚ *86 Christopher St, West Village*
⊚ *49 Franklin St, Greenport*
⊕ *cuevashop.com*

Menswear without creative limits is the name of the game at Cueva, a multi-brand shop that sells small labels from all over the world, with a focus on quality and individuality. There's no one style you'll find here, just a whole bunch of clothes that feel simultaneously original and highly wearable.

Kartik Research (MANH) **NEW!**

⊚ *61 Orchard St bet. Grand and Hester St, Lower East Side*
⊕ *kartikresearch.com*

New on the block from New Delhi, India, Kartik Research is a brand by designer Kartik Kumra, who makes clothes for people who want to tell a story through their style. Each piece utilizes a traditional Indian technique, whether it's block printings, kantha stitching, or intricate beaded embroidery. While the garments are culturally-informed and made traditionally, the cuts and styles are decidedly current and the experience in the store is a modern retail delight.

SEED Brklyn (BK)

⊚ *1217 Bedford Ave, Bed-Stuy*
⊕ *shop.seedbrklyn.com*

More accurately, SEED Brklyn is a concept store. This lime green creative hub is home to a leafy cafe, a technology-driven art gallery, and an epic selection of experimental fashion, shoes in every category, art books, and even collectible toys. With brands like Martine Rose, Ambush, and Saucony, you can expect to find streetwear with a serious fashion edge in this playhouse of interdisciplinary Brooklyn culture.

Ven. Space (BK) **NEW!**
369 Court St, Carroll Gardens
ven.space

People have been talking about Ven. Space since the minute it opened its doors in fall '24. In an unassuming Brooklyn brownstone, this serene shop features muted tones and a refreshing approachability — rare for a shop with a designer roster as stacked as what's on offer here. Find a slew of contemporary designers in the current zeitgeist, exciting brands you've never heard of, and deep cut mainstays — an amalgamation of carefully selected pieces that are guided by a point of view that's at once utilitarian and edgy. There's no web shop to peruse, so go see for yourself and be ready to experience the thrill of discovery.

fig. (BK)
121 7th Ave, Park Slope
shopfigbrooklyn.com

Part of local designer Christine Alcalay's mini fashion empire, fig. is where stylish Brooklyn dads shop. They want to run with the pack, but still feel like they've got their own style. There's something slightly British about the selection here, too, with lovely tweed jackets and chore coats in the winter.

Local Menswear Designers

Steven Alan (MANH) **MADE IN NYC** **NEW!**
511 W 20th St, Chelsea
stevenalan.com

Making a grand return to brick-and-mortar retail in late 2024, Steven Alan's signature twist on American style has been embraced by both old fans and a new generation. Since the '90s, Steven Alan has been dressing the downtown set in striped shirting, just-right slouchy trousers, and tailored knitwear that's the fashion equivalent of Ralph Lauren's cool, creative cousin. His Chelsea storefront is home to his eponymous line, as well as a stunning collection of jewelry and watches — vintage and new — and other trinkets that fit perfectly into the Steven Alan universe.

Harlem Haberdashery (MANH)
◉ *245 Malcolm X Blvd bet. W 123rd and 122nd St, Harlem*
⊕ *harlemhaberdashery.com*

The Harlem fashion scene isn't complete without Harlem Haberdashery. This shop sells its own brand of menswear, suits, a line of spirits, eyewear, and neighborhood-focused streetwear, and hosts an annual gala to benefit local organization Take Care of Harlem. Everything found here features the brand's regal crest, rich hues, and a nod to the neighborhood's streetwear sensibility.

The Cast (MANH) **MADE IN NYC**
◉ *72 Orchard St bet. Broome and Grand St, Lower East Side*
⊕ *thecast.com*

Since 2004, owner and designer Chuck Bones has been supplying rebels near and far with heirloom quality leather jackets that are made entirely in NYC. While you can stop by the LES store to try on readymade models in a rainbow of hides, you can also order a completely customized piece. Luxury leather, totally local, without the big designer mark-up. There's no better place to get dressed like a Ramone.

Knickerbocker (MANH)
◉ *375 Canal St nr. Wooster St, SoHo*
⊕ *knickerbocker.nyc*

Inspired by classic American sportswear, Knickerbocker is a brand for the youthful New York dude who appreciates looking put together but doesn't take himself too seriously. Slightly baggy pleated twill pants, boxy striped oxfords, and fly-fishing inspired khaki jackets hang on racks amid pale wood tables merchandised with gorgeous art books and stacks of neutral knits. Think early Ralph Lauren but with a slight aesthetic wink to 1950s baseball.

F.E. Castleberry (MANH)

◎ *246 W Broadway bet. Beach and N Moore St, Tribeca*
⊕ *fecastleberry.com*

Lavish and unapologetically Wes Anderson-esque, F.E. Castleberry is the designer for the downtown maximalist who still actually wears a proper suit. His pink atelier feels like the library of a well-read eccentric and the items sold there — suiting aside — including striped slippers, knits with artist references printed on them, and hand-painted monogrammed leather goods.

Linder Sport (MANH) NEW!

◎ *13 Christopher Street, West Village*
⊕ *lindersport.com*

Classic, effortlessly cool wardrobe staples by an independent brand with a store in the West Village — can you even believe it? Linder Sport specializes in well-tailored basics like solid tanks and tees, striped rugby shirts, everyday chinos, and great knitwear, all with a fresh, youthful flair. Oh, and the prices? A crewneck T-shirt costs $35 and jeans are under $100.

The Brooklyn Circus (MANH) (BK)

◎ *361 Canal St, SoHo*
◎ *150 Nevins St, Boerum Hill*
⊕ *thebkcircus.com*

This local brand has a vintage collegiate aesthetic with a Brooklyn streetwear spin. Notably, their hallmark is a line of weighty varsity jackets, with each edition inspired by a different figure or event in Black history. For a more subtle addition to your outerwear, their take on a chore coat is equally lovely.

Grown and Sewn (BK)

◎ *145 Columbia St, Brooklyn Heights*
⊕ *grownandsewn.com*

It's simple: clothes designed in Brooklyn, made in America from quality cotton. Pants, shirts, and a few accessories. Wham, bam, that's it! Good, well-made clothes for the man who cares where his stuff comes from and doesn't want any fuss. If only it was always this straightforward!

Corridor (MANH) (BK)
⊚ *245 Elizabeth St, Nolita*
⊚ *322 Bleecker St, West Village*
⊚ *165 Dekalb Ave, Fort Greene*
⊚ *145 Wythe Ave, Williamsburg*
⊕ *corridornyc.com*

Founded over a decade ago with the simple intent to make great shirts, Corridor has grown into the go-to brand for the brand of city guy who dabbles in exploratory fashion and is mostly just looking for a little fun. Garments and textiles are designed in-house and produced ethically by weaving, knitting, and sewing specialists. Patterned notch-collar shirts paired with '90s wash jeans and crocheted cardigans — a leisure uniform for the modern man.

Old-School Menswear

Rothman's (MANH)
⊚ *222 Park Ave S, corner of E 18th St, Flatiron*
⊕ *rothmansny.com*

They don't make independent shops like this one anymore. Hitting all categories of one's wardrobe, Rothman's sells sportswear, suiting, shoes, and basics all in one shop. For a dude with no idea where to start, this is the place. Expect to find popular brands like Billy Reid, Marine Layer, and Citizens of Humanity.

Vinny's Men Store (BK)
⊚ *307 Utica Ave, Crown Heights*

A Google review describes Vinny's as *'the place to go to get your "Grown Man" on,'* which is absolutely accurate. But grown men still have fun, as evidenced by the selection of shirting in wild patterns for sale at Vinny's. Unique sweaters and more casual clothes fill in the gaps between the extensive selection of suiting and shirts. Old-school but a little spicy, Vinny's is a Brooklyn gem.

104 | CLOTHING

The New Fashion District

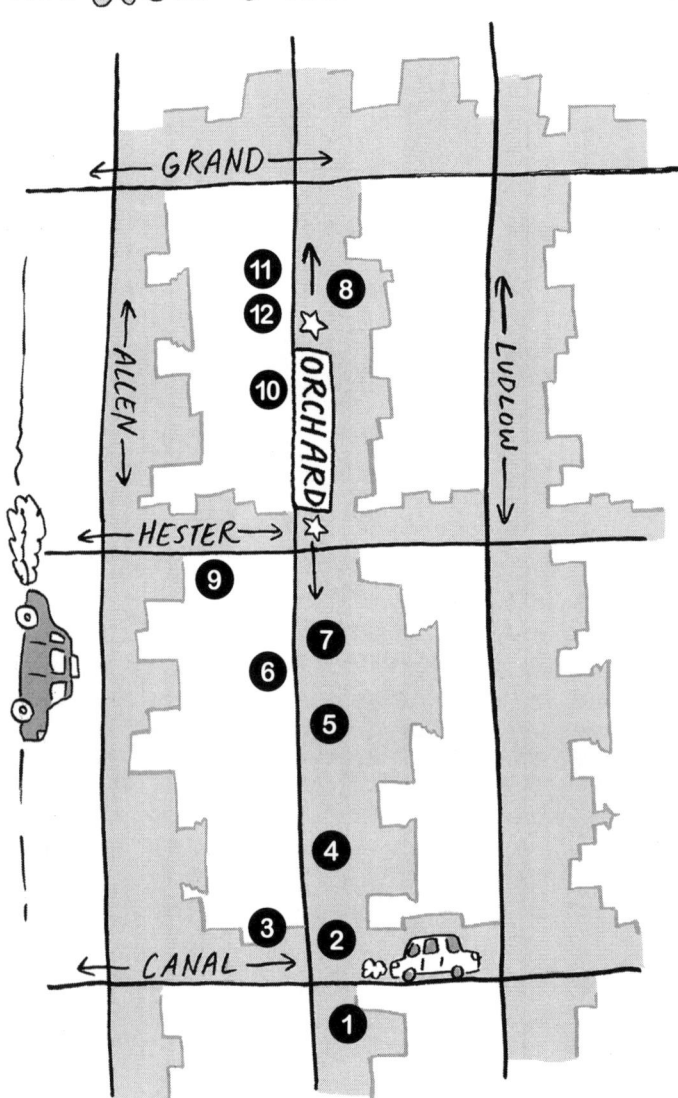

Over the past eight years, the stretch of Orchard Street between Canal Street and Grand Street has quickly become the beating heart of fresh, new local fashion. It started with the arrival of **Bode** in 2019, with **Sandy Liang** following shortly after in 2020 — but the catalyst was surely the 2014 opening of contemporary home goods store **Coming Soon**. Since the pandemic boom of "Dimes Square," there appears to be no stopping the popularity of this tiny sliver of this Lower East Side/Chinatown border. It's been decades since NYC has seen such a densely populated fashion hotbed, with almost every storefront occupied with a local business, most of which are exciting multi-brand boutiques featuring emerging brands, flagship stores of hot young designers, and scores of vintage dealers.

1. **Collina Strada**, avant garde womenswear
2. **Coming Soon**, maximalist home goods
3. **Fugazi,** ultra contemporary streetwear
4. **TUMBAO**, Latin American designers
5. **Sandy Liang**, playful womenswear
6. **Unisecon**, Chinese heritage-inspired
7. **Desert Vintage**, luxe archival vintage
8. **Pêche**, affordable cool girl style
9. **Bode**, vintage-inspired menswear
10. **Colbo**, neutral, minimalist menswear
11. **Wythe**, classic Americana menswear
12. **Kartik Research**, menswear from India

WANT MORE?

Venture north above Grand, or east towards Essex Street for dozens more. On a whole, the Lower East Side has more local fashion than any neighborhood in NYC!

W.M. Robins (BK)
⊚ *1112 Nostrand Ave, Prospect Lefferts Gardens*
⊕ *wm-robins.com*

For the dapper gentleman, W.M. Robins sells suiting, as well as a lovely selection of men's hats, casual linen pieces, polos, and knitwear for all seasons. This family-owned shop is tightly edited, but sells everything that a classic, well-dressed man might need for his wardrobe.

Suiting

Watson Ellis (MANH)
⊚ *80 8th Ave #1010, entrance on E 14th St, Chelsea*
⊕ *watsonellis.com*

Men's suits, women's suits, non-binary suits — Watson Ellis is a haven for folks who don't fit into a box, and also want something out-of-the-box. Creative tailoring and an endless selection of fabric options (including great vegan options!) make for custom suits that are wildly different in approach to more traditional studios.

New Era Factory Outlet (MANH)
⊚ *63 Orchard St bet. Grand and Hester St, Lower East Side*
⊕ *newdresssuits.com*

The last remaining on what was once a block full of old-school menswear dealers, New Era Factory Outlet is an incredible resource for well-priced suiting and tuxedos! Need a tux in a pinch? This is the place! It's a small shop with a vast inventory of suits and accessories of all sorts — including some truly wild colors. I'd go so far as saying that New Era Factory Outlet has the best inventory of ready-to-wear suiting in the whole city!

J. Mueser (MANH)
⊚ *19 Christopher St bet. Waverly Pl and Greenwich Ave, West Village*
⊕ *jmueser.com*

For classic suits and tailored ready-to-wear, J. Mueser has been a downtown favorite since 2008. With a penchant for fabulous fabrics and classic silhouettes, they offer an accessible, modern take on traditional tailoring. Visit to shop chic city-friendly jackets and impeccable shirting, or make an appointment for something bespoke. Tip: J. Mueser also hosts Clementina, a local brand offering classically tailored suits for women!

Robinson Brooklyn (BK)
◉ *209 Wythe Ave Unit 106, Williamsburg*
⊕ *robinsonbrooklyn.com*

Since 1998, founder Craig Robinson has been following the traditions of haberdashery, but with his own modern take on tailoring. There's no limit on customization here, though Craig's signature style has a dash of eccentric, British flair. While the specialty here is totally bespoke suits, there are off-the-rack options as well.

Esquire Menswear (QNS)
◉ *30-51 Steinway St, Astoria*
⊕ *esquirenyc.com*

Family-owned and decidedly old-school, Esquire Menswear has been a Queens staple for over 40 years due to its quality menswear and European suiting. Owner Frank takes great pride in expert tailoring and, while formalwear is the name of the game at Esquire (tuxedos, too!), they also sell shoes and have a mezzanine full of dapper sportswear. Come here for an updated suit and leave with something to wear to the country club too.

Womenswear

Lingerie & Loungewear

Azaleas (MANH)
◉ *140 2nd Ave bet. E 9th St and St. Marks Pl, East Village*
⊕ *azaleasnyc.com*

Finding a decent selection of swimwear in the city is a harrowing task, but Azaleas is a rare type of shop where you can find indie brand bikinis sold by lingerie experts who know a thing or two about quality and fit. Find lingerie brands like Clo and Fleur du

Mal, as well as swimwear by brands like Acacia and Araks. It's a playful assortment that strikes the perfect balance of sexy, but undeniably cool, and actually wearable.

Only Hearts (MANH) MADE IN NYC
- 230 Mott St, Nolita
- 386 Columbus Ave #1, Upper West Side
- onlyhearts.com

Lacy bralettes, cheeky loungewear, and organic cotton panties fill these shops. By the youthfulness and carefree vibe of the brand, you'd never guess that it's been around since 1978. Amongst the many things that keep Only Hearts at the forefront of the local lingerie biz is the fact that everything is made right here in NYC. From base layer camisoles to sexy mesh bodysuits and even underwire bras that cost less than $100, this brand is proof that it's possible, and sustainable, to keep things local.

Orchard Corset (MANH)
- 157 Orchard St bet. Stanton and Rivington St, Lower East Side

At this old-school lingerie shop, owner Peggy is a master at bra fitting, attracting customers from all over the city who — by word of mouth — know that she's got a catalog of inventory hidden in boxes at her shop. But, as the name suggests, Orchard Corset does indeed sell gorgeous authentic corsets made of satin and structured with proper boning. Swing by for a fitting and leave with something that feels like it was made just for you.

Elsi Intimate (MANH)
- 1214 St. Nicholas Ave nr. W 171st St, Washington Heights
- elsiintimate.com

Elsi is a tried and true staple for Colombian shapewear, affordable lingerie, and loungewear in Washington Heights, and sells everything you'd need to outfit your intimates drawer. The store is packed floor-to-ceiling with bras in inclusive sizing and a rainbow of colors, hardcore shapewear, and especially fun PJs. A couple of years ago, I was walking by when a pair of slinky leopard print lounge pants caught my eye — they cost less than $10 and are still my very favorite house pants.

Iris Lingerie (BK)

⊚ *323 Atlantic Ave, Boerum Hill*
⊕ *irislingeriebrooklyn.com*

When you want an old-school bra fitting experience, you go to Iris Lingerie in Boerum Hill. It's a no-nonsense place — you don't really come here to browse, you come here to trust Iris to know what you need. She's a real expert, so let her take the lead and find you something that *actually* fits.

The Rack Shack (BK)

⊚ *17 Thames St, East Williamsburg*
⊕ *therackshackbk.com*

Owner Laura Henny did an astonishingly difficult thing by opening a lingerie shop specializing in sexy lingerie for larger-busted women. While everyone needs a well-fitted nude t-shirt bra (they sell those here, too), colorful, lacy, provocative bras that actually fit and come in cup sizes larger than F are few and far between. You'd be hard-pressed to find a more unique, more empowering bra shop. With sizes 28AA–46O (and up!) and an extraordinary staff of experts, The Rack Shack really is for everyone.

The Fajas Store (QNS)

⊚ *81-25 41st Ave, Elmhurst*
⊕ *fajasstore.com*

The culture around shapewear and compression garments is a whole different game in Latin America. The Fajas Store in Elmhurst is a terrific example of one that does this category of undergarment especially well. Here you'll find smoothing pieces for wearing under regular clothes or eveningwear, as well as specialty post-op compression garments. What sets Colombian fajas apart from mainstream brands of shapewear is the specificity of the garments, the extensive size options and the tailoring options — yes, you can get your shapewear tailored here, too!

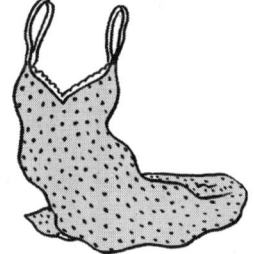

Local Womenswear Designers

Batsheva (MANH) `MADE IN NYC`
◉ *166 Elizabeth St nr. Kenmare St, Chinatown*
⊕ *batsheva.com*

Designer and former lawyer Batsheva Hay is all-in on her well-established ruffly, maximalist style. Her dresses are beloved in the world of indie fashion for their puffy sleeves, Laura Ashley florals, easy-wearing volume, and, frankly, because they make you feel like it's 1989 and you're playing dress-up in your stylish mom's closet.

Collina Strada (MANH) `MADE IN NYC` `NEW!`
◉ *52 Canal St bet. Orchard and Division St, Lower East Side*
⊕ *collinastrada.com*

Wild patterns, textural fabric treatment (think loose thread and artfully placed holes), and playful volume are the calling cards of Collina Strada — a cult-favorite brand amongst the city's most avant garde fashion girls. Most of what's available here is made in New York City, with an emphasis on sustainability. Opened in late 2024, this new flagship store is a feast for the eyes, with a groovy floral hand-painted floor — the perfect backdrop for trying on a dripping dress or pooling cargo pants

Dana Foley (MANH) `MADE IN NYC`
◉ *174 Ludlow St bet. Houston and Stanton St, Lower East Side*
⊕ *danafoleynyc.com*

Known for her slinky dresses, Dana Foley is where hot girls shop for evening wear. Now-timeless '90s silhouettes dominate this line, which also includes cargo pants, low-rise mini skirts, and gorgeous corsets. Better yet: everything is made locally, with sustainability in mind. Come here when you're ready to graduate from Reformation.

LOCAL Our city is full of designers without a storefront presence, and many of them are open to appointments, order pick-ups, and open studios. Here are a few made-in-NYC brands to check out:

NAOMI NOMI
⊕ *naominomi.com*
Delicious fabrics, meticulous details, and perfect tailoring are the specialties at this shirting brand. If you've ever wondered why perfect oxfords are hard to find for women — NAOMI NOMI is the answer to your prayers. Be sure to keep an eye out for open-studio events for in-person try-ons or book a private shopping appointment.

Rosie Assoulin
⊕ *rosieassoulin.com*
For high drama, deliriously fun dresses, this is the place. Patterns, stripes, layers, volume — whether you want to stand out at a special event, or seek a bold addition to your vacation wardrobe, a special piece from Rosie Assoulin will leave you excited to get dressed.

NOT
⊕ *notaligne.com*
Designer Jenny Lai makes clothes for men and women with movement in mind. In fact, one of her specialties is in making garments for live performers. At her Upper West Side studio, you can schedule an appointment to try on her colorful, sculptural pieces.

Kallmeyer (MANH) **MADE IN NYC**
◎ *83 Orchard St, Lower East Side*
◎ *1022 Madison Ave, Upper East Side*
⊕ *kallmeyer.nyc*

Think up a visual of the most enviably chic and effortlessly sexy Tribeca gallery girl you can imagine — she's probably wearing Kallmeyer. Known for her impeccable tailoring, ultramodern women's suiting, and drape-y dresses, Daniella Kallmeyer occupies a local fashion niche of her own. Everything is crafted in NYC and sold in an environment that makes customers feel like they're shopping in a private atelier. For the discerning minimalist looking for a forever fashion, this is an essential brand.

Maryam Nassir Zadeh (MANH)
◎ *123 Norfolk St nr. Rivington St, Lower East Side*
⊕ *maryamnassirzadeh.com*

On a quiet block of Norfolk St is a spacious, minimal space that's home to a curated selection of indie designers and the work of Maryam Nassir Zadeh. Her signature minimalist, perfectly disheveled, slightly offbeat style has been a downtown favorite for the past 15 years. Visit especially for the footwear, which is Italian-made and hits a sweet spot for high fashion that's actually practical.

Sandy Liang (MANH)
◎ *28 Orchard St, Lower East Side*
⊕ *sandyliang.info*

Sandy Liang's shining silver home for her signature brand of teenage nostalgia is something of an anchor shop on this bustling fashion block. Satin, bows, rhinestones, and Mary Janes abound; shoppers from all over the world flock for big brand collabs, schoolgirl skirts, and Peter Pan collars. Look around the city and you'll spot members of the new generation of trend-setters wearing her "Return to Sandy Liang" necklaces à la Tiffany & Co. in the early aughts.

Tamara Malas (MANH) **MADE IN NYC** INCLUSIVE SIZING **NEW!**
⊚ *143 Ludlow St bet. Stanton and Rivington St, Lower East Side*
⊕ *tamaramalas.com*

We dare you to name a shop for all sizes that's more fun than Tamara Malas! With a whopping range of sizes from 0 to 36, this brand of sassy separates *really* is for everyone. Expect prints galore, wild swimwear, and summer-ready dresses, alongside textured jackets and chunky sweaters. Responsible manufacturing is a serious priority here, with some pieces made right here in the Garment District.

Zero + Maria Cornejo (MANH) **MADE IN NYC**
⊚ *33 Bleecker St nr. Mott St, NoHo*
⊕ *zeromariacornejo.com*

Since 1998, this Chilean-born designer has been making timeless, artful clothes for real women. Her use of angles, volume, and creative tailoring makes for garments that are wearable and cool for all ages. And it's a good thing, too, because the attention to detail and quality of these pieces is bar none. Buy something and feel confident that you'll be wearing it forever.

Judi Rosen (MANH)
⊚ *198 Elizabeth St bet. Prince and Spring St, Nolita*
⊕ *judirosenny.com*

The queen of jeans! Downtown mainstay Judi Rosen is responsible for bringing ultra high-rise butt-lifting pants back, and thank god she did! This jewel-box of a shop is stocked with the full line of vintage-inspired jeans, as well as made-in-America essentials, eclectic knick-knacks, and accessories.

Still Here (MANH)
⊚ *268 Elizabeth St, Nolita*
⊚ *905 Madison Ave, Upper East Side*
⊕ *stillhere.nyc*

This relatively new denim label embraces what they affectionately call "the American uniform" — well-worn, well-fitted jeans and a perfect, timeless t-shirt. Their versions of both are exceptionally high quality and strike a chord often missed by denim brands that are more focused on chasing trends. For those who haven't been able to find that just-right pair of vintage Levi's, try Still Here for something fresh instead.

Rachel Comey (MANH) (BK)
◎ *95 Crosby St, SoHo*
◎ *220 Smith St, Cobble Hil*
⊕ *rachelcomey.com*

These are clothes for fashion people. With details that most brands wouldn't bother with, distinctive prints, surprising color stories, and separates that effortlessly work right into any existing wardrobe, Rachel Comey defines the aesthetic of the 21st century New York Woman. She's even collaborated with institutions like the New York Review of Books and MoMA to create prints highlighting cultural touchpoints. In addition to day-to-night separates, find surprisingly well-priced costume jewelry, distinctive footwear, and a show-stopping piece of evening wear or two. Check the labels, too, because some garments are made in New York and are proudly labeled as such.

Merlette (MANH) **NEW!**
◎ *18 Jay St bet. Greenwich and Staple St, Tribeca*
⊕ *merlettenyc.com*

Known for its easy, modern twist on classic feminine style, Merlette is a brand that's made with longevity in mind. At this newly opened Tribeca storefront, you'll find an abundance of gentle ruffles, artful ruching, and perfect pleats — just enough visual interest for a stylish gal about town, but classic enough to keep forever, through all ages. Visit for easy dresses for all-day wear, and effortless separates to help you feel put together with little effort. Ah, the magic of an intentional, well-made garment.

Fe Noel Little Caribbean (BK) **MADE IN NYC**
◎ *1133 Nostrand Ave, Prospect Lefferts Gardens*
⊕ *fenoellittlecaribbean.com*

Inspired by her Grenadian heritage, Brooklyn-native designer Felicia Noel designs celebratory, colorful womenswear. Her brick-and-mortar shop specializes in limited-run pieces made locally in an effort to repurpose deadstock fabric, while her online store exhibits her made-to-order high end pieces.

Kimera (BK) `MADE IN NYC`
◎ *400 3rd Ave, Gowanus*
⊕ *kimeradesign.com*

Since 1999, designer Yvonne Chu has been crafting classic dresses and totally custom pieces for discerning New York women. Most of her pieces are made-to-order from silk shantung and taffeta, and can be ordered in-person at her Brooklyn shop. Prices hover around $250–$300 for cocktail dresses, all of which are deceptively simple in design.

A Note on Maternity Clothing

Maternity clothing is a tricky thing to shop for, and while there are plenty of lovely big-brand shops in NYC specializing in this very important sub-category, there are very few independent retailers. Do you have a great recommendation? Please let us know! For now, here's one we know and love:

Emilia George (MANH)
◎ *325 Greenwich St, corner of Duane, Tribeca*
⊕ *emiliageorgeofficial.com*

Emillia George is perhaps best known for their in-house maternity clothing brand, which features more than just oversized tops and stretchy dresses. Cool moms from all over the city make the trip downtown to find stylish knits and well-cut pieces that translate seamlessly into postpartum life. Though this shop is self-described as "a motherhood boutique," the selection doesn't stop there — find postpartum essentials, fertility wellness products, and safe, natural baby goods.

Mature Womenswear

The Brownstone Woman (MANH)
◉ 24 E 125th St bet. 5th Ave and Madison Ave, Harlem
⊕ thebrownstonewoman.com

Owner Princess Jenkins is a Harlem legend for her character-filled lifestyle boutique. Laden with bold accessories, voluminous, and colorful jackets, and her own line of flowy linen pieces, this shop is for everyone, but especially suited for grown women who want to be comfortable, feel chic, and still make a statement.

Gabrielle Carlson (MANH) MADE IN NYC
◉ 1034a Lexington Ave bet. E 75th and 74th St, Upper East Side
⊕ gabriellecarlson.com

Beloved by the ladies of the Upper East Side, Gabrielle Carlson's timeless line of locally-made clothing comes in natural fibers, a rainbow of flattering jewel tones, and flowy shapes that suit anyone of any age. Wear one of her raw silk jackets from lunch to the museum to the ballet — they're as comfortable and functional as they are beautiful.

Lana's Loft (QNS)
◉ 114-04 Beach Channel Drive, Rockaway Beach
⊕ lanasonline.com

Bright and beachy, Lana's Loft is a quaint boutique and a much-loved member of the small biz community on the Rockaway Peninsula. Locals come here to buy comfy, casual clothes well-suited to the lifestyle of a chill beach mom. Billowy blouses, printed dresses, and plenty of beach-themed garb dominate the inventory here. Lana's Loft is open year-round and shifts to cozy knits with a fun assortment of holiday-specific pieces in the fall and winter. Come here for a floral linen dress in the summer, and return for a jack-o-lantern top in October.

Multi-brand Womenswear

Café Forgot (MANH)
⊚ *29 Ludlow St nr. Hester St, Lower East Side*
⊕ *cafeforgot.com*
Small but mighty fashion destination Café Forgot is globally known for being New York City's source for discovering the most interesting young designers out there. There's a reverence for the art here that's palpable and earnest, with racks stocked with fresh and colorful pieces for the youthful girl-about-town.

TUMBAO (MANH)
⊚ *20 Orchard St bet. Hester and Canal St, Lower East Side*
Occupying a discreet lower lever storefront in the new fashion capital of NYC, Tumbao touts the largest curation of Latin American fashion in the world. Spanning menswear, jewelry, accessories, shoes, decor, and especially womenswear, this shop shines a bright light on up-and-coming creatives. There's no website, and they have minimal social media, so you'll just have to go and see the magic for yourself.

Oroboro (MANH)
⊚ *217 Mott St bet. Prince and Spring St, Nolita*
⊕ *oroborostore.com*
For the slightly more grown-up cool girl, Oroboro sells brands like Rejina Pyo and Ulla Johnson alongside classics like pants by Jesse Kamm and lingerie from Araks. Don't miss the selection of skincare, home goods, and accessories, too — from hand-embroidered throw pillows to woven baskets and herbal tinctures, the curation here is tight, and tailored to the urban sophisticate with a bit of a hippie streak.

Sincerely, Tommy (BK)
⊚ *343 Tompkins Ave, Bed-Stuy*
⊕ *sincerelytommy.com*
Part cafe and part boutique, Sincerely, Tommy is a Black-owned community hub that serves great coffee, while also supporting emerging designers. The vibe is decidedly minimal, but the pieces that grace the racks pack a serious punch. Visit to

revamp your wardrobe with something surely no one you know will already have.

Outline (BK)
◎ *365 Atlantic Ave, Boerum Hill*
⊕ *outlinebrooklyn.com*

Like nothing else in the city, the naturally lit, airy space Outline occupies instills an immediate sense of calm — all the better for perusing the racks of designer womenswear, filled equally with brands you've never heard of and ones so rare and high-end you're surprised to see them outside of Bergdorf's; Dries van Noten and The Row mingle with contemporaries like Super Yaya and Wales Bonner. Outline was opened by three friends with complimentary areas of expertise who've somehow struck a balance any luxury retailer can only dream of finding: an environment that makes an aspirational lifestyle feel accessible and full of wonder.

Rue Saint Paul (BK)
◎ *313 Court St, Carroll Gardens*
⊕ *ruestpaul.com*

Colorful dresses and statement separates are what will catch your eye at Rue Saint Paul, but what locals know is that many of the garments displayed here are available to rent. Consider it your better, independent Rent the Runway, except the clothes are ethically manufactured and you can actually try them on. They also have a community pre-loved buyback program to resell your contemporary and vintage treasures.

TREND REPORT

This past year, **Outline** ditched their online store in favor of a gorgeous, intimate print catalog, which is also viewable on their minimalist website — a particularly well-executed example of something we've noticed: a newly invigorated reverence for analog sales tactics in the world of luxury and fashion.

Leif Home + Woman ⓑⓚ
⊚ *319 Graham Ave, Williamsburg*
⊕ *leifshop.com*

A well-edited lifestyle shop will do just that: sell you on an aspirational lifestyle. The lifestyle on display here is one of a gentle, curious Brooklyn woman, who's a little offbeat, but intentional about the objects she buys and fantasizes about their place in her cozy upstate retreat. It's a one-stop shop for hard-to-find indie designers like Maria Stanley and Rujeta Sheth, and an IRL place to find staples from popular brands like AGOLDE or Jungmaven.

Tangerine ⓑⓚ
⊚ *616 Lorimer St, Williamsburg*
⊕ *tangerine-nyc.com*

The multi-brand outpost from the owners of made-in-NYC swimwear brand Nu Swim, and ready-to-wear and accessories label Coming of Age, Tangerine also sells popular brands like Saks Potts and Maryam Nassir Zadeh. Niche, imported sundries can also be found merchandised alongside the minimalist womenswear — be sure to pick up an Italian toothbrush or a Japanese can opener when you stop by to try on some Super Yaya.

Hellenic Aesthetic ⓆⓃⓈ
⊚ *30-91 31st St, Astoria*
⊕ *hellenicaesthetic.com*

Aptly placed in the historically Greek neighborhood of Astoria, Hellenic Aesthetic specializes in independent Greek designers. Find flowy, embroidered dresses, a spectrum of blues, swimwear, and culturally-specific charms. If you can't make it to Greece, a day trip to Astoria and a new outfit from Hellenic Aesthetic will quell the craving.

Special Occasions

Spina Bride (MANH)
◎ *132 10th Ave nr. W 18th St, Chelsea*
⊕ *spinabride.com*

With an incomparable selection of independent bridal designers from all over the world, Spina Bride caters to women looking for something a little different. Unlikely silhouettes and embroidered works of art fill the racks here. You'll even find dresses selected specifically for all of the wedding adjacent events you might be hosting.

Amsale (MANH) **MADE IN NYC**
◎ *150 Wooster St nr. Houston St, SoHo*
⊕ *amsale.com*

Since the 1980s, Amsale has remained a haven for *very New York* brides looking for something elegant, classic, and impeccably tailored. What's for sale here is timeless, but not without dazzling details. Each dress is made in NYC with traditional couture techniques, but you'll also find a lovely collection of ready-to-wear for mothers, bridesmaids, or any other formal event.

Lee Anderson Couture (MANH) **MADE IN NYC**
◎ *975 Lexington Ave nr. E 71st St, Upper East Side*
⊕ *leeandersoncouture.com*

Since the early '80s, designer Lee Anderson has been outfitting the uptown crowd in timeless made-to-measure evening wear. For the sophisticate who wants to feel like they're dressing for the Black and White Ball, there's no place better than Lee Anderson Couture for a show-stopping heirloom.

Happy Isles Salon (MANH)
◎ *134 Spring St bet. Wooster and Greene St, SoHo*
⊕ *thehappyisles.com*

Popular LA-based vintage salon Happy Isles is an appointment-only treasure trove of carefully curated vintage occasionwear and even a little rare haute couture. With a selection of dresses mostly from the '60s–'90s by big name designers, most shoppers flock here to find something unique for a wedding or special event. Be sure to book at least a month in advance!

Lein Studio (MANH) `MADE IN NYC`
⊕ *leinstudio.com*
This appointment-only studio is where the most stylish under-40 brides in NYC go for the rest of their wedding wardrobe. It's a truly fresh take on wedding dressing, from slinky suits for a courthouse wedding to crystal minis for the after party. These made-to-order pieces are things you'll cherish and enjoy wearing long after the photos are printed.

Veka Bridal (BK)
⊚ *412 Atlantic Ave, Boerum Hill*
⊕ *vekabridal.com*
A very Brooklyn bridal boutique, Veka Bridal sells a selection of independent designers for a modern bride. Streamlined silhouettes and pretty lace details are favored over traditional, voluminous gowns and prices are surprisingly affordable for an NYC boutique, with most designers starting around $2k–$5k.

Desi Attire NY (BK)
⊚ *1074b Liberty Ave, Cypress Hills*
This specialist is beloved in the Cypress Hills South Asian community and sells a variety of traditional Indian occasionwear in varying levels of formality. Even the most dazzling, detailed outfits are still priced under $400. Consider this your one-stop shop for something gorgeous to wear to a wedding (jewelry, too!). Don't miss their growing menswear selection, and be sure to ask about in-house tailoring.

Noni Styles (BK) `MADE IN NYC`
⊚ *1215 Nostrand Ave, Prospect Lefferts Gardens*
⊕ *nonistyles.com*
Noni is well-known in her pocket of Brooklyn for creating masterpieces of African occasionwear. With a traditional framework, but keen eye on modern tailoring and details, she goes above and beyond to make something special for her clients, who come for wedding dresses and more.

Pashmina Fashions (QNS)
⊚ *7226 Broadway, Jackson Heights*
A South-Asian formalwear staple in Jackson Heights for the past 25 years, this WOC-owned shop is beloved in the neighborhood for their intricate designs for men and women, and their attentive help for customers who are new to dressing for an Indian wedding. Be sure to check out the accompanying jewelry and accessories.

> **IMPORTANT!**
>
> Occasionwear shops often require an appointment. Check before you go!

Secondhand Clothes

In my past three years of data collection, I've found that Vintage & Thrift is the most rapidly growing category in New York City retail. With new shops popping up in every shopping neighborhood on what seems like a weekly basis, it's a category that has gained popularity as younger folks are ravenous for unique pieces in a more eco-conscious way. That said, the line between what's **vintage** and what's **thrift** have become seriously blurred. Here's a breakdown of shops in every secondhand category that do their thing particularly well.

Designer Consignment

A consignment shop is different to a vintage shop because the owner of the clothes being sold gets paid *after* they're sold, with a percentage going to the shop selling them. Typically, consignment shops deal exclusively with higher-priced designer goods and utilize this system because it means they can take on more inventory without the burden of sinking too much cash into it.

Tokyo Joe (MANH)
⊚ *334 E 11th St bet. 2nd and 1st Ave, East Village*
⊕ *tokyojoenyc.com*

On a quiet block of the East Village is a tiny, crowded storefront that looks like any other independent vintage store, but once you go inside you'll find a bounty of rare and unique designer goods, sold there on consignment at prices much better than more visible competitors. The curation here tends to be more aligned with current vintage trends than most, making it an underground favorite of the fashion set since 1994.

Michael's Luxury Consignment (MANH)
⊚ *1125 Madison Ave nr. E 84th St, Upper East Side*
⊕ *michaelsconsignment.com*

Looking for a gown for a fancy wedding without breaking the bank? Or maybe a designer handbag at a fraction of the cost? Michael's is a wonderful place to start. The style of the clothing here is very Upper East Side, skewing feminine and grown-up.

Consignment Brooklyn (BK)
⊚ *371 Atlantic Ave, Boerum Hill*
⊕ *consignmentbrooklyn.com*

The style of a consignment shop tends to reflect the style of the people who live in the neighborhood it inhabits, because that's whose clothes are being sold here, and Consignment Brooklyn is no exception! Cool mom with a flexible budget and an eye for indie designers is the vibe here, with so much inventory it'd take hours to see all of it. If you're too overwhelmed to flip through the densely packed racks, be sure to check out the exceptional selection of jewelry.

Morph. (BK)
⊚ *1405 Coney Island Ave, Midwood*

Catering specifically to the surrounding Orthodox Jewish community, Morph is a unique consignment shop because though they, too, specialize in high-end designer clothes and accessories, the styles available here are decidedly modest. Gorgeous formalwear, Chanel accessories, and lots and lots of shoes line the walls here.

Thrift

In contrast to vintage stores, thrift stores stock clothing and items that generally arrive there by donation, the proceeds of which typically benefit a charity or some sort of community-focused cause.

Cure Thrift MANH
◉ *91 3rd Ave bet. E 13th and 12th St, East Village*
⊕ *curethriftshop.com*

This spot is popular for hosting celebrity closet sales with the likes of Amy Sedaris and Busy Phillips, but on a regular day it's packed full of quirky furniture, costume jewelry, and tons of clothes. They're discerning here and tend to sell things that are more vintage than thrift, as the prices most certainly reflect. Still, it's not-for-profit, as all sales benefit many different Type 1 diabetes charities.

Vintage Thrift Shop MANH
◉ *286 3rd Ave bet. E 23rd and 22nd St, Gramercy*
⊕ *vintagethriftshop.org*

Benefitting the non-profit charity United Jewish Council of the East Side, this little thrift shop is full of quirky knick-knacks and a nice selection of well-priced designer goods. The quality tends to be higher than most thrift stores, but the prices are better than you'd expect. Many come for the actually old vintage clothes, but the real secret is that there's usually a great stock of gorgeous, well-maintained vintage furniture and home decor.

Modify MANH **NEW!**
◉ *371 Malcolm X Blvd nr. W 129th St, Harlem*

After testing out her concept through pop-ups around the city, environmentalist Kadjatou took over her dad's Harlem storefront to open NYC's first thrift shop that specializes in modest clothing for those following Islamic principles of dressing. Her shop is full of affordable options to suit all styles from everyday-casual to formalwear.

Gotham Thrift Shop (QNS)

⊚ *61-01 Myrtle Ave, Ridgewood*
⊕ *gothamthriftny.com*

This family-owned neighborhood favorite requires a little picking through, just as any good thrift store does. They've got knick-knacks galore, cheap furniture, vintage comics, and the occasional designer accessory. Visit for inexpensive tableware and kitschy gifts.

*See **Every Thing Goes** in Secondhand Furniture on pg. 247 for an excellent selection of actually cheap vintage clothes on Staten Island.*

Vintage T-Shirts

Mr. Throwback (MANH)

⊚ *437 E 9th St bet. 1st Ave and Ave A, East Village*
⊕ *mrthrowback.com*

True specialists in the vintage t-shirt space are few and far between these days, but Michael at Mr. Throwback is a real expert in the niche world of vintage sport gear. His East Village storefront is packed with character and organized by team and color, with something for just about everyone, especially from the '80s through the '00s. Skip eBay and go here instead for something special to wear and rep your favorite team.

Metropolis (MANH)

⊚ *803 Broadway bet. E 12th and 11th St, Greenwich Village*
⊕ *metropolisvintageonline.net*

You'll find a little of everything here, but what Metropolis specializes in is rare band and tour t-shirts. For a music nerd, the collection is unparalleled, but expect to spend $100+ for the good stuff. Owner Richard has been keeping Metropolis stocked with expertly sourced treasures since the '90s and has been a fountain of knowledge in this specific corner of the vintage world.

Fantasy Explosion (BK)
◎ *164a Driggs Ave, Greenpoint*
⊕ *fantasyexplosion.com*

At its core, Fantasy Explosion is a vintage shop that specializes in menswear and extremely niche merch referencing cultural events from decades past, but what fashion folks keep coming back for are the limited-release sports and NYC culture-related t-shirts and hats that are designed and distributed in-house. It's a place full of surprises, and a general vibe that's significantly more welcoming than its obvious coolness might imply.

Well-curated Vintage

Every vintage shop is bound to house its share of hidden gems, but there's something to be said about the shops that are so tightly edited that they almost sell nothing. These are the real trend-setters — the ones who specialize in an era or subgenre of fashion, who cater to shoppers who are too discerning (or impatient) to do the searching themselves.

James Veloria (MANH) | NOW OPEN IN LA! |
◎ *75 E Broadway #225,*
Under the Manhattan Bridge, Chinatown
⊕ *jamesveloria.com*

Since opening in 2017, Collin James Weber and Brandon Veloria Giordano's eponymous vintage shop has taken the scene by storm. With a unique knack for sourcing experimental '90s and early aughts designer pieces, the selection here includes lots of Jean Paul Gaultier, Vivienne Westwood, and Comme des Garcons. Come for the Clueless vibes, stay for the fashion history lesson.

Duo NYC (MANH)
◎ *324 E 9th St bet. 2nd and 1st Ave, East Village*
⊕ *duonyc.com*

Owned by two sisters, Duo is a small shop with a tight curation of timeless womenswear and vintage denim. In addition to things like perfectly worn Levi's and mint condition 1980s cashmere, there's also an edited selection of current small-brand accessories and cosmetic products. Special, subtle, wearable womenswear that transcends the decades it's been worn through.

> **CONSIDER THIS**
>
> Heavily curated vintage shops require a lot of work and time to source, restore, and stock such specific and rare things, so *of course* they're more expensive than some rando on eBay. Save time, trust the experts!

Stock Vintage (MANH)
⊚ *143 E 13th St bet. 4th and 3rd Ave, East Village*

True vintage, pure Americana, and absolutely one-of-a-kind. Stock Vintage sells men's vintage dating from the early 1900s through the 1970s and is a reliable source for denim, leather, well-worn ringer tees, and pieces that you won't believe have survived as long as they have, given the life they appear to have lived. Try calling before visiting, as the listed hours aren't always accurate.

Desert Vintage (MANH)
⊚ *34 Orchard St bet. Hester and Canal St, Lower East Side*
⊕ *desertvintage.com*

Prestige vintage specialist Desert Vintage was first founded in Tucson in 1974, but was given a new life when it was taken over by experts Salima Boufelfel and Roberto Cowan in 2012. This second location is designed to make you feel like you've stepped back in time and into a dream wardrobe of pristine fashion confections dating back to the turn of the century. Expect a balance of big name designers (the true vintage, only!) and pieces of unknown origin that are special enough to make you think they're one-of-a-kind (and probably are). Visit especially for outerwear and evening dresses.

Edith Machinist (MANH)

⊚ *104 Rivington St bet. Ludlow and Essex St, Lower East Side*
⊕ *edithmachinist.com*

Since 2002, owner Edie has been lending her extensive vintage fashion knowledge to TV and film, but her shop is approachable for all. It's less about designer names here, and more about owning a small piece of another time. What you'll find is beautifully maintained shoes, accessories, delightfully quirky costume jewelry, and carefully selected true-vintage clothes that are treated with a reverence that's often lacking in today's vintage shops.

Treasures of NYC (MANH)

⊚ *69 Mercer St bet. Prince and Spring St, SoHo*
⊕ *treasuresofnewyorkcity.com*

It's labelmania at Treasures of NYC! As the name implies, this appointment-only vintage showroom is a fever dream closet of high-end designer treasures. Have you ever wanted to find a specific dress that Carrie Bradshaw wore? Or wanted to own a LV x Murakami piece from the early aughts? This is where you'll find it!

Old The Best (MANH) **NEW!**

⊚ *138 W 10th St bet. Waverly Pl and Greenwich Ave, West Village*
⊕ *oldthebest.com*

This charming little shop on a quiet block of the West Village is packed with hundreds of authentic designer handbags from every brand a collector could dream of. Colorful Chanel flap bags, a few Birkins, and hard-to-find styles from Louis Vuitton and Dior line the shelves, alongside a terrific selection of jewelry. For bag hunters, it's a shopping experience far more delightful than trolling eBay, but with prices that might surprise you (in a good way!).

Front General Store (BK)

⊚ *143 Front St, Dumbo*
⊕ *frontgeneralstore.com*

Arrive at Front General Store, and you'll find it crowded — both with shoppers and merchandise, because this place covers lots of bases. Moroccan house slippers, French glassware, and fancy candles fill the front of the store, but a walk to the back reveals their own brand of vintage-inspired knits, a reliable stock of Stan Ray pants, and extremely selective vintage. There's lots of knitwear and denim, but most exceptionally: a regular and rotating stock of Issey Miyake Pleats Please garments in mint condition.

House of Kellogg (BK)

◎ *65 Bond St, Boerum Hill*
⊕ *houseofkellogg.com*

You'd be hard pressed to find a more playful vintage store in Brooklyn. Owner Jennifer Kellogg fills her candy-colorful storefront with new, re-worked pieces, and designer vintage from the '80s and '00s, and all sorts of unexpected finds that fit her wacky, slightly punk, totally feminist vision. If you've ever fantasized about adopting the spirit of Mary from Party Girl, this is a good place to start.

Berriez (BK) INCLUSIVE SIZING

◎ *544 Park Ave Ste 510, Bed-Stuy*
⊕ *shopberriez.com*

With a focus on sizes L–5X, Berriez is a spacious studio for gals looking to feel good and make a statement with bright colors and wild patterns. The curation here is creative and exciting — featuring mostly vintage from the '90s–'00s, with an inspired selection of re-worked pieces and emerging designers. Berriez keeps regular weekend hours but is otherwise appointment-only.

Amarcord Vintage (BK)

◎ *223 Bedford Ave, Williamsburg*
⊕ *amarcordvintagefashion.com*

Colorful, mid-century, and European garments pack the racks at this beloved Brooklyn vintage spot. Amarcord is what a fictional movie version of a vintage store looks like. Shopping here is like visiting the costume closet of an entire century of history, and while their specialty is 20th century Italian designers, the selection is accepting of all archival quality fashion. In fact, the extensive Amarcord archive of fashion is open by appointment to industry professionals for rentals and reference.

10ft Single By Stella Dallas (BK)
◎ *285 N 6th St, Williamsburg*

With an extensive and decidedly American selection, you'll find tons of outerwear, military garb, varsity jackets, well-worn leather goods, and pretty vintage dresses here. What you should really come for, though, is the stacks and stacks of textiles like tablecloths, blankets, and rugs, which can be found at Stella Dallas Living, 281 N 6th St.

By Liv Handmade (BK)
◎ *293 Manhattan Ave, Williamsburg*
⊕ *bylivhandmade.com*

This isn't your typical vintage shop. Owner Liv has filled her storefront with light and lacy vintage, wares by other local makers, and her very own pieces made from reworked vintage, featuring her signature slinky but demure style. Think Victorian ghost meets hot Prairie girl. A favorite amongst the Brooklyn coquette set, By Liv Handmade is quite literally one-of-a-kind.

Plus BKLYN (BK) INCLUSIVE SIZING
◎ *671 Manhattan Ave, Greenpoint*
⊕ *plusbklyn.com*

Filling a serious void in the market, Plus BKLYN is a vintage and secondhand shop that's fully stocked entirely with garments in sizes 0X–6X. Owner Alexis made the shop she wished existed, and she did a damn good job of it! Colorful, sassy, and inclusive — this place rocks. Don't forget to style your new outfit with the fab accessories for sale, too.

grace land new york (QNS)
◎ *1882 Woodbine St, Ridgewood*
⊕ *gracelandnewyork.com*

This multi-hyphenate shop sells a house brand, vintage, and re-worked pieces, but what sets it apart from the many other gorgeous, contemporary fashion boutiques is their custom services. Here, you can commission something totally custom, or bring in something beloved to be repaired or reimagined. It's a circular and mindful way to build a creative wardrobe, and the type of shop that I hope we see more of in the future.

Desk

Contemporary Stationery

Niconeco Zakkaya (MANH)
◎ 263 E 10th St bet. 1st Ave and Ave A, East Village
⊕ niconeco.com

A true rabbit hole of cuteness, Nicoceco Zakkaya is a shoebox of a stationery store that's jam-packed with indie brand Japanese stationery, washi tapes, and craft supplies. For bullet journalers and letter writers especially, this is an incredible resource for pretty things to make it all a little more fun. The sticker selection here is unmatched!

> **NEW IN 2025!**
>
> **Niconeco Zakkaya** opened a darling new shop and cafe in Williamsburg called Loaf on Paper. Find it at 64 Grand Street!

East Village Postal (MANH)
◎ 151 1st Ave bet. E 10th and 9th St, East Village
⊕ eastvillagepostal.com

This family-owned postal shop has quietly grown into one of the city's best stationery shops over the past few years. Hard-to-find pens, a global selection of greeting cards, popular Japanese notebooks, and fancy gifts make this a one stop shop. Ship a package, find a great birthday gift, and replace the scissors you lost — all in one place! Hot tip: Jane, one of the owners, makes stunning life-like crepe paper flowers, which can be purchased here.

Goods for the Study (MANH)
⊚ *234-236 Mulberry St, Nolita*
⊚ *50 W 8th St, Greenwich Village*
⊚ *2105 Broadway, Upper West Side*
⊕ *goodsforthestudy.com*

Covering all of the stationery bases, Goods for the Study occupies three storefronts in two neighborhoods and sells just about every brand that's currently making paper goods. Especially if you're searching for a very specific type of notebook, or are on the hunt for a new favorite pen, you'll find an unbeatable selection here. Owner Sarah McNally is also the mastermind behind the McNally Jackson bookstores, which also stock a selection of what's available here.

Yoseka Stationery (BK)
⊚ *63 West St, Greenpoint*
⊕ *yosekastationery.com*

A true stationery nerd's shop, the heavily curated selection at Yoseka is driven by a very Japanese penchant for decorative journaling. Amongst the washi tapes, hard-to-find oil-based stamp pads, and tiny paper goods is the real draw: the pen testing bar, which is stocked with hundreds of mostly Asian pens and writing tools ranging from niche limited edition fountain pens to '90s-style glitter gel pens.

The Analog Stationer (BK)
⊚ *621 Vanderbilt Ave, Prospect Heights*
⊕ *theanalogstationer.com*

Filling a serious void in this area of Brooklyn, The Analog Stationer is a one-stop shop for carefully selected paper goods, desk tools, and writing instruments from all over the world. Find European art supplies, hard-to-find pencil models, unique desk decor, and paper to satisfy even the fussiest users. Owner Chaya knows what's good, and her extensive knowledge doesn't stop at the product selection — she also hosts workshops and puts a big emphasis on community.

FIELD TRIP!

Head down to the Seaport Museum in lower Manhattan to check out **Bowne & Co.** — a historic 19th century letterpress print shop with antique equipment on view and hand-printed stationery for sale.

Her Winter Flowers (BK)
◉ *283 S 5th St, Williamsburg*
⊕ *herwinterflowers.com*
This pretty little South Williamsburg shop specializes in gifts and paper goods by female illustrators and designers, with a decidedly sweet point of view. Swing by for floral notepads, lovely greeting cards, or a decorative Japanese letter-writing set to share with your pen pal.

Custom Stationery

City Papery (MANH)
◉ *23 W 18th St bet. 6th and 5th Ave, Flatiron*
⊕ *citypapery.com*
Occupying the cavernous storefront that once housed Paper Presentation, City Papery offers same-day stationery printing services and an incredible selection of envelopes in every size and color imaginable, which can be purchased individually or in packs. Find great gift wrap (boxes! ribbons!) and all of the pens, tapes, and things you'll need for addressing whatever it is you're printing.

Blacker & Kooby Vanessa (MANH)
◉ *1390 Lexington Ave bet. E 92nd and 91st St, Upper East Side*
⊕ *blackerandkooby.com*
Part art supply store, part custom invitation shop, Blacker & Kooby by Vanessa is a neighborhood stationer through and through. You can even get other custom things, like matchboxes and party cups, made here!

Plum Paperie (SI)

◎ *57 New Dorp Plaza N, East Shore*
⊕ *plumpaperie.com*

Staten Island's premier custom invitation shop has a lovely East Shore storefront that also functions as a gift and stationery shop. They're known for their personalized service, attention to detail and traditional style.

Fancy Pens

Altman Luggage (MANH)

◎ *135 Orchard St*
bet. Rivington and Delancey St, Lower East Side
⊕ *altmanluggage.com*

Yes, this is primarily a luggage store, but it's also a well-stocked retailer for current fancy pens by big name brands like Graf von Faber-Castell, Caran d'Ache, Parker, and Lamy. With prices ranging from $40–$1k+, there's something for everyone here. Visit to find a gift for a newly minted lawyer or college graduate.

Janoff's Stationery (MANH)

◎ *2870 Broadway bet. W 112th and 111th St, Morningside Heights*

I have a pen world friend who swears that Janoff's has one of the best selections of fountain pens in America. While most know this uptown shop as a quirky art supply retailer, take a peek in the glass case and you'll see just a fraction of the deadstock fountain pens hiding in this place. Ask nicely, and they'll show you some treasures.

Fountain Pen Hospital (MANH)

◎ *10 Warren St bet. Church St and Broadway, Tribeca*
⊕ *fountainpenhospital.com*

Renowned as America's most prestigious fountain pen shop, the Fountain Pen Hospital is where serious collectors go to talk shop, get pens serviced, and check out the latest limited edition. It might feel like a pen museum, and the conversations overheard might be mistaken for those of elite watch collectors, but don't be intimidated — the experts working here take pleasure

Greeting Cards

> **SHOPPING TIP**
>
> Stay on top of your card sending by buying your cards when you see ones you like — *not* when you need them. That way, you'll end up with a stash and will be more likely to actually send that congratulations or condolence card.

Greenwich Letterpress (MANH) MADE IN NYC
⊚ *15 Christopher St*
bet. Waverly Pl and Greenwich Ave, West Village
⊕ *greenwichletterpress.com*
Renowned for their own brand of funny greeting cards and stationery with niche pop culture and NYC references, the sister-owned Greenwich Letterpress is certainly the most eccentric stationery shop in town. While many visit for the epic sticker selection, what they do best is curate the most unique selection of greeting cards in town.

Measure Twice (BK)
⊚ *225 Court St, Cobble Hill*
⊕ *measuretwiceshop.com*
Owners Kimberley and Zach have been in the stationery biz for decades and have an unrivaled knowledge of the greeting card industry. The whole right side wall in their shop is densely covered with cards for every occasion and by independent card makers from all over the world.

Office & School

Essex Card Shop (MANH)
◎ *47 Ave A bet. E 4th and 3rd St, Alphabet City*

This is exactly what stationery shops used to be: packed to the brim with paper goods in every size and format, walls covered in craft supplies, displays stuffed with pens and pencils, and shelves of specialized office supplies. A general store, art and office supply, and stationer, this store sells any analog object your heart desires. Be sure to ask owner Muhammad for help because he possesses a wealth of knowledge.

Phil's Stationery (MANH)
◎ *9 E 47th St bet. 5th Ave and Madison Ave, Midtown*
⊕ *phils-stationery.com*

One online review says: "*I wasn't looking for 'Old New York' but I found it at Phil's.*" This is the type of shop stationery freaks tend to gatekeep, because it's full of deadstock supplies and IYKYK specialty tools. Locals bring their fountain pens here for troubleshooting, and office workers who prefer taking pen to paper stock up on quality notebooks.

Montgomery Stationery (BK)
◎ *5014 13th Ave, Borough Park*
⊕ *montgomerypens.com*

This old-school neighborhood stationer has a robust inventory of fancy pens but also functions as a vital local resource for school supplies, printing services, and general office supplies. It's the best-stocked general stationer and pen shop in Brooklyn.

Ink & Toner (BK)
◎ *2001 Ave U, Sheepshead Bay*

A whole storefront for ink and toner! I could hardly believe it when I happened upon it. Locals love this place for the friendly service and inexpensive (and eco-friendly) cartridge refills. You can even get your printer repaired here!

Tannens (BX)

◎ *363 E 149th St, Mott Haven*
⊕ *tannens149.com*

Education and teacher supply stores are few and far between, but this one fills the void nicely. Tannens sells everything a parent might find on a school supply list, plus education toys and classroom decorations for teachers.

Paper

Shulman Paper (MANH)

◎ *242 W 26th St bet. 8th and 7th Ave, Chelsea*
⊕ *shulmanpaper.com*

For 100 years, this family-owned paper distributor has been supplying printers and stationers with paper from mills like French Paper, Crane, Neenah, and Mohawk. Their storefront is stacked with reams to make a paper nerd's heart sing, and houses an incredible collection of printing equipment ranging from the latest in paper cutting technology to old-school Heidelberg letterpress. Most of what happens here is high-quality print work. Make an appointment to shop for great paper for a particular use, or inquire about custom work.

Typewriters

Gramercy Typewriter Company (MANH)

◎ *108 W 17th St bet. 7th and 6th Ave, Chelsea*
⊕ *gramercytypewriter.com*

Deserving of its own subcategory, Gramercy Typewriter is the very last place in New York City to buy these analog machines. It's no wonder this place is known as a favorite of the one-and-only Tom Hanks, because it's staffed by experts who are kind and generous with their specialized knowledge. Bring a machine here to be inspected and repaired, or stop by for a new ribbon. The models for sale come at a premium, but that's because they've been refurbished to be in perfect working condition. On the hunt for something specific? Ask for help! The folks at Gramercy Typewriters know the secondhand market better than anyone.

Electronics & Appliances

Audio/Visual

New Hi-Tech Corp (MANH)
⊚ *47 Canal St bet. Orchard and Ludlow St, Lower East Side*
⊕ *newhitech.net*

There's no way around it: Frank is an electronics repair wizard. As evidenced by the (mostly not for sale) analog models that line the walls here, he specializes in old school stereos, projects, TVs, tape recorders, camcorders, and radios. In fact, I've not personally heard a story of Frank not being able to repair something.

Audio46 Headphones (MANH)
⊚ *29 W 46th St bet. 6th and 5th Ave, Midtown*
⊕ *audio46.com*

A true specialist in headphones, Audio46 stocks all styles of headphones for every purpose. Whether you're a runner, a DJ, a gamer, an audiophile, or just a regular person with sensitive ears, you're sure to find the perfect match here. The professional staff offer hands-on help to demo different models and dispense advice.

In Living Stereo (MANH)
⊚ *2 Great Jones St bet. Broadway and Lafayette, NoHo*
⊕ *inlivingstereo.com*

For high-end stereo equipment, this is the spot! Shop amps, loudspeakers, turntables, and more in this well-designed temple of audio. A shop for audiophiles and aesthetes, I haven't encountered a more dialed-in selection of equipment in the city. Don't miss their Headphone Annex, where you can demo top-of-the-line headphones.

Stereo Exchange (MANH)

⊚ *23 E 17th St 2nd Fl bet. 5th Ave and Broadway, Union Square*
⊕ *stereoexchange.com*

By appointment only, Stereo Exchange is a purveyor and installer of fine audio equipment. From high-end brands to Sonos systems — take a big step up from Best Buy and pay a visit to Stereo Exchange to upgrade your home audio system.

Gadgets & TV

Bondy Appliances (MANH)

⊚ *40 Canal St nr. Division St, Lower East Side*
⊕ *bondyexport.com*

Come to this family-owned shop for all of the little appliances you need around your home, but especially if you're in need of 220v models for use abroad or in unusual circumstances.

MTV Super Sound (BK)

⊚ *747 Manhattan Ave, Greenpoint*
⊕ *mtvsupersound.com*

Packed full of small home appliances, this shop sells it all but specializes in more analog and often deadstock things like proper alarm clocks and vintage novelty landline phones.

Lucas Electronics (BK)

⊚ *886 Manhattan Ave, Greenpoint*
⊕ *lucaselectronicsnyc.com*

Clean, spacious, and well-stocked with small household appliances, as well as current model televisions, air conditioners (plus installation!), and high-end vacuums, Lucas Electronics also offers Amazon price matching!

Brooke's Appliances (BK)

⊚ *387 7th Ave, Park Slope*
⊕ *brookesappliance.com*

Brooke's is a one-of-a-kind appliance shop with a few specialties, including: air conditioners, vacuum cleaners from high end brands like Miele, and home sewing machines — all at compet-

Large Appliances

itive prices. Services include carpet and upholstery cleaning, as well as sewing machine and vacuum repair.

I can speak from experience when I say: do not invest in a large appliance without seeing it first and talking to a real person about it! Especially when these things have to be hoisted up stairs or down impossibly narrow hallways, it's simply not worth the risk. Here are a couple of great places to start the hunt.

Gringer & Sons (MANH)
⊚ *29 1st Ave nr. E 2nd St, East Village*
⊕ *gringerandsons.com*

You can find anything from gorgeous $40k ranges to window unit air conditioning units in this 100+ year old family-owned appliance shop. The 1st Ave showroom only displays a fraction of what's actually available, but just ask an expert and they'll help you find what you need.

Plug-ins (BK)
⊚ *4103 13th Ave, Borough Park*
⊕ *pluginson13.com*

I can't think of a place for home things in NYC that's more of a one-stop shop than Plug-ins is. Outfit your home with brand new large appliances, buy a new steamer for your wardrobe, and get a full set of dinnerware all in one place.

Richmond Appliance (SI)
⊚ *6308 Amboy Rd, South Shore*
⊕ *richmondappliance.com*

Skip the big suburban appliance store and visit family-owned Richmond Appliance to outfit your new home or find a thoughtful replacement for an old kitchen or laundry machine. Selling all major brands of appliances in a range of prices, it's a big box store variety with far superior service.

Photography

For current photography equipment and all of the technical accoutrement, it's hard to beat **B&H** and **Adorama** — both of which are independently owned and operated A/V superstores in Manhattan. However, for vintage cameras, analog photography equipment, and great resources for film, we have some ideas.

SOMETHING FUN

For their recent 50th Anniversary, **B&H** made a wildly detailed Lego kit of their iconic storefront! Available for purchase in-store and online.

Bleeker Digital Solutions (MANH)
◉ *85 Kenmare St nr. Mulberry St, Nolita*
⊕ *bleekerdigital.com*

Photographers love family-owned Bleeker Digital Solutions for their impeccable film processing and friendly service. Go for a great selection of fairly priced film and for the development, scanning, and retouching services that are professional, efficient, and no-frills.

Exposure Therapy (BK)
◉ *615 Marcy Ave, Bed-Stuy*
⊕ *exposuretherapy.nyc*

Since hitting the scene in 2020, Exposure Therapy has carved a niche as the coolest little film shop in the city. Find $10 development services, a great selection of specialist film, disposables, and vintage cameras for sale. Their social media presence lends itself to an attitude that's creative but not too serious, as does the occasional experimental product, like film pre-exposed with a Charli xcx BRAT border.

photodom. (BK)
◉ *1717 Broadway #3, Bushwick*
⊕ *photodom.nyc*

Is Photodom a film photographer's paradise? I think so. Find a range of cameras from Y2K point-and-shoots to pristine Rangefinders, darkroom chemicals, a special house-brand line of color treated film named like cannabis strains, and really creative merch. This vibrant Black-owned shop might appeal to experts, but provides an especially welcoming and fun entry point for beginners, too.

Brooklyn Film Camera (BK)
◎ *855 Grand Street, East Williamsburg*
⊕ *brooklynfilmcamera.com*

This vintage camera shop might as well double as a Polaroid museum, because the shelves are lined with models from all eras of their existence. You can even get an old Polaroid restored here, or hire a Polaroid photo booth for events! It's not all about Polaroid, though, because Brooklyn Film Camera also sells cameras of all types; common and hard-to-find film and offers workshops on obsolete types of photography.

Vacuum Specialists

Crown Machine Services (MANH)
◎ *2792 Broadway nr. W 108th St, Upper West Side*
⊕ *crownsalesandservice.com*

While they can repair any small electronic machine, Crown Machine services is known for being experts in vacuum cleaners and are also authorized dealers of Miele machines. Collectors can even trust these fine folks with their vintage models. *As seen on HBO's How To With John Wilson!*

M&M Vacuums `MOVED TO WESTBURY!`
◎ ~~*71-05 Metropolitan Ave, Middle Village*~~
⊕ *mmvacuums.wixsite.com*

Get your high-end vacuums here! This is the place you go when you're fed up with your Target vacuum cleaner losing its suction. Find brands that you've probably never heard of but are far better than what you're familiar with. You can also get your machines serviced and buy maintenance products and bags, too.

ELECTRONICS & APPLIANCES | 143

Shop Type: Variety Store

A shop that sells a little bit of everything. It's called a "variety store" because it stocks too many product categories to list. This is where one goes to stock up on kitchen and household essentials, novelties, random gifts, and seasonal items.

Synonyms: general store. Dollar stores, five and dimes, and discount stores are also types of variety stores.

3rd Ave Dollar and More (MANH)
⊚ *135 3rd Ave, Gramercy*
"I love stopping by to see their holiday decorations every few months. They go all out and cover the whole front of the shop with stuff for whatever holiday is coming next. I've never seen so much Thanksgiving decor in my life!"
– Camille J

DID YOU KNOW?

The everyday products sold at a good variety store are often cheaper than they are on Amazon or at Target, etc. Need a roll of packing tape? A new can opener? A box of q-tips? Try the variety store first!

Entertainment

Adults can shop for toys, too! The shops in this section were chosen because they sell unique modalities of entertainment for all ages and are especially great at reminding grown-ups that you're never too old to play.

Collectibles

Dashop Corp. (MANH)
◎ *6a Elizabeth St bet. Canal and Bayard St, Chinatown*

Dashop could easily fit into any category in this section because they sell a little bit of everything. Locals visit for the reliable selection of Gunpla kits, model kids, action figures, Funko POP! toys, and their counter full of gaming and trading cards.

Toy Tokyo (MANH)
◎ *91 2nd Ave bet. E 6th and 5th St, East Village*
⊕ *toytokyo.com*

A collectible toy enthusiast's dream — Toy Tokyo specializes in, but is certainly not limited to, Japanese toys. Find anything from rare KAWS toys to hard-to-find anime figures, plus a whole wall of ever-popular blind boxes. Be prepared to spend some serious time here, because every nook and cranny is packed full of curious objects.

Kidult Brick (BK)
◎ *269 Ave U, Gravesend*
⊕ *kidultbrick.com*

I did a double-take while walking through this quaint business area in Gravesend because I couldn't believe what I was seeing: a glass counter full of Lego mini figures lined up like little plastic soldiers. That's right: this is an independent dealer of Lego products, with a specialty in pre-owned mini figures. Come here for the set you can't find anywhere else, or for rare mini figs.

Museum of Nostalgia (QNS)

◉ *31-27 31st St, Astoria*
⊕ *museumofnostalgia.com*

Part museum, part shop — a visit to this quirky space is a field trip right back to the 1980s. Expert toy collectors Phebe and Jeff have created a delightful space for showcasing their treasures, some of which are for sale. From California Raisins to Trolls and Transformers, a person of a certain age is sure to find something they'd forgotten about from their childhood. And for the younger set, the museum has a play area and arcade machines. Check social media for current hours.

dAN's Parents' House (BX)

◉ *239 City Island Ave, City Island*
⊕ *dansparentshouse.com*

Revisit your pre-2000s childhood in this wildly fun 1860s house, packed full of toys, trinkets, and treasures. Owners Dan and Reina started at the Brooklyn Flea selling toys from Dan's own 1980s childhood, and have gone on to occupy a whole house full of delights that'll make you giddy for a different era. Figurines of niche characters, trading cards in their original packs, board games you forgot existed, an entire room full of vinyl, and plenty of bits and bobs to share with the younger generation — it's a nostalgia trip that's worth a day out in this special little corner of the Bronx.

Hobby Shops

This type of shop might not be part of the everyday retail vernacular anymore, but it's far from obsolete. Typically, you'll find tools and supplies for old-school hobby activities here, like model trains, RC vehicles, intricate model-making, as well as other small mechanical collectibles and toys.

The Red Caboose (MANH)

◉ *23 W 45th St bet. 6th and 5th Ave, Midtown*
⊕ *theredcaboose.com*

The Red Caboose is the most comprehensive stockist of general hobby supplies and tools in Manhattan, but what they really specialize in is model trains and cars, specifically an extensive collection of subway cars. It's a pilgrimage site for model train enthusiasts and features little notes throughout, annotating particularly useful, rare, or interesting items.

Rudy's Hobby & Art (QNS)
◎ *3516 30th Ave, Astoria*

Rudy's Hobby & Art is old-school. Get model-making kits, model trains and places, and plenty of supplies and paints for all of your own hobby projects here. Despite what the charmingly vintage signage and packed window displays imply, this shop isn't just a relic of the past — they retail current toys and kits, too.

Redline Hobbies (BX)
◎ *3192 Webster Ave, Norwood*
⊕ *redlinehobbiesny.com*

While cataloging a residential area of the Bronx, I was surprised and delighted to spot a group of grown men nerding out over their souped-up RC cars on a sidewalk. The shop they were standing in front of is Redline Hobbies, which is a true specialist in the world of radio-controlled vehicles. You can get parts for your existing vehicles, buy new ones, and also troubleshoot issues with the knowledgeable staff. Trucks, boats, places, helicopters — they have it all here.

Magic

Don't Blink Magic Shop (MANH)
◎ *336 W 37th St Ste 960 bet. 9th and 8th Ave, Hell's Kitchen*
⊕ *dontblinknyc.com*

Sure, you can buy your magic supplies online, but you won't get advice or a demo from Magick Balay, the expert owner of this unassuming magic shop. Find tools for card tricks, sleight of hand, and illusions here. While the selection is more tightly edited than it is at other shops in the field, you can trust that it's from a point of discernment and knowledgeable curation.

Tannen's Magic (MANH)

⊚ *45 W 34th St #608 nr. 6th Ave, Midtown*
⊕ *tannens.com*

For 100 years, Tannen's Magic has been operating as a one-stop shop for New York City magicians. From card tricks, to elaborate stage magic — everything you need can probably be found at Tannen's. You can even register your kid for their annual week-long magic camp, attend lectures by world-class magicians, and participate in a magic-themed book club here!

> **America's oldest magic shop!**

Movies

Night Owl Video (BK) **NEW!**

⊚ *288 Grand St, Williamsburg*
⊕ *nightowlvid.com*

Would you have guessed that a new shop for physical media would open in the year 2025? That's exactly what Night Owl Video is: a place for DVDs, Blu-ray, VHS, and all things movies. Even in the age of streamers, there are some titles that just can't be found online, and Night Owl fills the void of cult favorites and forgotten titles. There's no online catalog, so browsing feels akin to the thrill of going to Blockbuster to pick out something for a Friday night sleepover.

Table Games

The Compleat Strategist (MANH)

⊚ *11 E 33rd St bet. 5th Ave and Madison Ave, Nomad*
⊕ *thecompleatstrategist.com*

For over 45 years, The Compleat Strategist has been an integral resource for all things board games. Find the classics amid a full range of new, rare, and special edition games. They've got all of the *Dungeons & Dragons* books, a ton of puzzles, and great card games you've never heard of.

Chess Forum (MANH)

◎ *219 Thompson St*
bet. W 3rd and Bleecker St, Greenwich Village
⊕ *chessforum.com*

Want a reminder of why there's no place like New York? Visit Chess Forum. This charming storefront is home to rows of tables ready for a game of chess. Anyone can come play, no matter their skill level, for a mere $5/hr (free for kids! $1 for seniors!). Most folks come here to meet and play with other chess enthusiasts, but Chess Forum also retails a selection of incredible high quality, unique chess sets.

Art of Play (BK) **NEW!**

◎ *69 Atlantic Ave, Brooklyn Heights*
⊕ *artofplay.com*

What started as a line of design-forward playing cards is now a brick-and-mortar outpost for games and curiosities from all over the world, most of which are chosen for their functionality, uniqueness, and style. Find Japanese wooden puzzle boxes, kinetic sculptures, beautiful board games, and, of course, their signature card decks. There's plenty for all ages here, but Art of Play mostly stands as a reminder to adults that play is for everyone.

Twenty Sided Store (BK)

◎ *280 Grand St, Williamsburg*
⊕ *twentysidedstore.com*

Specializing in all things cards, Twenty Sided Store hits all genres: role-playing games, tarot cards, anything *Magic the Gathering*, family-friendly games, adult party games, and silly card games. This place is run by longtime Brooklynites whose passion for games is palpable from the minute you walk through the door. Visit for something specific you can't find elsewhere, or when you want to try something new and don't know where to start.

Gamestoria (QNS)

⊚ *42-11 Broadway, Astoria*
⊕ *gamestoria.com*

Gamestoria is an incredibly thorough stockist of popular table games, but what gamers love is that they can also use the store as a gathering place. Make a purchase of $20+ or pay $10 per person to bring your own game or utilize the shop's extensive board game library.

Trading Cards

Bleecker Trading (MANH)

⊚ *96 Christopher St, West Village*
⊚ *185 W 80th St, Upper West Side*
⊕ *bleeckertrading.com*

New, limited edition, and vintage sports cards fill these twin shops. You'll feel like you're a kid visiting a neighborhood card shop in the '70s here — it's family-friendly, the staff is ultra knowledgeable, and the selection is the right balance of new and vintage.

Royal Sports & Entertainment (QNS)

⊚ *96-11 Metropolitan Ave, Forest Hills*

Take a trip to Forest Hills for rare baseball cards and an incredible selection of sports memorabilia, autographs, and collectibles. It's the closest thing in the city to visiting an IRL auction catalog. This isn't just a place for old-school collectors — you can also find Pokemon and Yu-Gi-Oh cards here. Be sure to swing by their second store down the street for comics and figurines, too.

Video Games

Videogamesnewyork (MANH)
◎ *202 E 6th St bet. Bowery and 2nd Ave, East Village*
⊕ *videogamesnewyork.com*

Take a trip through the entire history of video games at Videogamesnewyork, a well-established dealer of new and vintage games and consoles. There's something for every type of system that's ever existed — even hard-to-find replacement parts for retro devices. Where else in the city can you get the hottest new PS5 games and rare original GameBoy games in the same store?

Brooklyn Video Games (BK)
◎ *6120 4th Ave, Bensonhurst*
◎ *6801 20th Ave, Bensonhurst*
⊕ *brooklynvideogames.com*

Brooklyn Video Games is a neighborhood favorite buy-sell-trade video game shop, but what's *really* special is their new second location on 4th Ave, which features a collection of awesome vintage arcade machines, by-the-hour console set-ups and group gaming tables.

Music Planet Games & Records (BK)
◎ *649 Manhattan Ave, Greenpoint*

This might be the last place in the city where you can buy records, CDs, and video games all in one place. Visit to feel like it's 1997 and you're hanging out at the mall with your friends after school.

K&P Games Express Inc (BX)
◎ *940 Southern Blvd, Longwood*

A top-notch Gamestop alternative, K&P is beloved by gamers in the Bronx for their mix of old, new, and special releases. The community vibes here are strong and the folks behind the counter are full of knowledge. Word on the street is that you can get games ahead of their release here.

Food & Beverage

This is where things get really specific! It'd be easy to write an entire guidebook on this category alone, but for now, here's a selection of favorites I've encountered while exploring, by asking around and talking to other New Yorkers and through my own shopping experience.

Alcohol

Beer

Alphabet City Beer Co. (MANH)
◎ *96 Ave C, Alphabet City*
⊕ *abcbeer.co*
With a focus on New York breweries, this bar and shop features an extensive menu of specialty brews on tap and in their stacked fridges. Visit for one of their popular trivia nights and leave with an exciting stash to stock your own fridge.

Top Hops Beer Shop (MANH)
◎ *88 Essex St within Essex Market, Lower East Side*
⊕ *tophops.com*
A longstanding LES favorite for hard-to-find craft beer, Top Hops is the kind of place where craft beer skeptics are converted and beer nerds find something new to try. Sit at the bar and enjoy something on tap before picking up a few cans to take home.

Eastern District (BK)

- *1053 Manhattan Ave, Greenpoint*
- *370 Bedford Ave, Williamsburg*
- *90 5th Ave, Park Slope*
- *easterndistrictny.com*

Beer! Cheese! Charcuterie! Get all of your picnic snacks at Eastern District — a shop that prioritizes selling local producers. Their Made in Brooklyn gift baskets and state-specific cheese selections make a great gift for a former New Yorker who's feeling homesick, or as a cooler, local alternative to Harry & David.

Grimm Artisanal Ales (BK)

- *990 Metropolitan Ave, East Williamsburg*
- *grimmales.com*

In just a little more than 10 years, Grimm Artisanal Ales has become a revered name in the world of beer for their creative, experimental brewing and history-informed approach. While they're most known for their sours and IPAs, they also have a sister brand, Physica Wines, on the premises, making whole-cluster (skin *and* stem contact) wine from local North Fork grapes. Pay Grimm a visit in East Williamsburg for drinks and pizza from their rooftop restaurant, Lala's Apizza, or to purchase wine and beer to take home.

Talea Beer (BK)

- *87 Richardson St, Williamsburg*
- *taleabeer.com*

Women-owned and renowned for their bright and modern taproom, Talea Beer's flagship location in Williamsburg is home to their production facility and retail counter for purchasing beer. Alongside more creative, often fruit-forward types, they do a rare thing for a craft brewery: they make an actually good light beer in a normal sized can!

Holiday Beverage (SI)

- *4569 Amboy Rd, South Shore*
- *holidaybev.com*

It's not easy to find craft beer on Staten Island, but it can be found at Holiday Beverage — a beer distributor with knowledgeable staff and a diverse selection, including a surprisingly good range of NA options.

Especially Good Wine & Liquor

Community Wine and Spirits (MANH)
◎ *140 10th Ave nr. W 19th St, Chelsea*
⊕ *communitywineandspirits.com*

Community Wine and Spirits is an emporium for the modern drinker. The spacious store is designed with a discerning minimalism that attracts a curious crowd of wine lovers and cocktail enthusiasts looking for something special, but still approachable. These enthusiastic experts host lively tastings on the first Saturday of every month and classes for learning about wines from particular regions, because the name isn't just for show — this shop is *really* about fostering a community around great wine.

Astor Wines & Spirits (MANH)
◎ *399 Lafayette St nr. E 4th St, NoHo*
⊕ *astorwines.com*

Astor Wines & Spirits has been an essential part of the wine retail scene for decades, but made headlines in 2022 when it became completely employee-owned. This is the store you visit (or order home delivery from) when you are shopping for a party and need lots of different things. It's also where you go when you need something specific and require a recommendation, or if you need something kind of rare. I suppose what I mean is: Astor Wines & Spirits has everything you could ever want or need and is a lovely, ethical small business. A win for everyone!

Grape Collective (MANH)
◎ *2675a Broadway nr. W 102nd St, Upper West Side*
⊕ *grapecollective.com*

Part wine shop, part editorial outlet, Grape Collective is all about storytelling. Their website regularly publishes interviews with winemakers, agriculture intel, and news about the wine industry, which translates to an immensely well-stocked and knowledge-driven shop. Find small-producer wines and even some locally made options here.

Henry Harde's Wines & Liquors (BK)

⊚ *9314 3rd Ave, Bay Ridge*
⊕ *henryhardeinc.com*

"Brooklyn's Fine Wine and High Spirit Store since 1933" is a charming little place — family-owned and well-stocked with just about everything. Stop by for one of their regular tastings, to peer into their elaborate window displays, or just to enjoy a genuine and welcoming wine shopping experience.

Corkscrew Wines (BK)

⊚ *489 Myrtle Ave, Clinton Hill*
⊕ *corkscrewbrooklyn.com*

"Honest Wines Made by Real People" is the motto here, and it's true! Owner Karin puts a serious emphasis on stocking wines by mostly female winemakers, with an ample assortment of wines from family estates and sustainability-focused indie producers. Come here for terrific wine, but leave knowing a thing or two about the inspiring folks who made it.

Black Cat Wines (BK)

252 4th Ave, Gowanus
blackcatwinesbk.com

Black and queer-owned, Black Cat Wines amplifies under-represented natural wine and spirit producers with their thoughtfully chosen inventory. It's the best kind of curated wine shop; basically every bottle is an awesome deep cut.

Dépanneur Wines (BK)

⊚ *242 Wythe Ave #2, Williamsburg*
⊕ *depanneurwines.com*

The wine shop component of the fancy pantry shop Dépanneur next door, this friendly and inclusive wine shop has a fabulous selection of bottles under $30 and regularly hosts tasting nights on Thursdays. This is a small producer-only zone, and a social one at that! Come for the neighborhood vibes, grab a few bottles, hit the shop next door for snacks, and you've got everything you need for a gathering.

Table Wine (QNS)

◎ *79-14 37th Ave, Jackson Heights*

What a charming little wine shop this is. Table Wine is beloved in Jackson Heights, as is owner Ernesto, who, along with his knowledgeable staff, labels every single bottle with a handwritten information tag. There's a shelf marked "Locals Only," featuring wine from all over New York State, and while the liquor selection is small, it includes many hard-to-find bottles from smaller brands.

Natural Wine

Pompette Wine (MANH)

◎ *420 Malcolm X Blvd nr. W 131st St, Harlem*
⊕ *pompettewines.com*

While not exclusively selling natural wine, Harlem favorite Pompette does place emphasis on their excellent biodynamic/natural/sustainable selection. It's just a really good neighborhood wine shop with a little European flair — the kind of place that you can go to knowing that you're in for a great recommendation at just about any price.

Magazzino (MANH) NEW!

◎ *83 Henry St nr. Forsyth St, Lower East Side*
⊕ *magazzinonyc.com*

Maggazzino offers a truly fresh perspective on old world wine. This bright space is merchandised for both efficiency and discovery, with uniform lines of bottles organized by region. Find France on the left side of the room and Italy on the right, with the common thread being their shared modus operandi: low intervention and small producers, only! Enter with curiosity, because each bottle has a story.

Radicle Wine (BK)

◎ *293 Greene Ave, Clinton Hill*
⊕ *radiclewine.com*

An absolutely rad wine shop, indeed. Radicle Wine is a unique natural wine retailer, but perhaps even more exceptionally, they do a great job of sourcing locally-made spirits. Keep an eye on their social media, too, because they occasionally host local bands for shows in their basement!

> *Check out **Radicle's** exclusive house wine made with their friends at Catch & Release.*

Thirst Wine Merchants (BK)
◎ *11 Greene Ave, Fort Greene*
⊕ *thirstmerchants.com*
With a deeply rooted interest in community, natural wine specialist Thirst also runs a CSA membership program for $98/month, which includes 4 specially selected bottles each month, in addition to a shop discount and access to events.

Forêt Wines (QNS)
◎ *6838 Forest Ave, Ridgewood*
⊕ *foretwineshop.com*
For the adventurous wine drinker, Forêt Wines is the brainchild of a pizzeria owner and a destination for environmentally conscious wine nerds. Their accessible approach to the most unusual and hard-to-find varieties of natural wine make it a popular spot for those looking for something extra special.

Specialty Spirits

Sakaya (MANH)
◎ *324 E 9th St bet. 2nd and 1st Ave, East Village*
⊕ *sakayanyc.com*
Opened in 2007 as NYC's first sake specialist, this peaceful and compact East Village storefront is a haven for fans of the Japanese spirit. On any given day, there's 100+ options to choose from and a staff member on hand to tell you all about them..

Ocean Star Wine & Spirits (BK)

◎ *1868 86th St, Bensonhurst*

Tucked into a residential area of multicultural South Brooklyn, what appears to be a nice, regular wine and liquor store is actually an incredible resource for baijiu, special Chinese herbal spirits, and a premium selection of sake.

Bin Bin Sake (BK)

◎ *29 Norman Ave #100, Greenpoint*
⊕ *binbinsake.com*

Sake is the main event at this specialty spirits hotspot, opened by the folks from nearby Japanese restaurant Rule of Thirds in 2022. Even so, there is also a meticulously curated selection of shochu, Japanese whisky, and niche natural wines on offer here.

Graham Wine Co. (BK)

◎ *303 Graham Ave, Williamsburg*
⊕ *grahamwine.co*

At first glance, Graham Wine Co. is just a nice neighborhood natural wine shop, but there's more to the story. The specialty here is in ethically produced wines and spirits — meaning union-made, fair-trade certified, and locally-made bottles that are vigorously researched and carefully selected. Amid small-producer natural wines, you'll also find name brand spirits like Four Roses bourbon and Herradura tequila, which have been verified as more ethical than the rest.

Beverages

Coffee

Porto Rico Coffee Importers (MANH)

◎ *40 St. Marks Pl nr. 2nd Ave, East Village*
◎ *201 Bleecker bet. 6th Ave and MacDougal St, West Village*
⊕ *portorico.com*

Family-owned for three generations, this local coffee powerhouse delivers a delightfully unique shopping experience and affordable freshly roasted coffee. Stand amid the bean-stuffed burlap sacks and get a fresh cup of coffee to sip while selecting your beans from the endless menu of options. You'll even find flavored varieties that are more natural and certainly more delicious than your run-of-the-mill grocery store alternatives. .

HOT TIP: *find pints of exclusive, locally-made French Italian Espresso ice cream here!*

Carmel Grocery (QNS)
64-27 108th St, Forest Hills

This wonderful Middle Eastern market is full of specialty sundries, fresh Israeli pastries, trays of baklava, and has been referred to as the "Israeli Zabar's." Most notably, Carmel Grocery is home to a big, old coffee roaster, which sits right in the middle of the store and churns out dark-roasted beans.

Cerini Coffee & Gifts (BX)
2334 Arthur Ave, Belmont
cerinicoffee.com

This Arthur Ave mainstay is a one-stop shop for Italian coffee supplies, a nice variety of kitchen tools, and hard-to-find imports. Find a variety of great beans for espresso, a range of machines for making it, all kinds of moka pots, and the parts and pieces you'll need to repair or restore them.

Non-Alcoholic

Spirited Away (MANH)
177 Mott St bet. Kenmare and Broome St, Nolita
spiritedaway.co

Touted as "America's First NA Bottle Shop," Spirited Away is stocked with non-alcoholic wines, beers, spirits, and creative alternatives. Notably, founders Douglas and Victoria also operate Dry Atlas, an incredible resource for industry folks and consumers to discover the best of what's going on in the NA space on a global scale.

Minus Moonshine (BK)

◎ *257 Driggs Ave, Greenpoint*
◎ *433 Sterling Pl, Prospect Heights*
⊕ *minusmoonshine.com*

If it's alcohol-free and available in America, it's probably for sale at Minus Moonshine. This queer, Indigenous-owned shop is an extensive library of functional beverages, beers, wines, spirits, sparkling teas, bitters, sodas, shrubs, and ciders — prepare to be overwhelmed in the best possible way.

Tea

Physical Graffitea (MANH)

◎ *96 St. Marks Pl nr. Bet. 1 Ave and Ave A, East Village*
⊕ *physicalgraffitea.com*

On the ground floor of the infamous St. Marks Pl address featured on the album cover for the Led Zeppelin's Physical Graffiti lies a shop by the same name, albeit with a cheeky spelling difference. 200+ varieties of single origin, medicinal, and creatively blended teas line the shelves here, and are available for purchase by the ounce or brewed for take away or to enjoy at one of the cozy tables in the front of the shop.

Grand Tea & Imports (MANH)

◎ *298 Grand St bet. Eldridge and Allen St, Lower East Side*
◎ *15 Eldridge St, Lower East Side*
⊕ *grandteaimports.com*

For all types of fine Chinese tea, Grand Tea & Imports is the place to go. Amongst shelves full of gifts, ceramic teaware, and heritage goods are jars and jars of labeled teas. You'll find aged pu-erh, small-batch oolongs, gorgeous floral blends, special teas from the "family reserves," and over 200 herbs and house-made blends in their traditional Chinese Medicine apothecary.

McNulty's Tea & Coffee Co. (MANH)

⊙ *109 Christopher St*
bet. Bedford and Bleecker St, West Village
⊕ *mcnultys.com*

A remnant of the Gilded Age, McNulty's Tea & Coffee deals in loose leaf tea and freshly roasted coffee from all over the world, and doesn't discriminate! There are few places in the city where you can get first flush Darjeeling by the ounce *and* your favorite British grocery store tea bags in the same place — McNulty's is one of them.

Bellocq Tea Atelier (BK)

⊙ *104 West St, Greenpoint*
⊕ *bellocqtea.com*

Tucked away on the edge of Greenpoint lies a sophisticated tea atelier that's home to local brand Bellocq — known for importing high-quality teas from all around the world, and for their thoughtful and unique blends sold in their signature yellow canisters. Find seasonal things like wine mulling sachets and cold brew iced tea bags, blends such as one inspired by the Stonewall Inn, a chocolatey tea for children called Little Dickens and Nocturne, a luxurious sleepytime tea.

Animal Products

Meat

Deluxe Meat Market (MANH)

⊙ *122 Mott St bet. Grand and Hester St, Chinatown*

This family business takes serious pride in providing the freshest meat tailored to the diverse variety of animal parts used in Asian cooking. That's not all though — Deluxe Meat Market also sells fresh fish, pre-sliced meats for hot pot, and prepared foods, including their highly regarded Chinese BBQ.

Esposito Meat Market (MANH)

⊚ *500 9th Ave on the corner of W 37th St, Hell's Kitchen*
⊕ *espositomeatmarket.com*

This beloved family-owned butcher shop looks like it's straight out of a movie. Sure, you'll find the standard fare here — all cuts of beef, pork, chicken, and lamb — but what's special about Esposito is their extensive stock of harder-to-find game. Looking for pheasant or squab? A dozen Cornish game hens for a dinner party? This is your best bet.

Hudson & Charles (MANH)

⊚ *555 Amsterdam Ave nr. W 87th St, Upper West Side*
⊚ *524 Hudson St bet. Charles and W 10th St, West Village*
⊕ *hudsonandcharles.com*

Owned by ex-vegetarians with a dedication to sustainability, all of the meat at Hudson & Charles is certified humanely raised, and all of the beef is grass-fed. These guys can tell you everything about the farmers who raise the animals they butcher and are setting the pace for a new wave of mindful butchers.

Atlantic Halal Meat (BK)

⊚ *282 Smith St, Carroll Gardens*

This barebones butcher shop is a favorite amongst Brooklynites who keep halal, and is well-known in the neighborhood for selling fresh goat and lamb at exceptional prices. You'll also find chicken, beef, veal, and a selection of accompanying dry goods.

Ends Meat (BK)

⊚ *254 36th St, within Industry City, Greenwood Heights*
⊕ *endsmeatnyc.com*

Inside Industry City is a whole-animal butcher with an immense variety of meat products for sale, including nearly a dozen types of house-made sausage, salami, and all cuts of mutton! Of course, you can get your standard fare here (chicken, pork, beef, lamb, duck), all while knowing that everything is local and nothing is going to waste.

Emily's Pork Store (BK)

⊚ *426 Graham Ave, Williamsburg*

You can't walk past this deliriously authentic Italian butcher shop without peeking into the jam-packed window display. Go inside and you'll find mountains of sausages, hanging cheese, stacks of mozzarella, and cases full of meat and antipasti. What locals know, though, is that this is the place to go for a legit Italian sandwich, packed so full of meat that you'll strain your mouth.

Seafood

Osakana (MANH)

⊚ *42 1/2 St. Marks Pl nr. 2nd Ave, East Village*
⊕ *osakana.nyc*

Sushi specialist Osakana sells top-quality omakase trays to take away, DIY sushi kits, and specialized Japanese groceries, but the primary focus here is on fresh Japanese fish for at-home sashimi. From slabs of fatty tuna to barbecued eel and delicate Hokkaido uni, Osakana is a place for sushi nerds and fish purists.

Aqua Best (MANH)

⊚ *276 Grand St bet. Forsyth St and Eldridge St, Lower East Side*
⊕ *aquabestnyc.com*

A Chinatown favorite amongst chefs and home cooks alike, Aqua Best is an impressively affordable source for all manners of seafood. Come for live lobsters, jumbo shrimp, and whole fresh fish, and especially for harder-to-find things like blue crabs and west coast oysters.

Tsar Caviar (BK)

⊚ *271 Brighton Beach Ave, Brighton Beach*
⊕ *tsarcaviar.com*

It's fitting that there'd be such an exacting caviar specialist in Brighton Beach, with its historically potent Russian population. Find kaluga, caspian, and osetra — all types of sturgeon and non-sturgeon caviar, at prices unmatched for the quality. This family-owned fancy food shop also stocks other luxury fish fare, truffle products, and caviar accoutrement.

FOOD & BEVERAGE | 163

Mermaid's Garden (BK)
◎ *644 Vanderbilt Ave, Prospect Heights*
⊕ *mermaidsgardennyc.com*

For a region that's known for its diversity of fish, it's startling how few fishmongers really prioritize selling locally caught fish. Mermaid's Garden specializes in sustainably caught fish, but typically stocks a great variety of fish from nearby waters. Check out their fish share, which has pickup locations across Brooklyn.

Metropolitan Fish Market (BK)
◎ *635 Metropolitan Ave, Williamsburg*

With charming signage advertising "LIVE EELS," this is a cash-only Italian-owned fish shop. They've got it all (including live lobsters and, yes, eels) at pre-gentrification prices. To the Italian-Americans reading this: visit next time you're tasked with the Feast of the Seven Fishes, because this place goes hard during the holiday season.

Fordham Fish Market (BX)
◎ *155 E 188th St, Fordham Heights*

An old-school favorite in the Bronx, Fordham Fish Market is popular for selling fresh, fairly priced fish, but is especially well-known for their crabs. Stone crabs, blue crabs, king crabs — they're all here, and they'll even steam and season them for you.

Geshmake Fish (BX)
◎ *513 W 236th St, Riverdale*
⊕ *riverdalekosherfish.com*

Get your freshly made gefilte fish here for Passover, or year-round. Geshmake Fish is a fully-stocked kosher fish market with a penchant for a polarizing fish loaf and a great selection of fresh, smoked, and prepared fish products.

Kosher Grocery Guide

I'm not qualified to recommend kosher grocery stores, so I tagged in Rabbi Mordechai Lightstone and his wife Chana for help! They're part of the Chabad community in Crown Heights, and are dedicated local shoppers with extremely discerning taste. Here are some of their favorite kosher certified shops:

Benz's Food Products, *332 Albany Ave* (BK)
Fully-stocked gourmet kosher grocery store with old world specialties, imported goods, and a noteworthy beer selection.

Uncle Edik's Pickles, *176-37 Union Tpk* (QNS)
Not your average pickle shop! The specialty here is Bukharian-style – a spiced, garlicky, vinegar-based Eastern European type of pickle.

Raskin's Fish Market, *320 Kingston Ave* (BK)
Find all types of fish here: fresh whole and fileted fish, house-made gefilte fish, and all kinds of amazing schmaltz herring.

The Boozery, *420 Troy Ave* (BK)
Pick up pre-packed cups and pints of alcohol-infused ice cream in fun flavors like passionfruit moscow mule and honeycomb whiskey.

Kingston Bake Shop, *380 Kingston Ave* (BK)
This beloved, no-frills neighborhood bakery is a Crown Heights staple for freshly baked bagels, cakes, cookies, and pastries.

The House of Glatt, *385 Kingston Ave* (BK)
For glatt kosher meats of all cuts and kinds, this butcher is full-service. Get what you need for dinner later, and pick up lunch from the hot bar while you're at it.

Crust Baker, *1149 Nostrand Ave* (BK)
Hot on the baking scene, even outside of the kosher food world, Crust Baker makes stunning sourdough that's so popular, it requires pre-ordering on their website (crust-baker.com).

Lubavitch Matzah Bakery, *460 Albany Ave* (BK)
Open seasonally from November through Passover, this specialist sells handmade artisanal Shmurah matzah, baked in wood-fired ovens. It doesn't get fresher or more authentic than this!

Weinstein's Hardware and Houseware (BK)
327 Kingston Ave
Chana's favorite everything store sells all the gear you need for keeping an organized, kosher kitchen, bits and bobs for around the house, and even hair bows for little girls made by the owner's wife.

Kettle & Cord, *390A Kingston Ave* (BK)
A kitchen store for the modern orthodox household, Kettle & Cord sells small appliances, color-coded kitchen tools, and pretty serveware.

Judaica Creations, *401 Troy Ave* (BK)
(By appointment only)
With a specialty in embroidered leather judaica, this small biz is the place to go for a customized tallis and tefillin bags or a luxurious challah cover.

Diet-Specific

Gluten-Free

Agata & Valentina Gluten-Free (MANH)
⊚ *1513 1st Ave nr. E 79th St, Upper East Side*
⊕ *agatavalentina.com*

Opposite the larger outpost of popular gourmet grocery store Agata & Valentina is a specifically gluten-free shop. Prepared foods, pastries, pantry items, and even fresh pasta are available here at the only dedicated gluten-free grocery store in the city.

Vegan

Orchard Grocer (MANH)
⊚ *78 Orchard St bet. Broome and Grand St, Lower East Side*
⊕ *orchardgrocer.com*

Part deli, part grocery, and entirely vegan. Orchard Grocer is a modern food shop tailored specifically to the vegan diet. Apart from produce, you can check everything off your grocery list here: dry goods, condiments, frozen meals, cheese, and snacks. Grab a sandwich or a truly terrific soft serve ice cream to go, too!

NEXT DOOR: *MooShoes, the city's preeminent vegan shoe and accessories store!*

Lily's Vegan Pantry (MANH)
⊚ *213 Hester St bet. Centre and Baxter St, Chinatown*
⊕ *lilysveganpantry.com*

Lily's is *the* OG downtown vegan specialty shop. For nearly 30 years, this woman-owned, Asian-led family business has been stocking the shelves with products you'd be surprised can even be made vegan. You'll find an unbelievable array of meat substitutes here, hard-to-find vegan versions of traditional condiments, and many things that are also gluten-free. Not in NYC? Lily's ships nationwide!

For A Greener Home

Earth & Me (BK)
⊚ *385 Kingston Ave*
⊕ *earthandme.co*

Appealing to aesthetes who want to keep a clean, sustainable home, Earth & Me stock refills for all types of cleaning and personal care products, as well as eco-friendly swaps for everyday household and personal care items, and a lovely selection of decor and vintage glassware.

A Sustainable Village (MANH)
⊚ *50 University Pl bet. W 10th and 9th St, Greenwich Village*
⊕ *asustainablevillagenyc.com*

This tiny shop is packed with everything you need to fill your cleaning cupboard and bathroom shelves with zero-waste alternatives. Passionate owner Em wills proves that it is possible to replace all of your everyday essentials with versions that are better for the planet. Check out her own brand of hand and dish soap!

Most Food

Bulk Foods Refillery

Traditionally a feature of health foods stores, a new wave of bulk food stores has arrived to help us shop a little more sustainably by buying just what we need without any unnecessary packaging. Bring your own containers (or use the recycled ones at the store) and stock up on everything from sushi rice to local pasta, and even specialty snacks!

Maison Jar (BK)

◎ *566 Leonard St, Greenpoint*
⊕ *maisonjar.nyc*

Don't let the slick branding fool you — this well-designed shop is still as crunchy as a bulk foods store gets. The breadth of options at Maison Jar is truly unmatched. In addition to all the dry goods you'd expect, there's a large selection of personal care products, and a fridge containing locally made alternative milks, cheeses, fermented foods, and a selection of in-season produce.

Precycle (BK)

◎ *593 Vanderbilt Ave, Prospect Heights*
⊕ *precycle.shop*

Traditional, bare-bones, and well-stocked — Precycle is a staple in both of the neighborhoods they occupy. Get grains, spices, eggs, dairy, and produce here, plus an exceptionally well-stocked selection of natural cleaning products and personal care goods.

Seed and Oil by Suryaside (QNS)

◎ *49-20 Skillman Ave, Sunnyside*
⊕ *suryasideseedandoil.com*

Located in a residential pocket of Sunnyside, Seed and Oil places a strong emphasis on local sourcing, with the vast majority of what's available here being grown or produced locally, or purchased from local distributors. The passion for their mission and the community they're serving is palpable here — they even offer a discount for neighbors in NYCHA housing.

Cheese

Formaggio Essex (MANH)

◎ *88 Essex Street, inside Essex Market, Lower East Side*
⊕ *formaggiokitchen.com*

The New York outpost of popular Boston-area cheese shop, Formaggio Essex focuses on small-producer cheeses from all over Europe and the Americas and also has an impressive selection of hard-to-find grocery items like beurre de baratte from France, tinned fish varieties you've never seen before, and Rancho Gordo beans.

Millport Dairy (MANH)
⊚ *2583 Broadway bet. W. 98th and 97th St, Upper West Side*

Beloved Union Square Greenmarket vendor Millport Dairy chose to move into a permanent storefront in 2024 when regulations for selling eggs outdoors changed. The friendly face of this PA-based Amish farm is John Stoltzfoos, who travels into the city 4 days a week to man the shop, which now offers an expanded range, including seasonal produce, all sorts of cheddar cheeses, bacon, cured sausages, fantastic butter, shelves full of pickles, baked goods, and, of course, the eggs that they're famous for. $6 for a dozen orange-yolked free-range eggs, sold to you by someone who can tell you all about the chickens they came from. What's better than that?

You'll also find Pennsylvania Dutch specialties like scrapple, a compressed pork and cornmeal concoction that's best sliced, fried, and eaten with breakfast. Or a fresh, chocolatey whoopie pie, which some say was invented by the PA Amish. It's hard to believe that we can live in New York City and still have access to direct-from-the-source delicacies from Amish Country without leaving the island of Manhattan.

MozzLab (BK)
⊚ *502 Henry St, Carroll Gardens*
⊕ *mozzlab.shop*

A newcomer to the scene, MozzLab has a singular specialty. Peek into their in-house mozzarella lab — or caseificio — to see the mozz masters hard at work. You can get fresh mozzarella in all its shapes and forms here, plus an assortment of antipasti, freshly made butter, and great sandwiches. Wanna get in on the action? MozzLab offers classes!!

Monger's Palate (BK)
⊚ *192 Driggs Ave, Greenpoint*
⊕ *mongerspalate.com*

Monger's Palate is a lovely little neighborhood cheese shop with a focus on extra special local producers and a delightful selection of gourmet pantry items and grocery staples. Locals love their pre-packed picnic baskets, which start at a mere $18.99, but you can also get charcuterie platters in a pinch and even cheese towers (you know, in lieu of a cake).

Stand Alone Cheese (QNS)
⊚ *79-07 37th Ave, Jackson Heights*
⊕ *standalonecheese.com*

Hidden away from the hustle and bustle of Jackson Heights lies the sweetest little cheese shop. Stand Alone Cheese has a serious European flair and is owned by Steffen and Jenny — who are married and met each other through their cheese work! Find an above-average selection of cheeses, charcuterie, pantry items, and great butter at this charming neighborhood staple.

Fancy Pantry

The above cheese shops could all very well fit into this category, but *Fancy Pantry* is more than a shop for cheese nerds who also love imported potato chips. These are the kinds of shops that are as much informed by the perspective of their owner as they are the type of product they're selling. It's about an aspirational lifestyle — one where even the interior of your fridge is gorgeous and everything you cook is effortless, because you don't have to try very hard; your carefully selected ingredients do the work.

Pop Up Grocer (MANH)

◎ *205 Bleecker St nr. 6th Ave, West Village*
⊕ *popupgrocer.com*

After years of hosting pop-ups showcasing new CPG brands all over the country, founder Emily Schildt settled into this punchy permanent home for her innovative grocery concept in 2023. The store operates as a valuable awareness tool for emerging brands, with stock shuffled seasonally. Swing by for a coffee and to try grocery items you've probably never seen off of the internet.

Dimes Market (MANH)

◎ *143 Division St bet. Ludlow and Essex St, Lower East Side*
⊕ *dimesnyc.com*

Run by the team from the ever-popular restaurant Dimes, this postage stamp-sized storefront sells Dimes-branded prepared foods, local produce, and a whole plethora of carefully sourced pantry and household items. Find cool brands like Tart Vinegar and Sisters Body, a smattering of fabulous gifts for the home, and a rotating selection of rare regional snacks.

Big Night (BK) (MANH)

◎ *154 Franklin St, Greenpoint*
◎ *236 W 10th St, West Village*
⊕ *shopbignight.com*

Katherine Lewin's dinner party empire is taking the food scene by storm. In fact, I heard the term "fancy pantry" from Katherine first. Her shops might be best known for their colorful and contemporary tableware, but what most regular visitors rely on is the meticulously edited selection of globally-sourced condiments, tinned fishes, NA beverages, spices, and more. Visit for ingredients you don't need, but that will inspire you to be a more adventurous cook. If you're lucky, you'll make it look as effortless as Katherine does.

Foster Sundry (BK)

◎ *215 Knickerbocker Ave, Bushwick*
⊕ *fostersundry.com*

Foster Sundry is a perfect, tiny neighborhood grocery store with a penchant for regional American specialties. Along the walls, you'll find a case with select in-season produce, a meat counter, a lovely array of cheese, and shelves stacked with everything from imported Italian pastes and pestos to beloved Michigan export Cream-Nut Peanut Butter. Stock up for a special dinner at home, and stick around for a great sandwich or an ice cream — they have It's-Its!

Great General Grocers

Did you know that even some big name grocery stores are independently owned and operated? That's the case for **Key Foods** and all of the brands under their umbrella. In addition to other small independent chains like **Westside Market**, **Morton-Williams**, and **Citarella**, we have no shortage of proper grocery stores to choose from. Here's one outstanding small biz general grocery store from each of the five boroughs:

Zabar's (MANH)
2245 Broadway nr. W 80th St, Upper West Side
zabars.com

Zabar's is more of a cultural institution than it is a mere grocery store. Come by for imported French teas, all of the cheese your heart desires, their famous selection of smoked fish, and a larger selection of jam and preserves than anywhere else in the city. Founded in 1934 by Ukrainian Jewish immigrants, and still owned by the original family, Zabar's has long imbued the many hallmarks of quintessential New York cuisine. Get pickles, black and whites, rugelach, smoked salmon, bagels, and a particularly good selection of merch. If you're like me, you come here for fun and marvel at the charm found in every little detail.

> **FUN FACT!**
>
> At the turn of the century, Essex Street on the Lower East Side was known as "pickle alley" for its abundance of folks dealing pickles out of barrels. To shop for pickles the real LES way, visit **The Pickle Guys** on the corner of Grand St and Essex St where you'll find barrels upon barrels of fermented delights.

The Greene Grape (BK)
⊚ *767 Fulton St, Fort Greene*
⊕ *greenegrape.com*

With two neighboring storefronts, one for groceries and one for wine and spirits, The Greene Grape has the bases covered, and with a spectacular focus on local and small producer brands. You might not find *everything* on your list here, but you will find an inspiring selection of seasonal, ethically sourced, especially regional things to spice up your regular rotation or make a special meal.

Horton's Market! (QNS)
⊚ *14-53 31st Ave, Astoria*

That's not a typo — this grocery store put an exclamation point in their name because they're that into what they do. This is, at its core, a really good version of a full-service neighborhood grocery store, and the folks who run this place certainly do it with as much enthusiasm and fervor you'd expect from a shop with an exclamation point in its name.

Ben's Market (BX)
⊚ *19 Knolls Crescent #B, Spuyten-Duyvil*

When you first happen upon it, Ben's Market is an unremarkable shop. At least, it seems that way until you talk to the people inside. No fewer than three people struck up a conversation with me the day I was there, and as evidenced by the signage throughout, this place is as friendly as it comes. Get all your basics at competitive prices here, but pay particular attention to the prepared foods. The brisket is well-known throughout the neighborhood for being extra special.

Top Tomato (SI)
⊚ *4045 Amboy Rd, South Shore*
⊚ *1071 Bay St, East Shore*

What began as a produce stand in Queens is now a beloved Staten Island grocery store. Though these shops are decidedly Italian, you can also find great produce, everyday groceries, and fresh baked goods here. Locals love the selection of prepared foods, made in-house, and the well-stocked deli counter, especially. To me, Top Tomato wins the award for Best Grocery Store Mascot for its peppy crown-wearing tomato guy.

Health Foods

There's a larger appetite for health food stores than ever, and as Whole Foods becomes less about organic and natural foods, shops like these become ever more important. And all of those buzzy health products you've seen on social media? These shops have been selling them all along. Magnesium, colostrum, chlorophyll, tart cherry juice — your local health foods store has a less price-inflated version of whatever you're after.

East Village Organic (MANH)
⊚ *124 1st Ave bet. St. Marks Pl and E 7th St, East Village*
Lebanese family-owned, East Village Organic is a friendly neighborhood market. They've packed everything you'd expect from a health foods store into this small space, but look for the prepared foods, truly excellent hot soups, and fresh juices.

LifeThyme (MANH)
⊚ *410 6th Ave bet. W 9th and 8th St, Greenwich Village*
⊕ *lifethymemarket.com*
One of the last remaining in the old guard of health food stores in Manhattan, LifeThyme is especially popular in the Village for their prepared food, particularly the extensive vegan options. This is a large, fully-stocked grocery store, and the massive vitamins and supplements sections shouldn't be missed. The overarching mission at LifeThyme is an admirable one: to bring the farm to the people by focusing on supporting regional farm communities and independent brands.

Forces of Nature (BK)
⊚ *1608 Sheepshead Bay Rd, Sheepshead Bay*
⊕ *eforcesofnature.com*
Forces of Nature is a surprising find on a hectic stretch of shops at the lower end of Russian neighborhood Sheepshead Bay. It's large and attractively merchandised with all of the mainstay

brands of a typical health foods store, and has an impressive collection of personal care products. Find the widest selection of meat alternatives and vegan-specific products available in this neck of Brooklyn.

Horseradish Market (BK)
⊚ *839 Broadway, Bushwick*
⊕ *horseradishmarket.com*

For anyone who thinks shopping sustainably is more expensive, this is the shop to prove you wrong. Horseradish Market sources most of what they sell in bulk and then repackage it in recyclable or reused packaging. The result is high-quality goods at a lower price than you'd typically see at a health foods store. You'll also find a great selection of affordable produce and other staples supporting the objective of providing an equitable, accessible avenue for eating well.

Produce

Get off the subway at Grand St and walk through Chinatown to find inexpensive greens and exotic fruits. Pay a visit to 5th Ave in Sunset Park for Latin American necessities like mountain peppers, stacks of cactus pads and perfect mangos. Or, just hit up the guy who sets up a stand in your neighborhood — that's almost always where produce is cheapest, even though it most likely comes from the same place as your local supermarket.

AAA Avocados (MANH)
⊚ *135 Chrystie St*
bet. Delancey and Broome St, Lower East Side

Walk down this slightly dismal block of Chrystie Street during the day and you might spot something curious: stacks and stacks of boxes containing pristine avocados. AAA Avocados is a specialized wholesaler that supplies the city's restaurants with avocados at the correct stage of ripeness, but regular folks can shop here, too! Prices vary day-to-day, but typically hover around $1 each. Be prepared to buy at least 4 or 5 and bring cash.

The Lowdown on Co-op Grocery Stores

A cooperative shop is a business that isn't owned by a person, but instead by a collective of members who pay for memberships and/or volunteer their time in exchange for discounted goods and ownership. This structure is typically found in the form of small neighborhood grocery stores, which are open to everyone and prioritize affordability and community support over profit. You'll typically find a commitment to local sourcing, healthy alternatives, and green practices, like bulk refills.

Park Slope Food Coop (BK)
◎ *782 Union St, Park Slope* ⊕ *foodcoop.com*
The mother of all co-ops, PSFC is one of the most highly regarded grocery stores in the city. One must be a member to shop here, and membership requires working one 2.75 hr shift every six weeks. This place is a well-oiled machine, and a Brooklyn staple for high-quality, affordable staples, a truly terrific cheese selection, seasonal niche condiments, and produce that's as local as it gets.

4th Street Food Co-op (MANH)
◎ *58 E 4th St, East Village* ⊕ *4thstreetfoodcoop.org*
Small in footprint but packed with character, the 4th Street Food Co-op doesn't require membership to shop, though membership does grant you a sizable discount. You'll find a small selection of produce here, but where this shop shines is in its selection of bulk grains, beans, snacks, and household products.

Greene Hill Food Co-op (BK)
◎ *1083 Fulton St, Bed-Stuy* ⊕ *greenehillfood.coop*
This lovely neighborhood co-op is just the right size to find everything you need without feeling overwhelmed. Get popular health food brands, great fresh produce, bulk goods, and natural household items, but also a small selection of regular products — because we can probably all agree that natural ketchup just isn't the same as Heinz.

CHECK IT OUT!

Brooklyn Terminal Market (BK)
◎ *5 S Market St, Canarsie*

This is a wholesale market that's open to the public! Don't be afraid to go in and shop the produce vendors, most of whom are cool with selling to regular folks, as long as you're willing to buy larger quantities. Most vendors here specialize in Caribbean and West Indian produce, but you'll find pretty much everything. The big tip, though, is that you can find an incredible variety of inexpensive garden plants here, like pumpkins in the fall and Christmas trees in December.

Neto's Market (MANH)
◎ *1391 St. Nicholas Ave bet. W 180th and 179th St, Washington Heights*

For Latin American specialties, Washington Heights residents love Neto's. The produce here is fresh, cheap and plentiful. This isn't just a place for plump jalapeños and fresh tomatillos, though — if it's an edible plant that's available in NYC, it's probably here.

3 Guys from Brooklyn (BK)
◎ *6502 Fort Hamilton Pkwy, Dyker Heights*

Imported specialty produce, inexpensive produce, local produce — it's all here at 3 Guys from Brooklyn, a family-owned shop. Get fancy Italian grapes, ripe mangos on sale, local greens, and top quality medjool dates all in one place.

Valentino Food Market (QNS)
◎ *66-64 Fresh Pond Rd, Ridgewood*
⊕ *valentinofoodmarketridgewood.com*

Touted as the oldest family-owned produce shop in Queens, Valentino Food Market maintains their charm with old-school hand-written signs posted everywhere. It's immediately apparent that this place is Italian, and while you'll find stacks of Italian peppers, fresh olives, citrus, and seasonal specialties, they've also got every other produce item under the sun.

This wouldn't be a section about produce if we didn't mention that we also have access to an incredible network of greenmarkets. Visit pg. 33 in the front of this book to learn more about where to find them and how to shop there.

Spices

SOS Chefs (MANH)
◎ *104 Ave B bet. E 7th and 6th St, Alphabet City*
⊕ *sos-chefs.com*

Feel like a kitchen alchemist at this venerable spice shop — a longtime favorite of city chefs for the carefully sourced global selection of spices on offer here. Owner Atef Boulaabi has been searching the world over and experimenting with different preparations for three decades, and her shop oozes care and attention to detail. Discover rare peppercorns, whole tonka beans, unusual fruit vinegars, and so much more.

The Meadow (MANH)
◎ *240 Mulberry St bet. Prince and Spring St, Nolita*
⊕ *themeadow.com*

Salt is the star of the shop at The Meadow. Well, that and a few of owner Mark Bitterman's other favorite things: chocolate, bitters, and flowers. These days, most of the salt here is from Bitterman's eponymous (and extensive) line of salts sourced from all over the world, whether it's flavored, pure, or in solid block form. There's even a fancy version of buttery popcorn salt!

Sullivan Street Tea & Spice Company (MANH)
◎ *208 Sullivan St bet. W 3rd and Bleecker St, West Village*
⊕ *onsullivan.com*

Step back in time at this quaint tea and spice shop in the West Village. Restock your spice rack or tea stash from the beautiful glass jars that line the walls, or pick up unique house-made blends and gifts, like their hilarious and adorable Pizza Rescue Kit.

Heatonist (MANH) (BK)

◎ *75 9th Ave, inside Chelsea Market, Chelsea*
◎ *121 Wythe Ave, Williamsburg*
⊕ *heatonist.com*

It's all about hot sauce at Heatonist, a decade-old shop selling spicy stuff from all over the world. Amid the small-producer craft hot sauces is a radically diverse range of Heatonist collabs, from the band Korn's sauce called "Here to Slay" to a line in collaboration with Bravo's Top Chef. You'll find the selection here to be more about flavor and less about burning your taste buds off.

> **FUN FACT!**
>
> **Heatonist** is the official hot sauce partner of the popular YouTube show Hot Ones!

Spice Professors (QNS)

◎ *69-30 Myrtle Ave, Glendale*
⊕ *spiceprofessors.com*

Though Spice Professors is popular for their annual stall at the Bryant Park holiday market, they've got a year round outpost in Glendale, from which they sell their signature spice blends and teas. Get fresh, nicely packaged spices here, and especially delectable blends for rubbing and marinating meat.

Tofu

Fong On (MANH)

◎ *81 Division St nr. Eldridge St, Chinatown*
⊕ *fongon.net*

The Eng family has been serving up specialty Toisanese tofu and rice products in Chinatown since 1933, and made a grand return to their original address in 2019. Everything here is made from scratch — soy milk, blocks of tofu, sticky and sweet rice cakes, and their famous tofu pudding. Visit to enjoy a fresh pudding on-the-spot and pick up provisions to take home.

Take A World Tour

Kalustyan's (MANH)
◎ *123 Lexington Ave bet. E 29th and 28th St, Kips Bay*
⊕ *kalustyans.com*

When you're on the hunt for a hard-to-find grocery item, your first stop should always be Kalustyan's. With a matrix of rooms and nooks over two stories, this shop is packed full of grains, spices, and specialty foods. While the shop was originally opened in 1944 by Kerope Kalustyan, who was Armenian by way of Turkey, it's now owned by cousins from Bangladesh Aziz Osmani and Sayedul Alam. Perhaps the greatest recent impact on the store is that of operations manager Dona Abramson, who is responsible for bringing in a mindblowing diversity of independent brands and niche specialties. A look at the curry powder section alone is evidence of how specific things can get here: Japanese, Jamaican, Sri Lankan, Malaysian, several specific regions of India — you can take a world tour by just walking the aisles. Here's an idea — by category — of what you'll find:

Dried fruit and nuts
Pistachios from at least three different countries, Indian snack mixes, and fruits you didn't know you could even get dried.

Grains and beans
Looking for a particular type of rice? They have it here. The same goes for beans — all of the niche varieties sold by fancy pantry brands can be found here cheaper. My favorite are the Christmas Lima Beans.

Spices
If you can't find it here, you probably won't find it in NYC. Spices from all over the world live here — whole, ground,

blended. This also includes a spectacular range of salts and dried chiles.

Tea and beverages
Tea nerds rejoice! Get no-frills bags of super niche, single-origin teas upstairs, along with any florals and aromatics you might want to blend them with. I visit to stock up on a super special purple tea from Kenya. Also find an unrivaled selection of beverage syrups and bitters.

Condiments
Niche condiments, local condiments, international condiments, and an overwhelming quantity of hot sauces — it's all here.

Fresh things
You won't find produce at Kalustyan's, but you can get fresh curry leaves, a few specialty chiles, and lemongrass. The dairy sections also sell things like great labne and mango lassi.

Everything else
Alternative flours, fabulous frozen samosas, green coffee beans, base oils, and ingredients for skincare, essential oils, flavor extracts, carefully sourced saffron... just go and see it for yourself!

Soybean Chan Flower Shop (QNS)

⊚ *135-26 Roosevelt Ave, Flushing, Queens*

Indeed, this is a flower shop, but the secret specialty is behind an unassuming counter. Soybean Chan is famous for its tofu pudding, which comes served in the traditional Taiwanese way: either sweet, with ginger syrup, brown sugar, and peanuts, or savory, with dried shrimp, scallions, and chili. Pick up a container of fresh soy milk and a bouquet of flowers on your way out.

Regional Specialty

Asian

New York City is home to three Chinatowns across three different boroughs. From the area between Broome and Canal St in Manhattan to 8th Ave in Sunset Park and the sprawling neighborhood of Flushing, produce vendors and hectic markets fill these vibrant shopping districts. This continent, though, is full of distinct cuisines that can't always be lumped together. Our list includes well-known favorites, and some items even specialists may not know of:

Hong Kong Supermarket (MANH) `Chinese` `Asian`

⊚ *157 Hester St bet. Elizabeth St and Bowery, Chinatown*

Once a national chain, this independently owned Asian supermarket is now one of only a few, occupying a sprawling storefront in Chinatown. The focus here is specialties and imported produce from mainland China, Hong Kong and Taiwan, but all sorts of Asian specialty foods can be found here. Folks from all over the city flock to Hong Kong Supermarket as a one-stop shop for regional foods at the right price.

Duals Natural (MANH) (BK) `Indian`

⊚ *91 1st Ave nr. E 6th St, East Village*
⊚ *321 Broadway, Williamsburg*
⊚ *764a Franklin Ave, Crown Heights*
⊕ *dualsnatural.com*

Indian specialty shop Duals Natural has three locations, all of which are friendly and filled with packets of spices, more dried lentil and split pea options than you've ever seen, house-made mango lassi (a vegan one, too!), and tons of ayurvedic health and beauty items. I go here to buy Vicco toothpaste — an herbal preparation that makes my teeth feel cleaner than anything else.

Yamadaya (MANH) `Japanese`

⊚ *450 6th Ave bet. W 11th and 10th St, Greenwich Village*

Take a little trip to Tokyo in this expansive shop. Japanese chain stores have been popping up all over the city the past couple of years, but this independently-owned neighborhood shop imbues a more authentic vibe, all while selling the same stuff — and more! Find Japanese pantry staples, skincare, home goods, cleaning products, as well as a great little stationery and office supply section. A few favorites include: soft Matomaru-Kun erasers, Morning Star incense for less than $5, and a gorgeous selection of fancy rice.

Myrtle Wombat (BK) `Asian` **NEW!**

⊚ *581 Myrtle Ave, Bed-Stuy*
⊕ *myrtlewombat.com*

New to the scene, Myrtle Wombat is a curious convenience store that sells Asian-leaning prepared foods like onigiri, egg salad sandos, and kimchi grilled cheese. The shelves are stocked with an array of Asian pantry staples and specialty food items, many of which are from independent-minority and women owned brands. It's a great place to scope out what's hot in the small-biz food scene, while also picking up lunch and getting a matcha fix. A win-win!

Guide to Chinatown*

"Greetings from **Welcome to Chinatown**, a nonprofit organization supporting the community of small businesses and entrepreneurs in Manhattan's Chinatown (and slightly beyond). It's a haven of niche small businesses that transport you to different worlds through very specific flavors, products, and experiences. We invite you to not just think of 'cheap eats' when coming here, but also think about worlds these small businesses are making for us — tourists and locals alike)!" – **Harry Trinh**, Head of Creative, **Welcome to Chinatown**

Grand Tea & Imports A jammed-packed store specializing in Chinese spiritual goods, with an extensive collection of Pu'er tea from Yunnan China) and teaware. It's one of the few places in the city where you can mix and match your teaware to your exact liking. ⊚ *298 Grand St.*

Bangkok Grocery Center Speaking of niche: tucked away on Mosco St is a true Thai staple. Come here for fresh Thai herbs, specific spice mixes and snacks that pack a flavor punch! ⊚ *104 Mosco St.*

New Kam Man One of the oldest Asian supermarkets in the US, this mainstay is a two-level store full of Chinese cooking staples, up-and-coming brands, and a whole lower level of homeware, tea, and more! And don't miss the Cantonese BBQ counter! The duck is their specialty and is sourced from Long Island. ⊚ *200 Canal St.*

EWA Trading Traditional Chinese Medicine is steeped in the principle of balancing the body. You can come here to grab some herbal supplements or have their in-house TCM practitioner prescribe a unique blend of herbs to better balance your body. ⊚ *80 Mulberry St.*

KK Discount Have you ever been in a mini maze of kitchenware? Well, this is it! Everyone from home chefs to restaurateurs comes here to get kitchen gadgets and tried-and-true-utensils. This place is perfect for anyone who is looking to fill out their home kitchen for the first (or millionth) time. ⊚ *78 Mulberry St.*

Albert Lam Bespoke Since 1978, Albert Lam has been mastering the art of tailoring and suiting. From celebrities to business owners, his suits give a completely tailored experience. The atelier looks and feels like Hong Kong's hey-day of suiting and you will come out (in a few weeks' time) with an impeccably made suit. ⊚ *800 Bowery, Ste 100.*

Hung Chong Imports This store reminds us of when the Bowery was filled with kitchen supply stores. This very neat and organized store boasts a very impressive collection of knives (and many other things)! ⊚ *14 Bowery.*

Lily's Vegan Pantry Chinese cooking has a very long history of vegan/vegetarian versions of classic dishes due to the Buddhist influence in China. Today, Lily's Vegan proudly carries Chinese specialties made with vegan ingredients. A personal favorite: the vegan cha siu! ⊚ *213 Hester St.*

Wing on Wo & Co. Over a century old, this store holds not just stories, but some of the best porcelain in the neighborhood. A thoughtful blend of old and new, this store is dotted with little fact cards to contextualize the traditional motifs! ⊚ *26 Mott St.*

To learn more about **Welcome to Chinatown**, *visit welcometochinatown.com or swing by their Small Business Innovation Hub at 115 Bowery, Ground Floor.*

Tashkent Supermarket (BK) (MANH) | Uzbek | | Asian |

◎ *713 Brighton Beach Ave, Brighton Beach*
◎ *678 6th Ave, Greenwich Village*

This fast-expanding local chain specializes in foods from Uzbekistan and other parts of Central Asia, and is known across the city for its large hot bar featuring regional dishes and flaky fresh-from-the-oven samsa. Brighton Beach is home to the enormous original location of this 100% halal supermarket, which is consistently packed with shoppers ogling freshly made desserts and scooping up pickled vegetables. Pick up pastries and fruit for a day at the beach here.

Dukan Syko (BK) | Korean | | Syrian |

◎ *214a Prospect Park W, Park Slope*
⊕ *dukansykomarketplace.com*

Dukan Syko is a mom-and-pop style grocer dreamed up by the team at beloved Syrian-Korean fusion restaurant SYKO. Here, all the heavy-hitter products from Middle Eastern and Asian markets come together to form a pantry department from multi-cultural heaven. You'll also find a prepared food section that's stacked with Halal offerings, kimbap, kimchi, and hummus straight from the SYKO kitchen.

Yun Hai Shop (BK) | Taiwanese |

◎ *170 Montrose Ave, Williamsburg*
⊕ *yunhai.shop*

Oh, this place is special! Owners Lisa and Lillian shine a light on small biz food producers in Taiwan and have a thoughtful approach that both highlights the traditional aspects of their native cuisine while imagining a very modern model for a specialty grocery. With great design, tight curation, and an emphasis on story-telling, they make shoppers feel like they're buying more than a bag of dried mushrooms or artisanal single-origin soy sauce. You can even find iconic Tatung electric steamers here!

3 Aunties Thai Market (QNS) [Thai]
◎ *40-08 61st St, Woodside*
◎ *64-04 39th Ave, Woodside*
⊕ *3auntiesthaimarket.com*

What do three enterprising retirees do with extra time and a desire for a place to hang out with their friends? They open their own specialty grocery store together! These social media-savvy aunties have a real following in this pocket of Queens, where they sell Thai specialty groceries that are otherwise difficult to find in the area.

MogMog Japanese Market (QNS) [Japanese]
◎ *5-35 51st Ave, Long Island City*
⊕ *mogmog.store*

Prepared sushi that's fancy restaurant quality is what most people pop into MogMog market for, but their exquisite Japanese groceries are not to be missed. Sure, they sell big brand snacks here, but you'll also find rice from local distributor The Rice Factory, small-batch condiments, really good dashi, and quality Japanese teas.

Lanka Grocery (SI) [Sri Lankan]
◎ *344 Victory Blvd, North Shore*

Sri Lanka is one of the most difficult Asian cuisines to find in New York City, and whether it be groceries or restaurants, most can be found on Staten Island, where the neighborhood of Tompkinsville is home to one of the largest diaspora in America. Lanka Grocery sells big brand dry goods, export specialties like cinnamon and cashew products, sacks of jaggery sugar, and traditional clay cooking pots. If you're visiting from another borough, stop at Lakruwana for dinner while you're there!

Caribbean & African

Pockets of Brooklyn neighborhoods Crown Heights, Flatbush, and Canarsie are home to tremendously vibrant Caribbean, African and West Indian communities. Take a stroll through any of these neighborhoods and you'll encounter no shortage of small grocery stores overflowing with produce, stacks of Milo tins, and dealers of raw shea butter and nourishing black soap. See below, a few standouts in neighborhoods less densely packed than those in central Brooklyn. 4

Flatbush Central Caribbean Market (BK) [Caribbean]
⊚ *2123 Caton Ave, Flatbush*
⊕ *flatbushcentral.com*
This indoor market is so much more than a spot for regionally-specific food! Flatbush Central Caribbean Market is a hub for locals, with vendors selling Caribbean products that run the whole gamut: handmade soaps, Haitian cookware, imported snacks, handmade clothing, and soccer gear. With over 27 vendors, a food hall, a bookable commissary kitchen, and a small business incubator program, it doesn't get more community-oriented than this.

Small Mommi African Market (BK) [African] [West Indian]
⊚ *583 Sutter Ave, East New York*
Members of the surrounding West Indian and Nigerian communities appreciate this friendly shop for the African exports and comforts of home to be found on the well-organized shelves. Find popular personal care brands, spices specific to African dishes, and nostalgia-inducing snacks and beverages.

SKKM West Indian Market (QNS) [West Indian]
⊚ *10-56 Beach 20th St, Far Rockaway*
Specifically Guyanese, but offering specialty foods covering all of the West Indies, this bustling grocery store stocks fresh produce, meats, non-perishable essentials, and is especially known for their homemade black and white pudding, which are rice-stuffed sausages popular in Guyana.

Eddie's Place African Market (BX) `African`

◉ *5 E 167th St, Concourse*
⊕ *eddiesplaceafricanmarketnyc.com*

This stand-out African grocer stocks even the most niche grocery items from West Africa. Fish, goat meat, produce, grains, packaged food, and excellent black soap fill this spacious store. The shop motto, "We make food feel like home," is apparent here.

European

French Wink (MANH) `French`

◉ *245 W 29th St bet. 8th and 7th Ave, Chelsea*
⊕ *frenchwink.com*

Francophiles, look no further — this one-stop shop even has an attached restaurant and wine bar. Filled with non-perishable food items, skincare and cosmetics' greatest hits, and harder-to-find artisanal brands, French Wink really has it all. From clean nail polish brand Kure Bazaar to Teisseire syrups and Opinel picnic knives, save the suitcase space on your next trip to Paris and just get it all here. No one will know.

Via Della Scrofa (MANH) `Italian`

◉ *60 E 4th St bet. 2nd Ave and Bowery, East Village*

By the same owners as neighborhood favorite Italian restaurant Via Della Pace, this small but mighty storefront makes a mean sandwich and also stocks some incredible niche Italian food products. This place is Italian-Italian, and regularly stocks both types of Sanbitter, Rossana pistachio candies, Firelli hot sauce, and Aquerello rice.

J. Baczynsky Meat Market (MANH) `Ukrainian`

◉ *139 2nd Ave bet. E 10th St and St. Marks Pl, East Village*
⊕ *eastvillagemeatmarket.com*

The interior of this charming shop has remained relatively unchanged since it opened in the 1970s as a butcher shop catering to this historically Ukrainian stretch of the East Village. Enormous kielbasa hang behind the checkout counter and the cases are full of prepared foods, homemade sauerkraut, soups, and fresh meat. Bags of pierogi can be found in the fridge alongside jars of homemade mustard strong enough to clear your sinuses.

Big Cheers (MANH) | British

◎ *287a Broome St nr. Eldridge St, Lower East Side*
⊕ *shieurasia.com*

Find imports from the British Isles in all categories here. Soft drinks, Walker's crisps, Quality Street tins, tubes of biscuits, and every possible candy bar an expat could crave. At Christmas time, brave holiday hosts come to Big Cheers for their beef suet — an essential ingredient for making a proper Christmas pudding.

Schaller & Weber (MANH) | German

◎ *1654 2nd Ave bet. E 86th and 85th St, Upper East Side*
⊕ *schallerweber.com*

Family-owned since 1937, this butcher shop and German grocery store is an Upper East Side staple, known for their own branded bratwurst, pâté, cured meats, and condiments like gourmet currywurst ketchup! Considering that Schaller & Weber has been growing and evolving for nearly 90 years, it's safe to say that if there's a German product that's not available here, you're probably not going to find it in NYC. Don't miss the salami snack sticks, made in collaboration with local brands such as Mike's Hot Honey, Hudson Whiskey, and Crown Maple.

Mani Market Place (MANH) | Greek

◎ *697 Columbus Ave nr. W 94th St, Upper West Side*
⊕ *manimarketplace.com*

A pair of Greek brothers, Taso and Taki, have been at the helm of this west side favorite for more than three decades. Mani Marketplace functions as a regular grocery store with fresh produce and any standard items you might have on your list, but what you really want to come here for are their Greek prepared foods, fresh feta and exclusive Wild Olives olive oil, made in Greece just for Mani Marketplace.

D. Coluccio & Sons (BK) `Italian`

◎ *1214-20 60th St, Bensonhurst*
⊕ *dcoluccioandsons.com*

Bensonhurst is a historically Italian neighborhood, and though it becomes more diverse with each passing year, there are still a handful of old-school joints here. D. Coluccio & Sons is a no-frills spot with an epic cheese and meat counter, antipasti selection, cooler full of polenta, and stacks of imported pastas and grains. Folks from outside the neighborhood come here to stock up because the prices are fair and the products come straight from Italy. Eavesdrop, and you might just think you're hearing Tony Soprano around the corner

Vanilla Gourmet Specialty Food (BK) `Eastern European`

◎ *287 Brighton Beach Ave, Brighton Beach*

The selection here actually spans several continents, with fancy foods and non-perishables from Turkey, Eastern Europe, and Russia. When a grocery store's ceiling is covered in decorative baskets, I always know I'm in for something good, and Vanilla Gourmet is no exception. Get jars of sour cherry preserves, above-average Turkish delight, and candies in gorgeous wrappers sold by the pound.

Mercado Central (BK) `Spanish`

◎ *354 Degraw St, Cobble Hill*
◎ *252 3rd Ave, Gowanus*
⊕ *mercadocentralnyc.com*

Boasting "the largest selection of tinned fish in NYC" this cozy, authentic Spanish grocery store specializes in gourmet goods from every region of the country. Pick up top-quality jamón to enjoy with potato chips fried in olive oil and manchego cheese-stuffed olives. New in 2025: a second location in Gowanus, featuring a tapas bar and a tinned fish plating service!

"The Real Little Italy"

Attracted by the job opportunities and construction of the new Bronx Zoo and the New York Botanical Garden at the turn of the century, droves of Italian immigrants flocked to the Belmont neighborhood in the Bronx in search of a more stable life. Naturally, a hub of commerce developed and over a century later, the Arthur Avenue area of Belmont is still thriving as the most vibrant center for Italian culture in New York City.

Start your day at the spectacular New York Botanical Gardens before hitting Arthur Ave for lunch and an afternoon of shopping. Be sure to explore the whole avenue, but if you want a hint, here are some of my favorite shops:

Borgatti's Ravioli & Egg Noodles, ⊚ *632 E 187th St*
It's not a trip to the neighborhood without picking up a box of ravioli from this charming 3rd generation family-owned pasta shop! If you're worried about refrigeration, you can also get freshly dried flavored pastas here — look to the back right of the shop and you'll see them drying on a rack!

Teitel Brothers Market, ⊚ *2372 Arthur Ave*
I've found things at this Italian grocery store that I've never seen elsewhere in NYC. For the really specific Italian-Italian stuff, there's nowhere else quite like it. Great antipasti, tinned fish, cans of olive oil, cheeses, and meats are all available here. For the bakers among us, you can also find a fairly priced bucket of almond paste here!

Cosenza's Fish Market and Randazzo's Seafood,
⊚ *both on Arthur Ave*
I'm not going to choose just one of these two rival fish markets, because it'd look like I'm playing favorites. The

truth is, they both offer a stunning array of seafood, from whole fish imported from Italy to every type of shellfish that exists. The best part: they both feature a sidewalk raw bar. Order a few oysters, watch as they're shucked, and slurp them down standing up.

Arthur Ave Retail Market, ⊚ *2344 Arthur Ave*
The heart of Arthur Ave is the indoor retail market. You'll find stalls selling overflowing crates of produce, cases full of meat, counters selling sandwiches, and barrels of antipasti. There's even a stall selling cigars that are hand-rolled on site. Don't forget to stop at the espresso bar on your way out.

Cerini Coffee & Gifts, ⊚ *2334 Arthur Ave*
Cerini Coffee & Gifts is a specialty shop for espresso machines and all of the things that go with them, but they also sell an impressive assortment of imported Italian goods from extremely specific kitchen tools to old-school toiletries and hard-to-find candies. Look for the gray cat!

Calabria Pork Store, ⊚ *2334 Arthur Ave*
Swing by to snap a photo of the famous Sausage Chandelier and stay for the wild selection of cured meats, cheeses, and southern Italian imports. This shop is the last remaining salumeria on Arthur Ave and stocks Calabrese specialties you won't find elsewhere.

HOT TIP

Don't miss the annual Ferragosto festival! Hosted by the Belmont BID, this is a traditional Italian summer event held at the beginning of September. For one day only, the streets fill with vendors, entertainment, and all things Italian.

Tavola Italian Market `Italian`

◎ 274 Court St, Cobble Hill
⊕ tavolamarket.com

Tavola Italian Market is a very well-stocked, very Italian grocery store, but I've included it here for this reason: they keep a reliable stock of Pocket Coffee. This Italian-Italian Ferraro treat is a rare find in the United States and only available between the months of October and April, as it's too risky to ship these espresso filled chocolates during warm months. Each one contains ⅓ of an espresso shot — a perfect mid-afternoon jolt. This alone is evidence enough that the stockists at Tavola know a thing or two about niche Italian groceries.

Mediterranean Foods `Greek`

30-12 34th St, Astoria
22-78 35th St, Astoria
mediterraneanfoodsny.com

The Greek community in Astoria is sprawling, and Mediterranean Foods is at the heart of this vibrant food culture. Aisles are filled with packaged imports, buckets of olives, and stacked baked goods at both of these neighborhood grocery stores, but what shoppers travel from other boroughs for is the incredible fresh specialties. Find no less than four types of feta here on any given day. You won't find a more extensive selection of Greek fare in New York City.

Latin American

You don't have to look very hard to find a small grocery store in New York City that stocks Mexican, Dominican, or Latin American pantry staples. In fact, most bodegas even have a nice selection. I'll admit — I don't feel equipped to call out anything in particular, because while I've encountered well over 100 such shops, they're typically equally well-stocked with standard fare. Do you know a shop that has a unique Latin American specialty? Please get in touch! For a diverse selection, check out any of the **Mi Tierra** supermarkets in Queens, which boast the flags of 11 nationalities on their signs. **Food Bazaar** is a much larger chain with a focus on Latin American specialities, and while it's certainly not a small business, it is still local and family-owned. In fact, the Korean founder arrived in New York by way of Argentina and has a deep understanding of the importance of finding the right culturally specific ingredients.

Búzios (MANH) `Brazilian`
◎ *19 W 45th St, 8th Fl bet. 6th and 5th Ave, Midtown*
⊕ *buziosnyc.com*

The idea of going to a grocery store in an office building may seem strange, but rest assured: take the elevator upstairs, open the glass door, and you'll forget you're in a dismal part of midtown. This small room is half Brazilian pantry items and half other important exports (Bikinis! Football gear! Regional home goods!). Búzios is stocked with restraint and discernment, but you'll still find luxurious Granado soaps here and everything you need to make authentic pão de queijo at home.

Tortilleria La Malinche (BK) `Mexican`
◎ *4202 5th Ave, Sunset Park*

This stand-out grocer is located on a vibrant, historically Mexican stretch of 5th Ave in Sunset Park and is well-known as one of the only retailers making fresh corn tortillas and masa in the area. The colorful store also stocks produce specific to Mexican cooking, homemade salsa, and a comprehensive selection of other Central American staple groceries.

Middle Eastern

Balady Market (BK) `Palestinian`
◎ *7128 5th Ave, Bay Ridge*
⊕ *baladymarket.com*

Owned by Muslim brothers who grew up in the neighborhood, this jam-packed halal supermarket is the largest in the area. I especially love that the copy on their website reads: "Balady is the inner child of supermarkets." Cases full of fresh cheese and halal meats, bins of mezze ingredients, shelves of terracotta tagines, and Middle Eastern sweets keep customers coming back to shop at Balady — a very fun grocery store, indeed.

Sahadi's (BK) `Lebanese`
◎ *187 Atlantic Ave, Brooklyn Heights*
◎ *52 35th St, inside Industry City, Sunset Park*
⊕ *sahadis.com*

With origins that go back to 1895, Sahadi's has outlasted every other old-world grocer in the city. Get Lebanese non-perishables here, Middle Eastern spices, bulk sweets, nuts, and dried fruit, as well as divine prepared foods including their famous hummus, manaquish, and baklava.

Edy's Grocer (BK) `Lebanese`
◎ *136 Meserole St, Greenpoint*
⊕ *edysgrocer.com*

Edy's Grocer is a breath of fresh air in the specialty food scene. Painted in bright pink and lime green, this peppy, modern deli adds a twist to traditional Lebanese food and stocks a nice range of spices, pantry items, and a big fridge full of housemade mezze. Be sure to check out owner Edy Massih's recently published cookbook, *Keep It Zesty*, for inspiration on how to use what you'll find here.

Sweets

Candy

Economy Candy (MANH)
◎ *108 Rivington St bet. Ludlow and Essex St, Lower East Side*
⊕ *economycandy.com*

NYC's oldest candy shop is also its most extensively stocked. Get old-school candy by the pound, hard-to-find imports like Italian candy chips, novelties like candy cigarettes, and local things like Cannoli Bars and Joyva Jell-Rings. This shop is so woven into the fabric of the Lower East Side that in 2023, the city named the nearest corner Morris "Moishe" Cohen Way after Economy Candy's founder.

BonBon (MANH) (BK)

- 130 Allen St, Lower East Side
- 1220 Lexington Ave, Upper East Side
- 119 Greenwich Ave, West Village
- 705 Driggs Ave, Williamsburg
- 66 Degraw St, Red Hook
- bonbonnyc.com

Long before it became a massive TikTok trend, BonBon had established itself on the Lower East Side as the only spot doing candy the Swedish way — sour, salty, and in long rows of bins, pick-and-mix style. Designed like a luxury store, and run by "real life Oompa Loompas," this mini-chain of sweet-scented shops make for a great experience. Grab a clean gold scoop and go to town on creating your own perfect mix, or pick up a few bags of the brand's very own sour fish in flavors like elderberry and wild strawberry.

Eugene J Candy (BK)

- 16 Wilson Ave, Bushwick
- eugenej.com

At this quirky candy shop, every day is Halloween. Eugene fancies himself a candy alchemist and is always experimenting with wacky new creations to sell to his curious customers, whether it's chocolate covered, freeze-dried, or his signature FJ Freaks, which are fruity candy clusters he describes as "Frankenstein Nerds." The shelves creak with nostalgic favorites and off-kilter novelties, perfect for curious tastebuds and candy lovers alike.

Williams Candy (BK)

- 1318 Surf Ave, Coney Island
- candytreats.com

A trip to Coney Island isn't complete without a visit to Williams Candy, a shop that's known for its window displays full of pristine candy apples arranged in straight lines. Covered in nuts and sprinkles, or caramel coated, both apples and marshmallows are available on sticks, but you'll also find bins of candy by the pound and truly terrific soft serve ice cream.

Chocolate

Roni-Sue's Chocolate Shop (MANH)
◉ *148 Forsyth St*
bet. Rivington and Delancey St, Lower East Side
⊕ *roni-sue.com*

The Roni-Sue's crew puts a whole lot of care into the chocolate she crafts at her chocolate emporium on Forsyth Street — owner Rhonda Kave even co-founded a chocolate company in Belize to source her socially responsible main ingredient! Shop the truffle case, pick up a bag of her famous Buttercrunch toffee, or maybe a box of Razzle Dazzle Bark. Can I tell you a secret? This shop has a magic little secret garden out the back. And if that's not enough, Rhonda offers a roster of great classes for chocolate lovers.

> **FUN FACT!**
>
> The name **Roni-Sue's** comes from Rhonda's mother's dress shop, from which she saved the neon sign that presently hangs in the window.

Confectionery! (MANH)
◉ *440 E 9th St bet. 1st Ave and Ave A, East Village*
⊕ *confectionerynyc.com*

No one does fancy vegan chocolate, macarons, and baked goods with quite as much flair as the ladies at Confectionery! Baker Maresa and chocolate maker Lagusta both have their own respective shops upstate in addition to this quirky little shared storefront right off Tompkins Square.

Fine & Raw Chocolate (BK)
◉ *70 Scott St, East Williamsburg*
⊕ *fineandraw.com*

For unique bars and better-than-Nutella chocolate spreads, look no further than Fine & Raw, a chocolate brand with a retail shop in their East Williamsburg factory. Come here for chunky nut butter bars, seasonal treats like s'mores kits complete with graham crackers by 7 Grain Army, and the best hot chocolate mix you've ever tasted — minus the refined sugar.

JoMart Chocolate (BK)
◎ *2917 Avenue R, Midwood*
⊕ *jomartchocolates.com*

On an unassuming, residential stretch of south Brooklyn lies a charming family-owned chocolate factory. JoMart has been around since the 1940s and specializes in traditional brittles, bars of all kinds, and chocolate covered everything. It's a sweet place to visit for gifts, after dinner treats, or just to see what they're experimenting with — all served up with a palpable human touch. A quote from current owner Michael Rogak: "The key to world peace is chocolate. Think about it."

Aigner Chocolates (QNS)
◎ *103-02 Metropolitan Ave, Forest Hills*
⊕ *aignerchocolates.com*

A sweet staple in Forest Hills, Aigner is currently run by its third generation of family owners. Find cases full of truffles, nutty barks, gift boxes, novelty chocolates, and my favorite: a lifesize solid chocolate pizza slice, decorated with white chocolate cheese and glossy red pepperoni. In 2025, Aigner Chocolates was added to the New York State Historic Business Registry!

MADE IN QUEENS

Do you know those decorative foil-wrapped chocolates? They're made in Rockaway Beach by **Madelaine Chocolate!** Find nostalgic mid-century designs for chocolate santas, sports balls, flowers, taxis, jack-o-lanterns, and colorful fish. The factory isn't open to the public, but you can find them at shops all around town and online at **candynation.com**.

Shop Type: Bodega

A bodega is what anyone anywhere else would call a mini mart. The term is Spanish and means "storeroom" or "warehouse," and was used by Spanish-speakers who immigrated to New York after WWII and used the term to describe the little shops they were opening all over the city. They sell basic grocery and household essentials, snacks, coffee, cigarettes, lotto tickets, and often have a deli counter or delicious prepared food specific to the ethnicity of the owners. Bodegas are typically open late or 24 hours, and are the cornerstone of any NYC community.

Synonyms: Corner store, convenience store, deli, superette, mini mart

RJJ Deli (BK)
194 Kingsland Ave, Greenpoint
"An old friend of mine once asked me what piece of New York I would take with me if I left and could never return. RJJ Deli Grocery would be that piece. It's the most well stocked deli in all of Greenpoint, and the family who owns (and works at) RJJ always treats you like one of their own. Greenpoint residents "in the know" refer to RJJ as "the avocado man place," because the owner consistently keeps ripe, delicious, reasonably priced avocados on the checkout counter."
– **Jo P.** in Greenpoint

Footwear & Accessories

Has anyone else noticed that it's strangely hard to buy shoes in NYC that aren't from a department store or directly from a big brand? You're not wrong — I've literally walked the whole city and feel the same way. Back in our Menswear and Womenswear section, many of the listed multi-brand boutiques have an exciting selection of current designer styles (get Margiela at **Outline**!), so be sure to check them out, too.

Belgian Shoes (MANH)
◎ *110 E 55th St nr. Park Ave, Midtown*
⊕ *belgianshoes.com*

Founded by Henri Bendel (nephew of *the* Henri Bendel) in 1955, Belgian Shoes is a New York City institution that specializes in a single style of slipper-style shoe that's made in Belgium and inspired by a style of shoe Bendel discovered on a trip there.

From their luxurious midtown boutique, Belgian Shoes sells these leather shoes in every color imaginable, with contrast piping and a tiny bow. Shoes can only be purchased in-person or by mailing in an order form (trace your foot on a piece of paper to determine sizing), and can be totally customized! They might be called Belgian Shoes, but I can't think of a single style that's more New York.

Shoes

Children's Shoes

For kids, who are constantly growing and probably can't express for themselves what they want in a shoe, a children's shoe specialist is an important asset for ensuring that you won't have to buy new footwear every two weeks. Here are three kid's shoe shops in three boroughs for help getting it *just* right:

Tip Top Kids Shoes (MANH)
⊚ *149 W 72nd St*
bet. Amsterdam and Columbus Ave, Upper West Side
⊕ *tiptopshoes.com*

The service here is old-fashioned but the styles for sale certainly aren't. Head uptown to Tip Top for a proper fitting and expert advice on sizing. Flashy Skechers, cool Vans, ergonomic On Running, and dressier shoes from Nina and Geox share shelves with Birkenstocks and even little tiny hiking boots from Keen.

Runnin' Wild Kids (BK)
⊚ *349 Court St, Carroll Gardens*
⊕ *runninwildkids.co*

Brooklyn parents rely on Runnin' Wild Kids to know how to *really* measure a child's foot. It's not all about shoes here, though. As evidenced by the plethora of mini sporting goods, scooters, and toys for sale, they understand that kids play *hard*. Additional services include balloon inflation and ice skate sharpening.

LISTEN UP!

New Yorkers wear their shoes HARD. The best thing you can do is get to know your neighborhood cobbler to keep your footwear fresh and pavement-ready. Get your soles replaced, revive worn leather, or have a designer pair re-heeled. Visit the Shoe Maintenance directory page on **thelocavore.com** to find one.

Da-Bar Too Shoes (QNS)
⊚ *70-05 Grand Ave, Maspeth*
⊕ *dabartooshoes.com*

Utility-minded Da-Bar Too Shoes stocks men's and women's orthopedic and athletic sneakers, alongside children's sneakers and uniform-appropriate school shoes. This includes little leather loafers, velcro Mary Janes, and white gym class shoes. Over 30 nearby Catholic and charter schools rely on this Queens mainstay to outfit their students.

Classic Brands

Tip Top Shoes (MANH)
⊚ *155 W 72nd St*
bet. Amsterdam and Columbus Ave, Upper West Side
⊕ *tiptopshoes.com*

Since 1940, Tip Top has been selling practical shoes to New Yorkers of all kinds. On a recent weekday visit, every chair was occupied with folks of all ages trying something on. Get your Blundstones, Dr. Martens, and Kork-Ease here — Tip Top really does sell all of the popular shoe brands (sneakers included), with one of the most comprehensive selections in the city. Kids shoes occupy their own storefront nearby, and the selection of socks by the checkout is worth a look.

Soula Shoes (BK)
⊚ *185 Smith St, Boerum Hill*
⊕ *soulashoes.com*

Former Barney's buyer Rick Lee opened up this Smith Street staple 20 years ago with the simple goal of creating a neighborhood-focused spot for Brooklynites to buy quality, hard-wearing shoes. Find boots by Sorel and Hunter, comfortable styles from Clarks and Camper, as well as smaller sustainability-focused ones like Coclico and Naguisa. Soula is a shop that understands that walking is an unavoidable part of living in New York City.

Shoe Market (BK)

◎ *197 Bedford Ave, Williamsburg*
⊕ *shoemarketnyc.com*

Since 1999, Shoe Market has been Brooklyn's most well-rounded source for stylish, functional footwear. Find men's and women's options by popular brands like Vagabond, G.H. Bass, Dansko, and Steve Madden, alongside a nice range of trendy sneakers. If you need to revive your shoe collection without breaking the bank, this is a great place to start.

Cowboy Boots

Zapateria Mexico (BK) (QNS)

◎ *4505 5th Ave, Sunset Park*
◎ *88-07 Roosevelt Ave, Jackson Heights*

Did you know that the cowboy culture of the American West was actually appropriated from that of Mexican vaqueros? Everything from the practice of cattle herding to the design of most Western wear came from our neighbors to the south. Zapateria Mexico is a pair of shops here in the city that deal in traditional Mexican Western wear, which is aesthetically similar to what you're used to. The boot selection here is unmatched — with an array of men's and women's boots in a variety of skins, colors, and levels of detail, customizable belts, stacks of hats, and racks stuffed with rodeo shirts and traditional guayaberas. Prices for boots here are under $300 and unmatched in value.

Great Women's Shoes

Miista (MANH)

◎ *69 Orchard St nr. Grand St, Lower East Side*
⊕ *miista.com*

The buzziest footwear shop to arrive in NYC in recent years is Miista, a London-based, Spanish-made brand known for square toes, lug soles, and statement boots. The interior of the store is a dramatic stadium of shoes: white-painted tiers lined with styles that range from pretty slingback to buckle-heavy sandals to chunky knee-high boots. I can't think of a better place to shop durable, trendy shoes that are as equipped for the trials of the urban jungle as Miista.

Coclico (MANH)
◎ *275 Mott St bet. Houston and Prince St, Nolita*
⊕ *coclico.com*

Designed in New York and made by a family-owned factory in Spain, Coclico specializes in sculptural silhouettes crafted from wood, cork, and buttery leather. And because they're designed by true New Yorkers, you can rest assured that a strappy pair of Coclico heeled sandals will keep you buoyant on that two-mile walk home from dinner.

Maguire Shoes (MANH) (BK)
◎ *198 Elizabeth St, Nolita*
◎ *190 Berry St, Williamsburg*
⊕ *us.maguireshoes.com*

Founded by two sisters, this Nolita outpost for Canadian-based Maguire Shoes is stocked full of playful and wearable women's styles that tap into current trends and are ethically manufactured in small factories across Europe. What's unique about this brand is that they carry cool styles across all categories of shoes — sneakers, outdoorsy boots, slick knee-high boots, chunky loafers, and even dainty wedding-appropriate heels. Most styles hover around $250 — a great price for the quality.

Daniella Shevel (MANH)
◎ *353 Bleecker St nr. W 10th St, West Village*
⊕ *daniellashevel.com*

She might be known for her colorful lace-up boots, but local South African-born designer Daniella Shevel's swanky West Village boutique is stocked with molded leather mules and woven sandals, too. You'll mostly find heels here, but every shoe features discreet memory foam padding and the heel heights are mostly 2" — boots that are quite literally made for walking.

EXTRA SPECIAL SPECIALIST

Cobbler Bushwick Co. is a very modern, woman-owned shoe repair shop that offers top-notch service on any type of shoe, in addition to classes on sneaker restoration and a selection of imaginatively designed upcycled sneakers. In 2025, they even added a coffee shop to their shop, which functions as much as a community space and education center as it does an extremely useful wardrobe maintenance resource.

⊚ *736a Evergreen Ave, Bushwick, Brooklyn*
⊕ *cobblerbushwick.co*

Paul Discount Shoes (BK)
⊚ *807 Utica Ave, East Flatbush*

This particular stretch of Utica Ave is a feast of activity. Grocery stores overflowing with tropical fruits, auto repair shoes, furniture dealers — it's an overwhelming area, and an important thoroughfare for vehicles. Amidst it all is a shop I wasn't expecting to find: Paul Discount Shoes, with its window displays lined with perfect rows of pumps. Need a particular color for a wedding or a prom outfit? This is the place. Most of what's for sale here are heeled sandals and classic closed-toe pumps in every possible color and pattern — I was particularly drawn to a pair in black and white polka dot satin — while still being comfortable, under $100 and with friendly service to boot.

Men's Dress Shoes

T.O. Dey Shoes (MANH) `MADE IN NYC`
⊚ *151 W 46th St, 3rd Fl bet. 7th and 6th Ave, Theater District*
⊕ *todeyshoes.com*

Professional dancers and performers go here for shoes made to their exacting standards, but T.O. Dey Shoes originally specialized in orthopedic shoes. An inkling of an idea and a little risk led this family-owned brand to experiment with incorporating orthopedics into custom shoes for the stage. This is where 85% of NYC's Broadway musicals source their shoes! Doctors send their patients here for custom footwear and average folks visit for better-fitting footwear, too. Everything is custom-made in New York City and costs $1,000+ per pair.

Leffot (MANH)
◎ *10 Christopher St nr. Greenwich Ave, West Village*
⊕ *leffot.com*

Exceptional leather goods are the specialty at Leffot, a well-stocked multi-brand men's shoe store in the West Village. You'll find made-in-America brands like Rancourt from Maine and Alden from Massachusetts, along with luscious British Chelsea boots from Cheaney and numerous customizable options While you're at it, round out your wardrobe with the lovely array of accessories available: belts, colorful watch bands, elegant socks, and expertly fitted gloves.

Cellini Uomo (MANH)
◎ *133 Orchard St*
bet. Rivington and Delancey St, Lower East Side,
⊕ *celliniuomo.com*

This stretch of Orchard Street was once home to dozens of menswear and accessory shoes — a history dating back to the turn-of-the-century immigrant culture of the Lower East Side. Recent years have seen record numbers of closures for these types of businesses, but a few remain. One of them is Cellini Uomo, a men's shoe store that specializes in Italian imports. Swaggy men from all over the city come here for exotic skins, wild colors and statement footwear. Everything is made in Italy, with prices ranging from $150 for suede driving shoes to over $2,000 for alligator skin boots.

See our Guide to Industry City on pg. 227 to learn about **Francis Waplinger***, a very special local shoemaker.*

Sneakers

Solestice (MANH)
⊚ *2115 3rd Ave bet. E 116th and 115th St, Harlem*

This woman-owned sneaker shop in Harlem features a slick, tunnel-like interior and a refreshing selection of collectible, limited edition sneakers, and ones for everyday wear — even for children! Rare new editions are available via raffle, but sneakerheads love Solstice for their discerning curation and large selection of women's styles.

West NYC (MANH)
⊚ *147 W 72nd St*
bet. Amsterdam and Columbus Ave, Upper West Side
⊕ *westnyc.com*

Sure, West NYC has a penchant for limited edition sneakers, but that's not all you'll find at this west side staple. Take a crunchy sporting vibe, mix in a little hypebeast sneaker culture, and add an undertone of heritage Americana aesthetic and you have West NYC. Get your Salomons, Tevas, and the freshest New Balances here.

Tākout (MANH) (BX)
⊚ *1401 St. Nicholas Ave, Washington Heights*
⊚ *2435 Grand Concourse, Fordham Heights*
⊕ *takoutny.com*

Tons of Dunks and Air Jordans line the shelves of these minimalist sneaker and streetwear shops, but Tākout delivers so much more to their loyal customers. Most anticipated limited editions land here, but you'll also find an extensive selection of Adidas classics and old standbys like Vans and Converse. Don't miss the cool streetwear for sale here, too — especially the coat selection in the winter.

Lee's Sneakers (BK)
⊚ *947 Pennsylvania Ave, East New York*

Located in an unassuming strip mall in East New York, Lee's Sneakers has a following for dishing out the hottest, newest name-brand sneakers and rare pairs, with a side of neighborhood spirit. The folks here are true sneakerheads and are generous in sharing their knowledge and intel. Wanna know the history of a classic model? Just ask! Looking for something specific? If they don't have it, they can probably point you in the right direction!

For athletic sneakers, visit the Running section on pg. 301, or **Paragon** *in Union Square. Shoes for specific sports can be found at many of the shops listed in our Recreation section starting on pg. 294 as well.*

Vegan Shoes

MooShoes (MANH)
⊚ *78 Orchard St bet. Grand and Broome St, Lower East Side*
⊕ *mooshoes.com*
Sister-owned MooShoes is an incomparable resource for vegan shoes and accessories. Eschewing the crunchy granola stereotype of vegan aesthetics, they stock shoes you might be surprised to learn aren't made of leather. Vegan Dr. Martens, men's dress shoes, high-heeled knee-high boots, wood-soled clogs, and the hottest brands of vegan sneakers, like Vejas and MoEa fill this little LES shop (which is next door to vegan food store Orchard Grocer). Bags from Baggu and Matt & Nat, small accessories, home goods, and even some clothes round out the selection at this one-stop shop.

Accessories

Bags

Big Bag (MANH)
⊚ *134 W 72nd St*
bet. Amsterdam and Columbus Ave, Upper West Side
⊕ *bigbagny.com*
Good, utilitarian bag shops like this hardly exist anymore. Big Bag sells mostly small European brands you've probably never heard of. In a city where it seems everyone is carrying the same

5 bags each season, Big Bag is a breath of fresh air if you prefer something unique, but still designed with function in mind. Most bags here run between $200–$500, and the accessories section is not to be missed — especially the packable hats by Italian brand Grevi.

HYER GOODS (MANH)
◉ *21 Greenwich Ave nr. W 12th St, West Village*
⊕ *hyergoods.com*

By industry veteran Dana Cohen, HYER GOODS is a thoughtfully designed, trend-forward line of handbags and accessories made from leftover fabric and leather from luxury goods manufacturers. The bucket bags, structured shoulder bags, and thoughtfully designed small leather goods are all classic enough to keep forever while mostly costing under $500. It's fashion you can feel good about!

Peter Hermann Leather Goods (MANH)
◉ *107 Thompson St bet. Prince and Spring St, SoHo*
⊕ *peterhermannleathergoods.net*

For the bag collector who isn't interested in big brands, Peter Hermann Leather Goods is a dream of a shop. Exquisite, handmade works of art fill the shelves in this charming storefront. Hand-beaded evening bags, big woven leather totes, luxurious hardware, and unusual leather treatments make the bags for sale here stand out. Visit often, because the stock here rotates and many pieces are very limited!

Looking for a truly bewildering selection of designer secondhand and vintage? See the listing for **Old the Best** *on pg. 128.*

Eyewear

Fabulous Fanny's (MANH)
◉ *335 E 9th St bet. 2nd and 1st Ave, East Village*
⊕ *fabulousfannysnyc.com*

There's no better source in New York City for vintage eyewear than Fabulous Fanny's. This tiny, beloved 9th Street storefront offers an impossible quantity of options, with drawers and cases organized with styles from just about every era. Most of the staff have an encyclopedic knowledge of what's in stock, so don't be afraid to ask for something specific. One of my most prized possessions, a pair of '90s gold-framed, pink-lens Dior sunglasses, was found here.

Caserta Eye (MANH)
⊚ *67 8th Ave bet. W 14th and 13th St, Meatpacking District*

Highly regarded as an if-you-know-you-know kind of shop, Caserta Eye is a playhouse of vintage, new, and unusual eyeglasses. Let the captivating window displays draw you in, and stay for a while as owner Paul shows you his hand-picked treasures and shares his expertise in fitting and repairing fine eyewear.

Silver Lining Opticians (MANH)
⊚ *92 Thompson St bet. Prince and Spring St, SoHo*
⊕ *silverliningopticians.com*

An astounding range of independent eyewear designers are stocked at this downtown optician. The eclectic selection includes their own line amongst other extraordinarily well-made Japanese brands, statement pieces by eyewear iconoclasts, and rare vintage frames from classic brands.

Selima Optique (MANH)
⊚ *7 Bond St, NoHo*
⊚ *899 Madison Ave, Upper East Side*
⊚ *59 Wooster St, SoHo*
⊕ *selimaoptique.com*

French-born, New York-based Selima Salaun has been designing glasses for the stylish urban wearer for decades. Go here for heirloom-quality frames that are classic enough to survive many style evolutions, but with an offbeat twist. Selima's oval-shaped Aldo frames were famously icon Carolyn Bessette-Kennedy's sunglasses of choice!

Hats

East Village Hats (MANH) [MADE IN NYC]
⊚ *80 E 7th St bet. 2nd and 1st Ave, East Village*
⊕ *eastvillagehats.nyc*

This is a hat person's hat shop. Owner Julia Knox is a milliner extraordinaire and sells classic styles like fedoras, boaters, newsboys, sculptural fascinators, and sisal sun hats, the majority of which are custom-made pieces created on-site using the extensive molding block collection started by original owner Barbara Feinman. Perhaps most notably, East Village Hats hosts a number of workshops for learning the ins and outs of working with materials like sinamay straw, cedar weaving, felt-making, cloche-draping, and more.

Esenshel (MANH) [MADE IN NYC]
⊚ *67 E 4th St #1 bet. 2nd Ave and Bowery, East Village*
⊕ *newyorkcustomhats.com*

Designer Rodney Patterson is known for his tall, bulbous, sculptural straw and hemp hats, which are made-to-order and on display at his East Village atelier. Exaggerated western hats, large and slouchy fedoras, and artful beret interpretations come in an array of colors and are great fun to try on. Each one is made in Brooklyn on an 1800s circular sewing machine, but come winter you'll find more options that are traditionally molded from wool.

City Hats (MANH)
⊚ *55 E Houston St bet. Mulberry and Mott St, Nolita*

I'm not going to even begin to list every type of hat sold at City Hats because the truth is: they pretty much have it all. Go here if you're looking for something specific, or if you're merely hat-curious and want to explore what's best for your personal style. You'll find a thoughtful selection of European and American-made brands, from big names like Kangol to independent milliners. Personally, this is my favorite spot for finding wool berets in any color.

Suzanne Couture Millinery (MANH) MADE IN NYC
◉ *136 E 61st St nr. Lexington Ave, Upper East Side*
⊕ *suzannehats.com*

Shop for a statement piece for your mother-of-the-bride look, something special for the derby, or something to display as a piece of art in your wardrobe at Suzanne Couture Millinery. Colorful fascinators and sculptural hats are adorned with exquisite details, from silk flowers to beaded embellishments. Each piece is made in the on-premises workshop and can be fully bespoke.

Al's Men Shop (BK)
◉ *1108 Fulton St, Bed-Stuy*
⊕ *alshatshop.com*

Get your panama hats, Kangol favorites, Stetson classics, and embellished fedoras at this old school Bed-Stuy haberdashery. Al's Men Shop is a favorite for the dapper gentlemen of Brooklyn looking for a proper hat at a fair price. With hundreds of styles to choose from, ranging from sporty to formal, Al's is a rare one-stop neighborhood shop for this dwindling category of menswear.

Leather Gloves

Sermoneta Gloves (MANH)
◉ *609 Madison Ave nr. E 58th St, Midtown*
⊕ *sermonetagloves.com*

The New York outpost of this family-owned Italian glove brand is a shopping experience right out of a black-and-white movie. Visit this tiny Madison Ave shop and be prepared to tell an expert clerk what you're looking for — most of the stock is hidden away, with samples of each style modeled on hand molds. Try your luck, though, because Sermoneta sells just about every style of leather glove, in every size and color, from suede driving gloves to sumptuous, long opera gloves. While not inexpensive, the gloves sold here are a great value considering the quality.

Wing & Weft Gloves (MANH) MADE IN NYC
◎ *265 W 37th St #11E nr. 8th Ave, Garment District*
⊕ *wegloveyou.com*

Call to make an appointment before visiting this lovely headquarters for Manhattan's most esteemed glove maker. Wing & Weft was established in 2017 by fourth-generation glove maker Katie Sue Nicklos and specializes in dramatic gloves for the stage, red carpet looks, and special occasions. Most of what's available here is opera-length and made of fabric instead of leather, though you can also get something totally custom made.

Neckwear

Fine & Dandy Shop (MANH) MADE IN NYC
◎ *445 W 49th St bet. 9th and 10th Ave, Hell's Kitchen*
⊕ *fineanddandyshop.com*

For those of good taste, this shop is a treasure trove of accessories, with piles of heritage British and old Americana vintage, and other especially unique neckwear. You'll find bowties, ascots, neckties, and everything you need to go with your formal look, like eclectic cufflinks, suspenders, lovely socks, and collar bars. Many pieces are vintage, but much of what's for sale at Fine and Dandy is designed in-house and made in NYC. I often send frustrated shoppers here to find surefire gifts for difficult dads.

Seigo Neckwear (MANH)
◎ *1248 Madison Ave bet. E 90th and 89th St, Upper East Side*
⊕ *seigoneckwear.blogspot.com*

The distinguished Seigo brand of neckwear can be found exclusively at this Madison Ave boutique. Everything is made entirely in Japan from the most decadent silks sourced from small mills in Kyoto, which are hand-printed in Niigata and sewn near Tokyo. Proprietor Mr. Katsuragawa is as much a specialist as one can be. Novelty patterns, stripes, florals, and traditional Japanese motifs can be found here, as well as a small selection of scarves and hats.

Hosiery & Socks

The Sock Man (MANH)

⊚ *99 St. Marks Pl bet. 1st Ave and Ave A, East Village*
⊕ *thesockman.com*

One of the last remaining shops in the area upholding the eclecticism St. Marks is known for, The Sock Man might seem like a place just for wacky novelty socks, but go inside and you'll learn that this is not the case. While you can indeed find any number of themed socks here, there's also a tremendous selection of crew socks in every color, athletic socks, colorful tights, all sorts of netted stockings, and even a little fetishwear. I can't think of another indie shop where you can stock up on everyday socks, complete a Halloween costume, and find a thoughtful, inexpensive gift all in one place.

Elegance NYC (MANH)

⊚ *2 Penn Plaza, inside Penn Station, Midtown*
⊕ *elegancenyc.com*

Indeed, this is a hosiery shop within Penn Station, as commuters in a hurry are liable to snag their stockings. Come here for quality socks in a pinch and to browse the extensive selection of tights, varying from inexpensive fishnets to high-end brands like Wolford.

Jewelry

Contemporary Fine Jewelry

SHW (MANH) **MADE IN NYC**

⊚ *307 E 9th St bet. 2nd and 1st Ave, East Village*
⊕ *shwjewelry.com*

Lithuanian-born designer Urte Tylaite has a knack for designing minimalist engagement rings and fine jewelry that still ooze personality through sculptural bezels, unusual use of prongs, and geometric shapes. Her 9th Street shop functions as a showroom, but is also merchandised with a lovely selection of understated Japanese porcelain and Brooklyn-made dinnerware.

Love Adorned (MANH)

◎ *269 Elizabeth St bet. Houston and Prince St, Nolita*
⊕ *loveadorned.com*

Formerly a popular East Village tattoo parlor with a side of jewelry, Love Adorned is thriving in its second life as a multi-brand indie jewelry dealer and home goods shop. First-time shoppers might find this space overwhelming, with its eclectic selection of merchandise, but start with the jewelry cases, because that's what they do best here. Find vintage gold charms, discover trendy young designers from all over the world, marvel at colorful semi-precious stones, and try on an endless number of statement rings.

Muse Shop (MANH)

◎ *605 Hudson St bet. W 12th and Bethune St, West Village*
⊕ *musexmuse.com*

A destination for discovering independent jewelry designers, Muse Shop serves a tightly edited selection including candy-colored squiggle rings by Bea Bongiasca, and precious stone-framed, hand-painted earrings by Silvia Furmanovich.

Page Sargisson (MANH) (BK) **MADE IN NYC**

◎ *1250 Madison Ave, Upper East Side*
◎ *347 Atlantic Ave, Boerum Hill*
⊕ *pagesargisson.com*

"Fine Jewelry for Fun People" is how Brooklyn-based designer Page Sargisson describes her work, and I agree. She's become known for her hand-carved gold signet rings, which feature a signature brush stroke texture. It's all in the details here. Gold cuffs have colorful stones pressed into them and hoop earrings are delightfully lumpy and irregular.

Tarin Thomas (MANH) **MADE IN NYC**

◎ *92 Perry St nr. Bleecker St, West Village*
⊕ *tarinthomas.com*

The West Village girls love Tarin Thomas for her ubiquitous stone- and mother-of-pearl-inlaid signet rings, geometric gold-plated earrings, and unique chains bedecked with colorful stone rings or birthstone plates. Fans of the brand love shopping here for classic pieces with a twist that won't break the bank. Most items hover between $150 and $250, and Tarin's popular signets and chains are also available in larger men's sizing!

Bernard James (BK) MADE IN NYC
◉ *181 Franklin St, Greenpoint*
⊕ *bernardjames.com*
Taking hints from nature and the world around him, Brooklyn native jewelry designer Bernard James has carved a special niche for himself in the fine jewelry scene. Floral-bedecked Cuban chains, solid gold friendship bracelets, and customizable canvas pendants are a few of the signatures you'll find in this minimalist, USM-clad storefront

Mociun (BK) MADE IN NYC
◉ *683 Driggs Ave, Williamsburg*
⊕ *mociun.com*
Designer Caitlin Mociun is something of a legend for her contemporary engagement rings and unbelievably detailed food charms (get a tiny diamond-studded slice of mushroom pizza for $4,500). She also recently launched CRZM, a "younger sister" brand featuring wacky, sculptural sterling silver and gold chains, mostly. This brand epitomizes Brooklyn cool girl style and the accompanying selection of gifts and home goods by independent brands fits the bill. I especially like to visit Mociun for a wedding or housewarming gift the recipient will have never seen before.

Fashion Jewelry

iGirl (MANH)
◉ *166 Orchard St, nr. Rivington St, Lower East Side*
⊕ *igirlworld.com*
iGirl is the new East Village home of Depop superstar Bella McFadden's fashion and accessories brand, inspired by Y2K emo subcultures. Ultra-femme and halloween goth styles mingle in her jewelry, bag, and hair accessory lines to create a look that's distinctly iGirl.

FOOTWEAR & ACCESSORIES

Laura Lombardi (MANH) MADE IN NYC
◉ *16 Clinton St bet. Houston and Stanton St, Lower East Side*
⊕ *lauralombardi.com*

Designer Laura Lombardi's LES studio is stocked with rhodium- and gold-plated jewelry that features chunky motifs that hark back to the statement styles of the '90s. Irregular chain-link necklaces, two-tone hoop earrings, and ball chains are priced from around $150–$250.

Susan Alexandra (MANH) MADE IN NYC
◉ *33 Orchard St bet. Hester and Canal St, Lower East Side*
⊕ *susanalexandra.com*

Designer Susan Korn made a name for herself with her structured beaded handbags, but lately it's her bar of enameled charms (dubbed "The Charmacy") that's drawing crowds. Choose from wiggly letters or an eclectic selection including martinis, pigeons, and pizza. Whether you're here for the charms, bags, decorative tissue box covers, or fabulously playful Judaica, you're guaranteed an ample dose of candy-colored girlhood. Don't miss the regularly scheduled after-hours bead nights!

Poetry Of Material Things (MANH)
◉ *220 Columbus Ave nr. W 70th St, Upper West Side*
⊕ *poetryofmaterialthings.com*

Dozens of indie designers covering just about every current style of jewelry fill this Upper West Side shop, making it a great place to buy a gift for a friend whose style you can't quite describe, or something unique to round out your own collection. Find colorful stone pieces by Rachel Comey and elaborate beaded earrings by Olivia Dar. Most pieces here hover in the $150–$450 range.

Haricot Vert's Dreamworld (BK) MADE IN NYC
◉ *119 N 1st St, Williamsburg*
⊕ *haricotvert.shop*

Founder Kelsey Armstrong's wonderful world of charms opened IRL in 2024 to great fanfare. For the past several years, she's become known for her Picto-Charms™, featuring vintage images and photos of everyday items. In her shop, affectionately called the Dreamworld, shoppers can select charms from the thousands on offer, design their piece and have it assembled on-site by skilled "Charmers." Be sure to try a Lucky Charm latte from the DreamBean café and check out the workshop and open studio schedule.

Traditional Jewelry

This is a highly personal category of jewelry, because everyone seems to "have a guy" who they'll fiercely defend as the best in the city. I'm not here to tell you who your "guy" should be, but here are a couple that I appreciate.

Oro Latino Jewelry Inc. (MANH)
◉ 82 Bowery bet. Hester and Canal St, Chinatown

Chinatown has no shortage of gold dealers. Just walk along Canal Street and you'll find little malls full of stalls, each with their own specialty. Most of these are family-owned and friendly places to shop for gold at good prices, and Oro Latino is no exception. Friendly second-generation owner Tommy Fung owns this compact counter and is well-known in the downtown community for selling unique chains, custom nameplates and New York-specific charms — including solid gold jewelry for repping your favorite local sports team

Kathe's Jewelry (MANH)
◉ 226 1st Ave bet. E 14th and 13th St, East Village
⊕ kathesjewelry.com

Named for the owner's daughter, this unassuming 1st Ave jeweler is a quiet neighborhood favorite for repairs and well-priced classic jewelry. I come here regularly for charm bracelet maintenance and love exploring the cases packed with vintage pieces — flashy rings, cabochon bracelets, all sorts of chains, dazzling hoop earrings, and quirky vintage charms.

Greenwich St. Jewelers (MANH)

◎ *93 Reade St nr. Church St, Tribeca*
⊕ *greenwichjewelers.com*

A perfect model for what a contemporary fine jewelry shop can be, Greenwich St. Jewelers is a family-owned, multi-brand store that's rich with sophistication. Shop here for an heirloom piece by an independent designer or to seek out any number of services you'd expect to find at a neighborhood jeweler, from repairs and redesign to appraisal. For those on the hunt for a high-end engagement ring with no idea where to begin: go here first!

Watches

For intel on where to shop for watches, I looked to tastemaker **Brynn Wallner** of Dimepiece:

Dover Street Market, ◎ *160 Lexington Ave.*
Shop a selection of pieces curated by Brynn herself, in collaboration with watch dealer Foundwell.

Material Good, ◎ *120 Wooster St 2nd Fl*
Visit this ultra luxe Soho boutique for high-end brands like Audemars Piguet and Richard Mille.

For a wide selection and thrilling shopping experience, Brynn recommends a visit to the **Diamond District** on 47th St: "Go around from booth to booth, storefront to storefront and try things on to get a taste of some real vibrant NYC life as well as a selection of luxury watches. Be prepared to barter."

Check out Brynn's work on Instagram **@dimepiece.co** and her website **www.dimepiece.co.**

Gifting

A type of shop that appears to be thriving in NYC is the gift shop. In pre-internet times, a gift shop was a place to go for a selection of universally appreciated things that one could gift to another person. What they sell might seem random, but a well-stocked gift shop typically follows a careful formula to ensure that the shopper will always leave with something. These shops are light on necessities, but chock full of things you'd enjoy receiving as a gift. While most neighborhoods have a great general gift shop, here are a few that have unusual or notable specialties.

Culturally Specific Gifts

You don't have to get on a plane to shop for special imports from far away places! Here are a few shops that'll momentarily transport you to an exotic place.

Irving Green (MANH) NEW!
⊚ *321 E 9th St bet. 2nd and 1st Ave, East Village*
⊕ *irvinggreennyc.com*

New on one of NYC's most stacked shopping blocks, Irving Green is a gift shop that specializes in Irish-made goods. Because of the singular sourcing focus, you're sure to find a selection unlike anything else in the city, including books, prints, kitchen tools and home decor. Get a housewarming gift for a friend who's proud of their Irish heritage, and deliver it in one of their signature tote bags (there's one with Sinéad O'Conner's face on it!).

Tribes of Morocco (MANH)
⊚ *346 E 9th St bet. 2nd and 1st Ave, East Village*

Recently relocated to a newer, bigger storefront, Tribes of Morocco has been selling handmade homewares imported from the North African country since 1992. Shop dozens of types of incense, woven rugs and textiles, colorful glass light fixtures, and hand-painted ceramics.

E. Rossi & Company (MANH)
◉ *193 Grand St nr. Mulberry St, Little Italy*
⊕ *erossico.com*

What was originally founded as a shop for Italian music, the last remaining Italian specialty gift shop in Manhattan's Little Italy sells far more than the CDs in their extensive collection. This family-owned business sells things like Modiano playing cards, cooking tools, decorative espresso cups, Italian horn charms and amulets, and, most notably, an incredible selection of retro deadstock Little Italy souvenirs. Want a real relic of New York City's Italian culture? This is the place.

Pearl River Mart (MANH)
◉ *452 Broadway bet. Grand and Howard St, SoHo*
⊕ *pearlriver.com*

A superstore of various Asian cultures, there is no Lower Manhattan Chinatown without Pearl River Mart. Find traditional silk qipao tops, the loveliest selection of house slippers, Mahjong sets, decorative nylon parasols, colorful ceramic rice bowls... I could continue this list for paragraphs. You'll even find several brands by young AAPI entrepreneurs here, like Fly by Jing, Tochi Snacks, Simply MKO, and Honey Belle.

Mexico In My Pocket (BK)
◉ *415 Court St, Carroll Gardens*
mexicoinmypocket.com

Owner Luisa Navarro has a palpable passion for the work of Mexican artisans and fills her shelves with hand-painted ceramics, silver jewelry, cookbooks, hand-blown glassware, and overflowing piles of paper flowers. Luisa's POV is unique and design-focused, and will inspire you to take advantage of her travel consultation services to book a trip for yourself.

Pick up a copy of Luisa's new book Mexico's Day of the Dead: A Celebration of Life Through Stories and Photos!

Kyichu Tibetan Handicrafts (QNS)
⊚ *45-53 47th St, Sunnyside*

I blinked to make sure my vision wasn't deceiving me before entering this beautiful shop, located in an unexpected part of Sunnyside, Queens. Here, you'll find traditional clothing and homewares from Tibet, piles of stone jewelry and beads, everything you might need as a practicing Tibetan Buddhist, and an incredible selection of woven rugs

---

HOTEL GIFTS, RE-IMAGINED

Take Me With You (BK)
⊚ *63 Bond St, Boerum Hill*
⊕ *takemewithyou.co*

Attached to the Ace Hotel, this is a true traveler's gift shop. Need an umbrella or hand sanitizer for the subway? You'll find them here! Or a dazzling pair of earrings for an event you're running late to? They've got those, too! Owner Casey has a worldly and unique design sensibility, sourcing her stock from places near and far. Somehow, she's found a balance between novelty and necessity, selling things worthy of the suitcase space of a discerning explorer.

Locally Made Gifts

Brooklyn Made Store (BK)
⊚ *445 Albee Square W, inside City Point, Downtown Brooklyn*
⊚ *51 35th St, Building 5 in Industry City, Greenwood Heights*
⊕ *brooklynmadestore.com*

Operated by The Brooklyn Chamber of Commerce, the Brooklyn Made Store is a locavore's dream. Find great brands from all over Brooklyn in one place here — from candles, pantry items, and skincare, to Brooklyn-themed souvenirs and gifts.

The WonderMart (BK)

⊚ *141 India St, Greenpoint*
⊕ *thewondermart.shop*

All it takes is one conversation with owner Perri Salka to feel completely enveloped in the community she's created around her shop, The WonderMart. Everything she sells is made by independent, local brands and the passion with which she gushes information about each and every item is infectious. Pick up popular stained glass butts, artist-designed press-on nails, quirky jewelry, and plenty of greeting cards to accompany your gift. On my last visit, I picked up a pair of handmade espresso cups with lemon and lime slices as handles.

ART GIFTS

Leroy's Place (BK)

⊚ *353 7th Ave, Park Slope*
⊕ *leroysplace.com*

If Pee Wee's Playhouse was a gift shop, it'd be Leroy's Place. Founded by illustrator Serene Bacigalupi in collaboration with puppet maker Jacques Duffourc, this quirky, checkered storefront is home to work by local artists and whimsical gifts. Serene's monster prints fill the walls, Mother Pigeon's stuffed birds hang out on shelves, and a variety of other creative creatures are perched throughout the store.

RIDER Gifts (BK)

⊚ *1016 8th Ave, Park Slope*
⊚ *347 5th Ave, Park Slope*
⊕ *ridergifts.com*

Though not exclusively local, RIDER Gifts is a gold star example of what a modern gift store can be. Owner Alma Lacour lives in the neighborhood and has a crystal clear idea of what her neighbors want and need. Prioritizing local brands, or at least independent ones, the selection is focused on really good stuff instead of as much stuff as possible. Locals trust Alma to supply them with unique things like embroidered pillows, made-in-

Brooklyn fancy candles, great chocolates, swirly resin decor objects, and that just-right pantry item for the host you're on your way to see.

Upstate Stock (BK)
◎ *2 Berry St, Williamsburg*
⊕ *upstatestock.com*
This multi-hyphenate shop is a cafe, a general store, and retailer of locally-made goods of the same name. Don't let the coffee line keep you from walking through the whole store — it's stocked full of local products with utility in mind and their namesake winter knits (made in New Jersey!), and scented products (soaps, candles, incense, etc.) made to smell like specific upstate woods! The shop was recently taken over by new owners, though they still sell the full Upstate Stock line.

NYC Souvenirs

Memories of New York (MANH)
◎ *206 5th Ave bet. W 26th and 25th St, Flatiron*
⊕ *memoriesofnewyork.com*
In certain parts of town, it seems that every other shop is hawking ugly magnets and I <3 NY shirts, but this one is so much more than that. A mix of new, deadstock, and locally-designed NYC-themed goods fill this Madison Square shop. Alper Tutus is the charismatic owner of this special little place, where you'll find quirky enamel ashtrays, fun keychains, and the best selection of postcards. You'll feel like it's 1999 and you're visiting the city for the first time.

Theater Circle (MANH)
◎ *268 W 44th St #1 nr. 8th Ave, Theater District*
Here's a tip: did you know that there's a specific type of binder designed for storing your Playbill collection? You can buy them here, at Theater Circle, along with merch from Broadway shows current and past, play scripts, Broadway-themed knick-knacks, and more.

Finding Your Way at Industry City

Located on the west side of the BQE in Sunset Park, Industry City is a former industrial complex turned shopping center and office park. Constructed in the early 20th century, this series of buildings was the first and largest multi-tenant industrial property in the United States. After a $450 million makeover in the 2000s, it's now home to coworking spaces, outlet stores, design firms, restaurants, and independent shops.

Navigating the complex can be tricky. The main campus is made up of eight identical buildings connected by long courtyards. Be sure to download the QR code map posted at entrances and remember — the private floors are only accessible by key card. Everything else is fair game!

AMAZING GROCERY SHOPPING!

Visitors to Industry City are never short on great food. **Sunrise Mart**, in Building 3, has an impressive selection of Japanese groceries and imported snacks. It also shares a space with a Japanese food court where you can grab everything from onigiri to ramen. Pay a visit to **Ends Meat,** a whole animal salumeria in Building 2, for an incredible breakfast sandwich, house-made sausages, and farm fresh eggs to take home! Building 4 is home to the new location of **Sahadi's**, the legendary Lebanese market on Atlantic Avenue — order from their mezze menu or pick up items for a courtyard picnic.

Nazz Forge and Adventurers Supply, *Building 6*
Follow the sound of blacksmiths hammering to Nazz Forge, where you can take knife-making and chainmail jewelry classes.

Next door is The Adventurers' Supply, a Dungeons & Dragons-themed supply shop. Get knives forged by pros and stock up on gear for your next tabletop game night, all in one spot. *nazzforge.com* and *theadventurerssupply.com*

Tailored Industry, *Building 4*
Up in The Loft at Japan Village is the showroom and shop for Tailored Industry, Industry City's resident 3D-knitting factory. Shop gorgeous knits and browse the bargain bin of sample pieces. *tailoredindustry.com*

Taro's Origami Studio Shop, *Building 4*
Tucked behind a patchwork noren curtain, this origami supply shop and studio has everything you need, whether you're a beginner or an expert. Shop a selection of American and Japanese origami instructional books, all kinds of paper, and even specialty tools like carrying cases for origami paper. *tarosorigami.com*

St. Mark's Comics, *Building 5*
This beloved East Village comic shop is thriving in its new home on the ground floor of Building 5. Shop recently released graphic novels, vintage comics, deadstock action figures, and more. Co-owner Mitch Cutler has been in the biz since he was 19 and can answer literally any question! *stmarkscomics.com*

CUSTOM GOODS, BY APPOINTMENT

Upstairs in Building 5 is **The Makers Guild**. Navigate a narrow hallway and peek into the shops, galleries, and studios of creatives who make their goods on the premises. Here you'll find **Bios Apothecary**, a fragrance lab lab where you can schedule an appointment to concoct your own perfume and beauty products with top-of-the-line botanicals. You can even have custom shoes made at the atelier of shoemaker **Francis Waplinger**!

Coney Island USA Gift Shop (BK)
⊚ *1208 Surf Ave, Coney Island*
⊕ *coneyisland.com*

It's not a Coney Island adventure without a visit to 1208 Surf Ave, home to the Coney Island Museum, the Coney Island Circus Sideshow, and the Coney Island USA Gift Shop, which is attached to an offbeat and well-air-conditioned bar called Freak Bar. Visit this very official gift shop for handmade gifts, Mermaid Parade merch, artwork featuring niche iconography, and more. Catch a show, learn a thing or two at the museum, hit the gift shop, and then settle in for a cold, local beer. Sounds like a perfect outing to me!

Gift Man (BK)
⊚ *176 5th Ave, Park Slope*
⊕ *giftmangifts.com*

Manhattan might be full of cheesy souvenir shops, but what about Brooklyn? For borough-specific mugs, hats, and more, Gift Man in Park Slope is the best-stocked option. Find Brooklyn Dodgers onesies, Park Slope-specific garb, and, of course, I <3 NY shirts. New service: get your goods custom embroidered on the spot!

VINTAGE TOBACCIANA

Zaidi's NYC (MANH)
⊚ *139 Division St nr. Canal St, Lower East Side*
⊕ *zaidisnyc.com*

Formerly known as Biggie's Bodega, Zaidi's is a singular specialist in (restored and working!) antique lighters, ashtrays from a bygone era, tableside cigarette carousels, and gorgeous cases for whatever it is you're smoking. Most of what's for sale here is tobacciana, but don't miss the rest of the oddities in this very special antique collection.

Pop Culture Gifts

Friends NYC (BK)
⊚ *56 Bogart St, East Williamsburg*
⊕ *friendsnyc.com*

A splashy shop for the chronically online, Friends NYC knows you're on TikTok and looking for that random thing you saw a niche influencer post about. You'd be hard pressed to find a gift shop in NYC that's more colorful and more fun to shop than this one. From pasta shaped pipes to socks with rats on them, there's kitsch around every corner. For the millennials among us: visit Friends NYC to get a jolt of nostalgia for Fred Flare (RIP).

Newtown HQ (QNS)
⊚ *36-12 34th Ave, Astoria*
⊕ *newtownhq.com*

Mexican-American owner Cindy has a serious penchant for Japanese anime culture. Enter her world in Astoria and find yourself immediately entertained by the collection of toys to be found. I say toys, because though much of what she stocks does, indeed, include blind box toys, Sonny Angel, Monchhichi, Tokidoki Unicorno, and such — she has a way of making everything feel like a toy, whether it be a notepad or a Miffy plush. And sticker collectors rejoice: the extensive collection of illustrator-made vinyl stickers is a real treat to sift through. It's Cindy's creative and vibrant world — an important part of which includes one-of-a-kind pieces from Mexico, each carefully selected to showcase the incredible talent found in her homeland.

Lockwood (BK) (QNS)
⊚ *98 Greenpoint Ave, Greenpoint*
⊚ *485 Driggs Ave, Williamsburg*
⊚ *32-15 33rd Street, Astoria*
⊚ *77-13 37th Ave, Jackson Heights*
⊚ *46-06 Skillman Ave, Sunnyside*
⊕ *lockwoodshop.com*

This wouldn't be a section about gift shops without including Lockwood, owner Mackenzi Farquer's local empire. The buyers here move fast, so you can bet you'll always find an object made to meet a cultural moment, such as celeb-themed prayer candles, borough-specific gifts, the latest skincare trends, cheerfully merchandised seasonal items, not-annoying kids stuff, as well as the cards and gift wrap you'll need to complete your gift..

CULT FAVORITES

Top Hat (MANH)
◎ *245 Broome St, Chinatown, Lower East Side*
⊕ *tophatnyc.com*

With no online store and hardly any social media presence, Top Hat is a mysterious place and a downtown gift-giver's best kept secret. Owner Nina Allen has — and I don't say this lightly — *impeccable* taste. Minimalist and utilitarian but slightly cheeky, everything at Top Hat is well-designed, but nothing is too precious. Find stationery from niche Japanese brands, intriguing accessories from independent makers across Europe, hard-to-find perfumes and toiletries, chic powder-coated tool boxes, and larger decor items like intricately woven blankets and statement lamps. Does anyone remember Kiosk? This is the closest thing we've got to something *that* singular in its dedication to surprising and objectively good design.

Annie's Blue Ribbon General Store (MANH)
◎ *232 5th Ave, Park Slope*
⊕ *blueribbongeneralstore.com*

Artfully merchandised tables stacked with seasonal delights, thoughtful last-minute treats for literally anyone, and a roster of community events are what keep neighbors hooked on this beloved Brooklyn shop. Annie's is the kind of place you go when you're on your way out of town and need a spot-on host gift, or when you're throwing a dinner party and looking for inspiration for your tablescape. Even better: owner Ann Cantrell puts an emphasis on stocking local brands! Shopping here, you get the sense that you've entered Ann's closet of favorite things — a colorful, friendly place that reminds you how fun shopping can be.

Home

Clocks

Sutton Clock Shop (MANH)
◉ *218 E 82nd St bet. 3rd and 2nd Ave, Upper East Side*
⊕ *suttonclocks.com*

This lower level storefront, with its carved wood sign and meticulous gold painted front window is the workshop of an expert horologist. Sebastian Laws's clock shop is a decades old family business, and one of the last of its kind in New York City. Currently, the shop deals mostly in by-appointment repairs, but the walls are lined with clocks for sale, and many of them are over 100 years old.

Decor

John Derian Company (MANH)
◉ *6 E 2nd St, bet. Bowery and 2nd Ave, East Village*
⊕ *johnderian.com*

Acclaimed designer John Derian is best known for his made-in-NYC decoupage objects, which take many forms — letter trays, pencil cups, paper weights — featuring vintage images of all sorts, from old NYC maps to botanical illustrations. Three neighboring storefronts on East 2nd Street make up this little enclave of interior delights. The first, John Derian Company stocks small decor items like decoupage, Astier de Villette products, food-shaped decorative candles, and stationery from London shop Choosing Keeping. The second, John Derian Drygoods is where you'll find larger items like rugs, textiles, mirrors, wall art, and planters. Finally, the third acts as a showroom for the John Derian line of furniture. A well-rounded universe, indeed, and one that is aesthetically gentle, floral and quaint in a way that's more New England than it is British. Imagine a lived-in country house owned by the most effortlessly stylish person you know. This person shops at John Derian.

*Visit **John Derian** in December for an epic selection of hand-blown glass Christmas tree ornaments!*

Household by Nickey Kehoe ⟨MANH⟩
◉ *49 E 10th St bet. University Pl and Broadway, Greenwich Village*
⊕ *nickeykehoe.com*

At Nickey Kehoe's twin stores, you can buy an entire lifestyle — and the fact that they're located in a classic Greenwich Village townhouse makes it even easier. The first floor is full of furniture in lush fabrics and fine woodworking, in a style that's an amalgamation of the frills of classic British style and the airy earthiness of California living. But downstairs, at Household by Nickey Kehoe, you're invited into the spaces where the real magic happens: the kitchen, the back patio, the mudroom, the den — there are objects for all aspects of life, from shiny lanterns to cozy quilts and old-fashioned brooms. These are the things that make a house a home.

Coming Soon ⟨MANH⟩
◉ *53 Canal St nr. Orchard St, Lower East Side*
⊕ *comingsoonnewyork.com*

The technicolor, maximalist, offbeat Memphis-adjacent aesthetic that's swept the design world in the past several years originated here, at Coming Soon on the Lower East Side. Visionary shopkeepers Helena and Fabiana opened their shop in 2013 with a perspective towards design objects that doesn't take them too seriously. For the past 10 years, they've stocked their shop with surprising objects that make unexpected gifts, and even better conversation pieces. Wiggly Gaetano Pesce vessels, bulbous '80s-esque ENTLER Studio light fixtures and a ceramic bowl with shoe-wearing legs by Chen and Kai live amongst more earnest things like milk glass from old-school Ohio-based Mosser Glass and ever-popular Sabre flatware. Many have tried, but no one does it quite like Coming Soon.

November 19 (MANH)

⊚ *37 Orchard St nr. Hester St, Lower East Side*
⊕ *november19market.com*

Clark Chung's shop fits into any number of categories, but what I love it for most are the home goods. Clark's taste is rugged, but gentle — quirky, but without even a twinge of kitsch. Bordallo Pinheiro food-shaped ceramics, patchwork quilts, speckled Japanese glass, and minimalist hand-turned wooden bowls adorn the rustic fixtures here. You'll also find a small section of beautiful children's things, french hand creams, Japanese bath products, carefully sourced vintage womenswear, and the Mr. Chung house brand of candles, incense, and socks.

Creel & Gow (MANH)

⊚ *131 E 70th St nr. Lexington Ave, Upper East Side*
⊕ *creelandgow.com*

If there was ever a shop for the person who has everything, Creel & Gow is that shop. A visit to this discreet storefront opens up a world that may make you feel like you're entering an eccentric collector's personal museum. An articulated blue lobster shell hangs in a glass vitrine, there are hinged boxes carved entirely from bright blue lapis, as well as taxidermy and sea shells dipped in silver. It's a surprisingly friendly place, and they sell something for everyone: a lovely, life-like pewter cast wishbone comes nestled in a little box for a mere $20.

Salter House (MANH) (BK)

⊚ *34 E 2nd St, East Village*
⊚ *119 Atlantic Ave, Brooklyn Heights*

Before there was the term "cottagecore," there was Salter House. In seven short years, Sandeep and Carson Salter have firmly established their twin outposts as the finest shops for heirloom quality, old-fashioned goods that are inspired by the past, but are firmly rooted in the present. There are no gimmicks here, just fine clothing made in the Garment District, hand-painted plates that will still look gorgeous when you inevitably chip them, Appalachian-style brooms, and really cool garden clogs.

21 Tara (BK)

⊚ *217A Smith St, Boerum Hill*
⊚ *88 Myrtle Ave, Clinton Hill*
⊕ *21tarabrooklyn.net*

Globally sourced linens are the specialty at 21 Tara, with shelves stacked high with block-printed bedding from Jaipur, decorative pillows made of woven ,textiles from Morocco, intricately painted Kashimiri enamelware and Senegalese woven baskets.

Michele Varian (BK)

⊚ *400 Atlantic Ave, Boerum Hill*
⊕ *michelevarian.com*

It's Michele Varian's world on this corner of Atlantic Avenue. You could outfit a whole home with the contents of her shop, with its sturdy, minimalist furniture, earthy textiles and linens, and contemporary lighting. It doesn't stop there — there's also gold jewelry in subtle, organic shapes, alongside gorgeous wooden toys and even high-class smoking paraphernalia. Many brands found here are local, and Michele Varian brand items are made in-house or nearby.

Slope Home (BK)

⊚ *229 5th Ave, Park Slope*
⊕ *slopehome.com*

Replete with all of the small things that make a home feel like a home, this Park Slope favorite is a big proponent for local sourcing and has shelves stocked with wooden kitchen tools, a stunning array of handwoven baskets, brushes for all purposes, stacks of classic table linens, delicious soaps, and cast iron skillets. Think shaker, not country.

Framing

Framing shops are all over the city, with L-shaped samples velcroed to the walls and big tables for plotting out jobs of all sizes. Most shops these days are well-equipped to take on even the most complicated jobs, but sometimes it's not so simple. Below are two recommendations that are beloved by artists for when something extra special is in order.

Ziello (BK)
⌖ *1382 Atlantic Ave, Crown Heights*
⊕ *ziello.com*

Ziello is where galleries and big time artists send work to get framed. You don't come here to simply pick out a frame and a good-enough matt board — it's a collaborative process, with tremendous skill and creativity involved. All frames are made in-house here, and they even restore antique frames!

San Art Framing & Supply (BK)
⌖ *254 3rd Ave, Gowanus*

There aren't a lot of framing shops that operate to the standards of true fine art framing while also remaining accessible to neighbors who just want something nice for their favorite Grateful Dead poster, but San Art Framing & Supply is not your average framing shop. No job is too strange nor too simple for these pros, who have a serious reputation for quality craftsmanship and for never upselling their loyal customers.

> **GREAT GIFT!**
>
> Stop by **NuFrame** on W 10th St. in the Village for properly framed photos of vintage matchbooks from iconic NYC restaurants, in collaboration with **Matchbook Diaries**!

Lighting

Historically, New York City's lighting district ran down Bowery between Houston and Canal St in Manhattan, but it's a dwindling species of specialty shop these days, and it's getting harder and harder to buy lighting IRL. Your best bet is still to take a stroll down Bowery, or pay a visit to the vendors at the New York Design Center and the shops in the Design District of Midtown for something more high-end.

A&E Bowery Lighting (MANH)
◎ *131 Bowery nr. Grand St, Lower East Side*

One of the last remaining Bowery light shops, and the one that I've been shopping at for the past 10 years, A&E sells every standard type of ceiling and wall lighting you could desire. Flush mounted lights, pendants, tracks, recessed lighting — you'll find all of it here, and with a range of lightbulbs. This is what I go here for: lightbulbs more specific than what I can find at the hardware store. If you have a vision for how you want a space lit, come here and ask for help — you can test and compare any of the options available.

Just Shades (MANH)
◎ *230 E 59th St bet. 3rd and 2nd Ave, Midtown*
⊕ *justlampshades.com*

That's right, this place sells lamp shades only. For more than 50 years, these experts have been selling stacks of designer lampshades and facilitating custom pieces for their discerning customers. Especially for reviving and re-styling an antique lamp, this shop is an incredible resource. Find hardware and decorative finials in addition to pleated lampshades, chic string shades, and ones covered in colorful silk dupioni or even kraft paper. Accent lighting certainly isn't an afterthought here.

Carlos de la Puente Antiques (MANH)
◎ *241 E 60th St nr. 2nd Ave, Upper East Side*
⊕ *delapuenteantiques.com*

As the first stop for a skilled antiquer in search of lighting, Carlos de la Puente specializes in extraordinary chandeliers. Crystal masterpieces, colorful Murano glass, and quirky mid-century pieces cover the ceiling, and surfaces are laden with table lamps.

Colony (MANH)
◎ *196 W Broadway bet. Franklin St and Leonard St, Tribeca*
⊕ goodcolony.com

A very contemporary co-op for designers, the showroom at Colony displays the freshest furniture, lighting, and textiles work around. You could furnish and style an entire home here and guarantee that it'd be truly one-of-a-kind, but what I want to call out is the exceptional selection of spectacularly stylish lighting. In a city where it's getting harder and harder to find unique but timeless fixtures IRL, Colony is a valuable and inspiring resource.

Also see **Assembly Line** *in New Furniture, pg. 244 for a terrific selection of stylish, minimalist lighting.*

Linens

Schweitzer Linen (MANH)
◉ *1010 Lexington Ave, Upper East Side*
◉ *1097 Madison Ave, Upper East Side*
◉ *457 Columbus Ave, Upper West Side*
⊕ *schweitzerlinen.com*

For luxury linens that are a little more local than the European standards you'll find at a department store, look no further than Schweitzer Linen. This family-owned business has been supplying the upper echelons of Manhattan society with deliciously luxurious bedding and all other manners of home linens for decades, and while you'll find simple sets here, the printed and embroidered ones are stunning.

Down & Quilt Shop (MANH)
◉ *527 Amsterdam Ave nr. W 85th St, Upper West Side*
⊕ *downquiltshop.com*

Feel like you're decorating a cozy cottage and not a cramped NYC apartment at this lovely old-school linens shop. You're not going to find boring white sets here — come for colorful coverlets, printed sheet sets, and embroidered throw pillows. Tip: this is a terrific place for a sweet gift for a new baby's nursery.

Duman Home (BK)
◉ *213 Court St, Cobble Hill*
⊕ *dumanhome.com*

Think you can't find ethically made sheets that aren't from an enormous DTC brand (you know the one) for less than $200? You haven't been to Duman Home. This shop is stocked with neutral-toned organic cotton bedding, Turkish-made towels, duvets, and home decor in a gentle color palette. And big news for those who don't believe in flat sheets: sets come without them! Still, a queen-sized Signature Hemstitch organic cotton sheet set plus a separate flat sheet comes out to $198.

> ### MADE IN NYC
>
> Manufactured in Sunset Park, Brooklyn since 1975, **Downright** is a brand of luxury comforters and pillows made of European goose down and hypoallergenic alternatives. Queen-sized comforters start around $180, and pillows start at around $40. See for yourself at **downrightltd.com**.

Mattresses

Charles P. Rogers Bedmakers (MANH)
⊚ *26 W 17th St bet. 6th and 5th Ave, Union Square*
⊕ *charlesprogers.com*

Made in New Jersey and sold in a beautiful showroom near Union Square, Charles P. Rogers has been New York City's premier bedmaker since 1855. Everything here is made by hand, and while the company seems old-school, each mattress features top-of-the-line technology in materials and construction techniques. Expect prices upwards of $2,000, but know that you're getting the highest quality, Made-in-America sleep that money can buy.

Organization

Organicer (BK)
◎ *4802 13th Ave, Borough Park*

Nothing made me smile while cataloging Borough Park more than the fact that this shop exists.* For all the little bits and bobs you find go to the Container Store for, come here instead! Organicer is well stocked with bins and boxes, acrylic fridge and pantry organizers, airtight OXO containers, hangers, makeup trays, and more.

*That, and an abandoned sign for a shop called Couch Potato depicting an anthropomorphized potato lounging seductively on a couch.

Prints & Wall Art

Archie's Press (MANH)
◎ *220 E 10th St bet. 2nd and 1st Ave, East Village*
⊕ *archiespress.com*

Owned by printmaker Archie Archambault for selling the circular maps and charts he's well-known for, this little shop is also a showcase for independent printmakers from all over the country. I don't know of another shop in NYC with a more diverse selection of affordable prints by current artists. Many styles of printmaking are showcased here — letterpress, risograph, and everything in-between, with most prints in apartment-friendly sizes. Visit for a housewarming gift, to fill your walls with something special, or for the unusual collection of greeting cards.

The Old Print Shop (MANH)
◎ *49 W 24th St, 2nd Fl bet. 6th and 5th Ave, Flatiron*
⊕ *oldprintshop.com*

Since 1898, this antiquarian print shop has maintained a reputation as an irreplaceable resource for American artifacts and antique maps. You might be surprised by how accessible the collection is, though. 19th century hand-colored French fashion illustrations for $35 and maps costing well over $5k live in harmony here.

Posteritati (MANH)

◎ *239 Centre St, 4th Fl bet. Broome and Grand St, SoHo*
⊕ *posteritati.com*

A cinephile's paradise, this unassuming 4th floor showroom is home to over 20,000 posters from 30+ countries. Sam and Stan are experts, and help visitors navigate the tremendously diverse collection. Large one sheet posters range from $50 into the thousands for rare, older movies like *Taxi Driver* or *Some Like It Hot*, but you'll also find smaller poster sizes and ones for more contemporary, niche films. Also available: rare posters for opera, music, advertising, festivals, and exhibition posters, too.

Philip Williams Posters (MANH)

◎ *122 Chambers St bet. W Broadway and Church St, Tribeca*
⊕ *postermuseum.com*

Doubling as a poster museum, Philip Williams is a must-visit for anyone with an interest in graphic design and advertising. Every possible category of poster can be found here, dating back to the 1800s, but I especially love the extensive collections of food and drink ads, and antique travel posters.

Picture Room (BK)

◎ *117 Atlantic Ave, Brooklyn Heights*
⊕ *pictureroom.shop*

For people with good taste who are ready to dabble in art collecting, Picture Room is the perfect place to start. Works here are sourced directly from the artists by the discerning eye of owner Sandeep Salter, who's been scouting emerging talent for over a decade. Over 100 artists making mostly works on paper can be found here, in a diverse range of styles — sold both framed and unframed. Though the storefront is next door to sister shop Salter House, it's advisable to make an appointment to shop at Picture Room. Prices start around $150.

Rugs

Kermanshah (MANH)
⊚ *57 5th Ave nr. W 13th St, Greenwich Village*
⊕ *kermanshahrugs.com*

An unfathomable quantity of traditional oriental rugs can be found in this Greenwich Village storefront. For three generations, the Kermanshah family has been sourcing antique rugs in traditional styles from all over the world. Handmade rugs are expensive, but the prices here are fair, and come with a history lesson.

Carpet Culture (MANH)
⊚ *392 Broome St nr. Mulberry St, Nolita*
⊕ *carpet-culture.com*

If you're in the market for something contemporary and new, Carpet Culture is your small biz best bet. They've got their own collection of rugs, and also retail designs that are traditional, overdyed or historically inspired. Like any high-end rug shop, everything here that's not woven is hand-knotted and will cost you a pretty penny. Be sure to make an appointment to view the rugs in-person, and call these experts next time you need your heirloom rug cleaned or restored!

Heirloom (BK)
⊚ *81 Grand St, Williamsburg*
⊕ *heirloombk.com*

Rug hunter Zach Zaman has traveled the world in search of the most unique works of hand-knotted art. Chinese deco, Mongolian pictorial rugs, Navajo rugs, and subgenres of antique rugs you (and I) have never even heard of. Antique tapestries and 19th century quilts are also on display here, as well a fabulous selection of work by contemporary fiber artists.

For woven Tibetan rugs, visit **Kyichu Tibetan Handicrafts**, *listed in the Gifting section, pg. 223.*

Furniture

Vintage Furniture

Horseman Antiques (BK)
◎ *351 Atlantic Ave, Boerum Hill*
⊕ *horsemanantiques.net*

This behemoth of a shop occupies multiple floors and is undoubtedly the largest retailer of mid-century furniture in NYC. Be prepared to spend hours getting lost in the stacks of furniture and objects. Get pairs of funky chairs and well-cared for wood pieces here. The prices do, rightfully, reflect the fact that this shop exists on a main shopping thoroughfare and includes designers like Nakashima, Eames, and Knoll. Horseman Antiques is also a dealer of new, made-to-order Milo Baughman furniture and offers upholstery services.

Harlequin Vintage (BK)
◎ *1033 Flushing Ave, Bushwick*

Owners Chloe and Jordan have a bold approach to sourcing the wacky and maximalist pieces that fill their shop. They've got a penchant for printed sofas and quirky accessories, a selection of mostly 80s vintage clothing, and a close eye on the current interior design trends amongst the younger crowd that fills the neighborhood.

Yesterday's News (BK)
◎ *428 Court St, Carroll Gardens*
⊕ *yesterdaysnews.biz*

Yesterday's News is a tchotchke person's dream, containing organized chaos in the form of curious vintage objects. Pay a visit on any given day and you're sure to encounter a sidewalk full of furniture and an interior with bins, baskets, and cases full of tiny objects, as well as stacks and stacks of pretty plates. What's great about this shop is that it strikes a perfect balance of being "curated," while still leaving room for the shopper to feel like they've discovered something.

ELPÍDA NYC (BK) ONLINE FOR NOW!
◎ ~~951 3rd Ave, Greenwood Heights~~
⊕ *elpidanyc.com*

In 2024, Elpída opened this expansive two-story antique and vintage furniture store with a specialty in 20th century designer furniture through the 1980s. Most of what you'll find in this sprawling space is for sale, but a slice of owner Esther's business is dedicated to prop rentals and staging. Contemporary art lines the walls and frequent partnerships with local brands and makers keeps things fresh and inspired.

Dream Fishing Tackle (BK)
◎ *59 Norman Ave, Greenpoint*

The weirder the better at Dream Fishing Tackle. Animal print! Oversized! Velvet! This is an eclectic vintage furniture store with a collection of outrageous objects that are sure to start a conversation. I dream of decorating my own '70s-inspired stoner den entirely with the things I find here.

Renewfinds (BK)
◎ *80 Oak St, Greenpoint*
⊕ *renewfinds.com*

Renewfinds has actually been around for over three years now, but in early 2024 they moved their collection of vintage furniture and design objects from a warehouse loft to a ground floor shop! The new space has a coffee cart operated by Eighty Oak Coffee, a back room for their in-house custom framing services, and plenty of space for 20th century design treasures.

Steppe (BK)
◎ *1341 Prospect Ave, Windsor Terrace*
⊕ *steppe.nyc*

Though the specialty of this vintage dealer has expanded beyond just rugs, you can find Turkish, Chinese, and Tibetan antique pieces amongst the well-edited selection of mid-century chairs, maximalist '70s sofas, and design objects. This multi-disciplinary design practice offers services as far-ranging as a full gut renovation to an interiors refresh.

New Furniture

It's not difficult to find new furniture in New York City if you're decorating purely for function, but the truth is — and I hate to say it — that most furniture showrooms in the five boroughs sell outdated, bulky furniture that's not the kind of stuff that'll last in a hectic household. It's not impossible though, and here are a few places to visit for quality goods and a little inspiration.

Jensen-Lewis (MANH)
◎ *969 3rd Ave nr. E 58th St, Midtown*
⊕ *jensen-lewis.com*

This might be the last old-school multi-brand furniture showroom in Manhattan. Jensen-Lewis started in the 1950s as a maker of canvas furniture and evolved to become a distinguished retailer of heirloom-quality furniture. Many of the brands found here are made in America, including contemporary wood furniture by the Vermont-based Copeland, and classic sofas made in Texas by American Leather.

Assembly Line (BK)
◎ *373 Atlantic Ave, Boerum Hill*
⊕ *assemblyline.co*

Owned by the same folks behind local design firm General Assembly, the furniture and design accessories for sale here reflect a shaker-inspired, city-suited sensibility that's both utilitarian and playful. Wood furniture made using traditional joinery techniques, lime wash paint, and upholstered furniture by Hudson-based brand Fern are amongst the highlights at this special shop. Folks with outdoor spaces come here for colorful Fermob outdoor furniture, and neighborhood moms visit for actually cool kids' room decor.

BEAM (BK)
◎ *272 Kent Ave, Williamsburg*
⊕ *beambk.com*

Independent, contemporary European brands are most of what's on display at BEAM — a furniture store fit for the young crowd found in North Brooklyn. With a full range of furniture, decor, rugs, and lighting, you could furnish and decorate an entire home in this single store. Find Scandinavian shelving, paint from Backdrop, colorful shower curtains, and sculptural coffee tables.

Collyer's Mansion (BK)
◎ *307 Henry St, Brooklyn Heights*
⊕ *shopthemansion.com*
The selection here is eclectic and reflects a global approach to sourcing. Piles of printed linens, colored glass, and over-stuffed sofas from Cisco Home Essentials round out this very Brooklyn home goods store.

Custom Furniture

Gothic Cabinet Craft (MANH) (BK)
◎ *2652 Broadway, Upper West Side*
◎ *160 Empire Blvd, Prospect Lefferts Gardens*
◎ *58-77 57th St, Maspeth*
⊕ *gothiccabinetcraft.com*
Made in New York since 1969, this wood furniture and cabinetry specialist should be a household name. Get basic bookcases, beds with drawers underneath, and simple, classic chests of drawers. Everything is made-to-order, and while nearly two dozen stain options are available, you can also get everything in unfinished pine for finishing however you'd like. The best part: the prices are only slightly higher than IKEA.

Classic Sofa (MANH) (BX)
◎ *200 Lexington Ave Suite #421, Midtown*
◎ *728 E 136th St, Mott Haven*
⊕ *classicsofa.com*
Did you know that you can get a totally custom upholstered sofa made in the Bronx? Classic Sofa has been around since the '80s, and was rescued by current owner Blake Anding in 2012. Sophisticated sleepers sofas, sumptuous leather Chesterfields and everything in between can be made in about 4 weeks here. Visit the Manhattan showroom and take a little trip

to the industrial area of the south Bronx where everything is made by in-house craftsmen.

Brooklyn Queens Furniture & Things (BK)
⊚ *329 Knickerbocker Ave, Bushwick*
Sure, this looks like a regular furniture store at first glance, and while you can come here for a new mattress or dining set, you can also have custom furniture made to your specifications! Get custom-made dog beds with underneath drawer storage (seriously!), shelves made for that odd nook in your living room corner, or a desk to fit into your closet-turned-office.

Secondhand Furniture

City Opera Thrift Shop
⊚ *513 W 26th St bet. 11th and 10th Ave, Chelsea*
⊕ *cityoperathriftshop.org*
In support of the New York City Opera, this thrift shop is a wonderful place for unusual, affordable secondhand furniture, with a few proper antiques to be found. You'll find clothing merchandised amongst the furniture, which you should shop carefully — it's not unusual to find a shocking designer treasure hiding in these racks! Don't miss the downstairs — this is where a lot of the good stuff hides.

Furnish Green (MANH)
⊚ *132 ½ W 24th St bet. 7th and 6th Ave, Chelsea*
⊕ *furnishgreen.com*
Good deals are the name of the game at this old-school vintage furniture shop. Colorful 60s tableware, mid-century coffee tables, peculiar decor objects, and a few surprises hide behind this lime green storefront. Visit often, because the eclectic inventory rotates quickly!

HOME | 247

The Big Reuse (BK)

⊚ *1 12th St, Gowanus*
⊕ *bigreuse.org*

Sales at this jam-packed warehouse benefit The Big Reuse, which is an incredible organization dedicated to fighting climate change on a grassroots level. If you're an avid DIY-er, or desire a little home refresh on a budget, there is no better place to start than here. Great, cheap chairs, architectural salvage, and offbeat home goods fill this humongous space. Don't miss the book and clothes, which are typically vintage store quality at thrift store prices.

Every Thing Goes Furniture & Clothing (SI)

⊚ *17 Brook St, North Shore*
⊕ *etgstores.com*

Every Thing Goes is worth the trip to Staten Island alone. They've got a separate bookstore and community space down the street, but their main store is a labyrinth of rooms with an outdoor storage full of great, cheap, and colorful vintage clothes, and even more furniture. So. Much. Furniture. For a DIY-er especially, this place is full of pieces that would make for great projects.

EXTRA SPECIAL SPECIALIST

Veteran's Caning at 465 Baltic Ave in Gowanus is your one-stop shop for repairing and replacing chair caning, rattan, or woven rush. This family-owned business has been at it since 1899 and can help you reimagine an old piece of furniture, or restore something special.

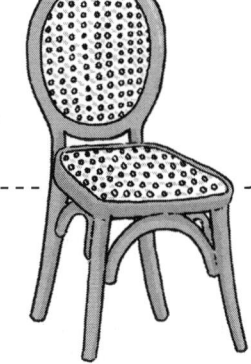

Health & Beauty

Fragrance

Aedes Perfumery (MANH)

16a Orchard St bet. Hester and Canal St, Lower East Side
aedes.com

Aedes Perfumery is the shop you visit when you're tired of smelling the same five scents every time you go out. Since 1995, this sensuously decorated shop has been stocking the finest, most niche fragrances from brands all over Europe, like Astier de Villatte and Santa Maria Novella, plus a tremendous array of hard-to-find candles and home fragrances.

Scent Bar NYC (MANH)

244 Elizabeth St bet. Houston and Prince St, Nolita
luckyscent.com

Scents by popular brands and indie perfumers alike fill the shelves behind the counter at this no-frills fragrance destination. Ask for something specific or seek advice, and someone will help you find the perfect match. It's not an ideal scenario for an introvert, but if you trust that the staff here are experts, you'll leave with something transformative that you likely wouldn't have chosen on your own.

Enfleurage (MANH)

237 W 13th St nr. Greenwich Ave, West Village
enfleurage.com

Fragrance folks come to Enfleurage for rare wildcrafted absolutes — potent fragrance oils made using a complicated extraction process. A few are even made using the ancient technique of enfleurage, which involves soaking plant matter in animal fat until it's saturated with scent. Another specialty includes frankincense essential oil from the shop owner's distillery in Oman. The comprehensive, alphabetized library of oils on display is a welcome place for even the most novice shopper to explore the 150+ options for home and body.

Stéle (MANH) (BK)
◎ *179 Mott St, Nolita*
◎ *339 Bedford Ave, Williamsburg*
⊕ *stele.nyc*

Nestled into a quiet block on Bedford Ave. is a new boutique fragrance specialist called Stéle. The shop's generous marble surfaces display indie and emerging perfumes accompanied by a smattering of other scented products for the bath and home. Founders Jake and Matt began as marble sculptors and came into the fragrance world as they searched for the perfect items to adorn their carved vessels and trays.

MAKE YOUR OWN CUSTOM FRAGRANCE!

The Fragrance Shop in the East Village is a quirky little spot for help blending something unique to you. Sniff hundreds of scents and seek expert help in combining them.

Exotic Fragrances in East Harlem stocks shelves upon shelves of fragrance oils, designer-inspired scents, and all sorts of bottles for blending and assembling them.

Bios Apothecary in Greenpoint and Industry City offers comprehensive classes on the ins and outs of perfume science, but you can also make an appointment to visit the all-natural perfume bar to create your own.

Nose Best in East Williamsburg is a sassy local candle brand whose evening speakeasy-style candle classes make for a lively alternative night out.

Apotheke in Red Hook has a stylish, spacious candle studio that's perfect for large group classes for bachelorette or birthday parties.

Herbal Medicine

Flower Power Herbs & Roots (MANH)
⊚ *406 E 9th St bet. 1st and Ave A, East Village*
⊕ *flowerpower.net*

Just entering this library of medicinal herbs will make you feel like you've been welcomed into the lair of mother nature herself. Large jars are alphabetized and full of dry herbs for making healing teas, but you can also find tinctures, syrups, and flower essences here, too. If you're new to herbalism, ask for advice or pick up a book to do a little reading on the subject.

Zola's Original Herbal Remedies (BK) (QNS)
⊚ *734 Nostrand Ave, Crown Heights*
⊚ *166-28 Jamaica Ave, Jamaica*
⊕ *ohremedies.com*

Master herbalist Zola Kojo is the matriarch of this natural medicine destination. You'll find loose herbs by the ounce and Zola's own brand of products, including concentrated capsules, various bitters, syrups, and proprietary powder blends. Book a one-on-one consultation to discuss your health goals and gain a better understanding of the benefits of herbalism.

Sacred Vibes Apothecary (BK)
⊚ *717 Coney Island Ave, Flatbush*
⊕ *sacredvibeshealing.com*

This small but mighty apothecary is the brainchild of herbalist Karen Rose, whose own blends of herbal teas and tonics are the main draw here. Also find loose herbs, condition-specific tinctures, and healing salves. Sacred Vibes is an ideal place to start, because you don't need an encyclopedic knowledge of individual plants to find something helpful. But if you do want to learn more, you can book a consultation or even sign up for the apprenticeship program.

Sex

Purple Passion (MANH)
⊚ *211 W 20th St bet. 8th and 7th Ave, Chelsea*
⊕ *purplepassion.com*

Check everything off your BDSM wishlist at Purple Passion, a fun and friendly mainstay for fetish gear, latex and leather clothing, shoes, and props for whatever your wildest kink might be. The staff here are knowledgeable, welcoming and inclusive, and can give you hyper-specific advice, or help newbies navigate the extensive inventory of toys with ease.

The Pleasure Chest (MANH)
⊚ *810 Lexington Ave, Upper East Side*
⊚ *156 7th Ave S, West Village*
⊕ *thepleasurechest.com*

For name-brand vibrators, strap-ons, dildos, better-than-drugstore condoms, and specialty lubes, The Pleasure Chest is the place to go. The selection of kink supplies for more creative sexual pursuits is well-edited but covers all the bases. Also find: wedge pillows, novelty butt plugs, and a fun selection of games.

Please (BK)
⊚ *635 5th Ave, Park Slope*
⊕ *pleasenyc.com*

With the tagline "An Educated Pleasure Shop," Please is a sex-positive place for folks who might not think they belong in a sex shop. Explore modalities for pleasure, connectivity, and relationship-building here, with the extensive collection of books and games alongside beautifully merchandised massage oils, lubes, electronic toys, and a table of dildos complete with information cards to explain the differences. And when you're ready for something more hardcore, they've got cuffs, clamps, and whips, too.

Shag (BK)

◎ *108 Roebling Ave, Williamsburg*
⊕ *weloveshag.com*

Art and intimacy converge at this pretty storefront, where erotic works by emerging artists are on display and sex is something that's playful and creative. Find everything from vibrators to lingerie, candles to cuffs, and books to butt toys. With a curated selection of gorgeous gifts, and work by local designers, shopping here is a boutique experience that offers a unique point of view and a friendly access point.

Skincare & Cosmetics

Senti Senti (MANH) (BK)

◎ *81 Mott St Store 2, Chinatown*
◎ *66 Ainslie St Store B, Williamsburg,*

Formerly known as oo35mm, Senti Senti has long been popular for their extensive range of Korean beauty products and baffling selection of sheet masks. You'll find popular brands like Dr. Jart and Cosrx in addition to smaller ones you've never heard of. While they sell all categories of skincare and cosmetics, their sunscreen selection alone is worth a visit!

Pretty Well Beauty (MANH)

◎ *185 Greenwich Ave Fl C1, in the Oculus, Financial District*
⊕ *prettywellbeauty.com*

Founded in 2019 by industry veteran Jazmin Alvarez, this clean beauty specialty store is a hidden treasure inside the Oculus mall. The list of 60+ independent brands found here features a huge roster of BIPOC founders, tried-and-true classics like Dr. Alkaitis and Sun Potion, cult haircare from Nuele and MFlorens, and hard-to-find makeup from Ere Perez and Axiology. Let Jazmin apply her expertise to helping you build a new routine from head to toe — even including sleep aids, herbal teas, and menstrual care. As she says: "Beauty is an inside job."

Takamichi Beauty Room (MANH)

◉ *125 E 17th St nr. Irving Pl, Gramercy*
⊕ *takamichibeautyroom.com*

The shop is tiny and the merchandise on offer is minimal, but you can be sure of one thing: everything is there for a reason, and the reason is that it's an objectively amazing product, and likely one that's hard to find in NYC. I visit regularly to buy a German brand of natural deodorant called Fine, which I swear is the only one that works. You'll also find innovative French sunscreen brand Seventy-One, Sicilian soaps by Ortigia, and cult Japanese itch relief product Kinkan Cool Liniment.

C.O. Bigelow (MANH)

◉ *414 6th Ave nr. W 9th St, Greenwich Village*
⊕ *bigelowchemists.com*

NYC's oldest pharmacy is also home to over 100 brands of skincare, haircare and cosmetics! You'll find a makeup counter with brands like Westman Atelier, Ritual de Filles, and Deborah Lippmann, as well as skincare and haircare ranging from your regular drugstore brands to high end ones like Dr. Haushka, Augustinus Bader, and Malin + Goetz. Don't miss the hair accessory counter, which has an amusing selection of French novelty hair clips!

Pasteur Pharmacy (MANH)

◉ *53 E 34th St, Midtown*
◉ *806 Lexington Ave #1, Upper East Side*
⊕ *pasteurshaving.com*

When I first told an older gentleman friend of mine about this guide book the first thing he said was "Do you know Pasteur Pharmacy?" While Pasteur looks like your average charm-filled uptown pharmacy, they actually specialize in old-school shaving products. All types of shave soaps, handmade brushes, blades, and aftershave products are for sale here, many of which are made exclusively for Pasteur. They even host an annual Oktobershave Meet-Up where shaving enthusiasts gather to share their mutual interest in niche shaving goods. Even if you have no use for these sorts of things, visit to marvel at the packaging design found on these jam-packed shelves.

Marché Rue Dix (BK)

◉ *1453 Bedford Ave, Crown Heights*
⊕ *ruedixbrooklyn.com*

A string of shops on Bedford Ave in Crown Heights is home to a special small biz ecosystem from masterminds Nilea Alexander and Lamine Diagne. Their vibrant world of cultural delights includes Café Rue Dix, a beloved Senegalese-French restaurant, and a salon offering hair, nail and facial services with their own line of natural products. Marché Rue Dix rounds out the trio of businesses, and sells an extensive range of locally made skincare, cosmetics, and hair products designed with Black beauty needs in mind, a funky selection of independent designers and private label goods including a collection made in Senegal, and gorgeous made-in-Senegal housewares. Get a manicure, do some shopping, and have a long, spicy dinner — get lost for a day in this unique little slice of Senegal, right in the middle of Brooklyn.

Thompson Alchemists (MANH)

◉ *132 Thompson St bet. Houston and Prince St, SoHo*
⊕ *thompsonalchemists.com*

A cult-favorite SoHo pharmacy, Thompson Alchemists is known for their extensive and reliable stock of French pharmacy favorites from brands like Nuxe, Embryolisse, Klorane, and Biafine. Don't sleep on their private label brand, especially the hairbrushes, which are Mason Pearson quality at a fraction of the price.

Zitomer Pharmacy (MANH)

◉ *969 Madison Ave nr. E 76th St, Upper East Side*
⊕ *zitomer.com*

Zitomer is indisputably the bougiest pharmacy in the city, and has become a well-known local alternative for traditional department store brands. If you're trying to quit big box cosmetics, this is the place! In addition to luxury brands like Chanel and YSL, they also sell their own line of makeup products amidst higher-end drugstore brands like Mario Badescu.

Big Love for Small Pharmacies

You don't need me to tell you where to find your nearest neighborhood pharmacy, so instead I'd like to remind you to give it a chance if you aren't shopping and getting your prescriptions filled there already. Here, a few New Yorkers share why they love theirs:

Nature's Prescriptions (QNS)
◎ *5-29 5th Ave, Long Island City*

"My art studio is just a couple of blocks away, but I only discovered this pharmacy relatively recently. It's tucked away on a side street and is a goldmine – well-stocked with high quality brands of supplements, body products, band-aids, snacks, socks, toys, and more! It's a few doors down from a very elegant torn-of-the-century police station, circa 1903."
– **Sonya G.** in Long Island City

Preferred Pharmacy (BK)
◎ *1771 Broadway, Bushwick*

"Preferred Pharmacy has never let me down. They are always so patient and caring, and especially sweet with elder customers. You can tell they know all their regulars by first name, and check in on how their families are doing."
– **Jackie D.** in Bushwick

FUN FACT!

The current shop cat at **C.O. Bigelow** is named Ozzy, short for Ozempic. Ozzy's predecessor was a beloved feline named Allegra, after the allergy medication.

Mumu Bath (BK)

◎ *72 Jay St, Dumbo*
⊕ *mumubath.com*

Mumu Bath is a bath and body shop that sells vegan, house-made products influenced by owner Sasha's Taiwanese heritage. Originally founded during the pandemic, and after years of participating in markets all over the city they opened their first permanent retail location in Dumbo in 2024.

Zoe's Beauty (BK)

◎ *119 Greenpoint Ave, Greenpoint*
⊕ *zoesbeauty.com*

Housed inside a Greenpoint hair salon, Zoe's stocks an impressive section of niche skincare and haircare brands like Eminence, Mad Hippie, Davines, and Oribe. You'll even find a selection of makeup, beauty implements, fancy hair brushes, and Marvis toothpaste — a true one-stop shop for a bathroom cupboard restock.

Millo (BK)

◎ *423 Ave U, Gravesend*
⊕ *millojewelry.com*

Tucked away on the western end of Avenue U in Sheepshead Bay is a surprising treasure trove of skincare and cosmetics. In addition to selling jewelry and other fashion items, Millo stocks skincare brands like Augustus Bader, Natura Bissé, Dr. Dennis Gross, and Dr. Barbara Sturm. You'll even find fragrance brands like Diptyque and Byredo!

Brooklyn Herborium (BK)

◎ *275 Columbia St, Columbia Heights*
◎ *1301 Prospect Ave, Windsor Terrace*
⊕ *brooklynherborium.com*

Everything sold here is concocted at Brooklyn Herborium's Windsor Terrace botanical-filled laboratory. They don't believe in cookie-cutter skincare routines here, and have specialized systems for different skin types that utilize powerful plants and advanced distillation and emulsification processes. This isn't your hippie aunt's skincare.

Tattoo Supply

Unimax Supply Co. (MANH)
◎ *269 Canal St 2nd Fl bet. Broadway and Lafayette, SoHo*
⊕ *store.unimaxshop.com*
Supplying tattoo artists and piercers all over town, Unimax is a tremendous resource for tools, inks, sterilization supplies, and even furniture specifically made for tattoo studios. But you don't have to be a professional to shop here. Pop in to shop for books about tattoo history and design, and check out the cases upon cases of dazzling body jewelry.

Vitamins & Supplements

The best selection of vitamins and supplements is always going to be found at a well-stocked health foods store. Visit our Health Foods section on pg. 174 for some recommendations.

TOTALLY HOLISTIC!

Elm Wellness
◎ *56 7th Ave nr. W 14th St, West Village*
⊕ *elmdrugs.com*
This proper health foods store sells everything you need for a well-stocked fridge and pantry, but what's unique is the friendly full-service pharmacy tucked into the back. With an understanding that good health requires balance, you can get your prescriptions filled while also shopping the 100+ brands of vitamins, naturopathic supplements, and herbal remedies.

Kids

Baby Stuff

Carriage Suite (MANH)
◉ *172 104th St bet. Lexington and 3rd Ave, East Harlem*
⊕ *carriagesuite.com*

This luxe baby goods shop in East Harlem is a terrific place to find cute and giftable baby clothes and accessories, but most exceptionally, Carriage Suite is a dealer of Cybex strollers and car seats. It's a lively Black-owned shop that's the only of its kind in this part of town.

Albee Baby (MANH)
◉ *715 Amsterdam Ave nr. W 95th St, Upper West Side*
⊕ *albeebaby.com*

With the widest selection of strollers and car seats in Manhattan, Albee Baby has been a valuable resource for generations of West Side moms. Set up your registry here, or visit to stock up on nursery essentials — they've got everything you'll need to keep your baby clothed, organized, and safe.

Everything But the Baby (BK)
◉ *371 Kingston Ave, Crown Heights*
⊕ *ebtbfamily.com*

This hectic little shop is packed to the ceiling with furniture, strollers, linens and — as described — everything *but* the baby! It's part of a family of shops in this area of Brooklyn including a nearby home furniture outlet and a specialized mattress showroom, so you can trust that this small business knows a thing or two about furnishing for a new member of your family.

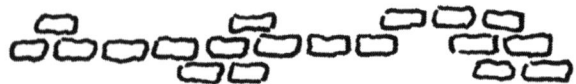

The Wild (BK)
⊚ *105 Grand St, Williamsburg*
⊕ *shop-thewild.com*

Organic and all-natural clothes, as well as carriers and baby products, fill this tightly curated baby shop, which also plays host to popular classes for moms and babies pre- and post-partum. For expectant parents concerned about chemicals and synthetic fibers, this is the place to shop for anything from safe cleaning products to breast pumps.

Children's Clothing

Jane's Exchange (MANH)
⊚ *191 E 3rd St bet. Ave A and B, Alphabet City*

Manhattan's only specialized children's thrift store has been serving the East Village since the early '90s. The founder's daughter, Jane, now runs the shop and sells maternity/nursing clothes, gear (strollers, car seats, etc.), furniture, and toys, in addition to kids' clothing. It's reliably stocked with clothes in great condition and all sizes, making it a perfect first stop for outfitting fast-growing kids.

an.mé (MANH)
⊚ *328 E 9th St, East Village*
⊚ *249 Bleecker St, West Village*
⊕ *anmeshop.com*

Lately, this pair of cute and colorful shops has become best known as a reliable stockist for the ever-popular Sonny Angel toys, but their original specialty is vibrant, contemporary and hard-wearing baby and kids' clothes by indie brands. Playful bedroom decor, unique baby gifts, and Japanese toys round out the selection of curious children's things at an.mé.

Makié (MANH)
⊚ *109 Thompson St bet. Prince and Spring St, SoHo*
⊕ *makieclothier.com*

With locations both in SoHo and Tokyo, this refined clothing store stocks mostly French and Japanese brands for babies, children and mothers. Everything is luxurious in a subtle way — made in neutral colors with sumptuous cashmere and organic cotton. It's the most expensive children's clothing retailer on this list, but the quality and commitment to classic design makes the pieces found here worthy of being continuously passed down. For gifting: find pre-wrapped baby outfits that include cute little elephant rattles.

Lucky Wang (MANH)
◎ *82 7th Ave nr. W 15th St, Chelsea*
⊕ *luckywang.com*

Wild and crazy patterns dominate the selection at Lucky Wang, which has been a staple in this design-y neighborhood for nearly 30 years. Get play clothes with personality for all ages, and don't miss the shop's eponymous brand, which includes gorgeous pint-sized kimonos.

Misha & Puff (BK) **NEW!**
◎ *349 Atlantic Ave, Boerum Hill, Brooklyn*
⊕ *misha-and-puff.com*

By designer Anna Wallack, Misha & Puff is a brand of children's clothing that's bold and colorful, but features retro prints so stylish you'll want to wear them — and lucky for you, the brand has a line for adults, too! Quirky knits and statement accessories are big standouts here, but don't skip the quality basics, like a rainbow of warm ribbed tights and durable denim.

WOODstack Treehouse (BK)
◎ *190 E 98th St, Brownsville*

WOODstack is a streetwear powerhouse with locations all over the city, but this storefront in their original neighborhood is special because it sells only sportswear and streetwear for children! Find tons of sneakers and comfy clothes here from big brands like The North Face, Nike, and Adidas, in addition to the sassiest limited edition styles.

Owl Tree (BK)

◉ *376 Court St, Carroll Gardens*
◉ *350 Flatbush Ave, Park Slope*
⊕ *owltreekids.com*

Affordable, stylish, and current — the stock at Owl Tree tends to be high-end and hardly worn. This consignment store has two locations and is popular with eco-conscious moms who still want their family to look cool. On the day I visited, I was especially impressed with the selection of occasionwear, but it's not just about kids here — there's also a small selection of maternity clothing, too.

Parachute Brooklyn (BK)

◉ *151 Norman Ave, Greenpoint*
⊕ *parachutebrooklyn.com*

As a buy-sell-trade kids clothing retailer, Parachute carries gently used contemporary and vintage clothing for kids 12 years and under. The overarching goal is to give children the opportunity to develop their own personal style in a sustainable and affordable way. You'll also find a curated selection of new accessories, gifts, and collaborations from small makers. For creative families, the zany and diverse assortment here makes shopping anything but a chore.

Kidstown (BK) (BX)

◉ *749 Broadway, Bed-Stuy*
◉ *220 E 161 St, Concourse Village*
◉ *1026 Westchester Ave, Longwood*
◉ *100 E 170th St, Mt. Eden*
⊕ *kidstownusa.com*

Skip the department store and visit one of these unbelievably well-stocked kids' stores for furniture, toys, and, especially, affordable name-brand clothes and school uniforms. Kidstown has been family-owned and operated since 1969 and fills a big void that currently exists in the world of small biz kids shopping: good, regular clothes at competitive prices. With sizes up to a kid's size 20, you can outfit the whole family for both school and play at Kidstown.

Education and School Supplies

Unfortunately, few education and teacher supply stores exist IRL in NYC these days, but we've got one great option and a selection of well-stocked general office supply and stationery shops listed in Desk on pg. 131.

> **FUN FACT!**
>
> America's oldest pencil factory is right across the river in Jersey City, NJ! General Pencil Co. was founded in 1889 and is still owned by the original family. They made a better-than-Ticonderoga yellow school pencil called the Semi-Hex #2 and a whole range of drawing and writing supplies. Find them at **The Locavore Variety Store,** 434 6th Ave, Manhattan.

Toys

Grandma's Place (MANH)
◎ *84 W 120th St nr. Malcolm X Blvd, Harlem*
⊕ *grandmasplaceinharlem.com*

Grandma's Place is the only proper toy store in Harlem, and boy, is this place beloved! Everything here is chosen with great care by Grandma Dawn, from classic games to piles of plush toys, and books centered around Black and Hispanic stories.

Kidding Around (MANH)
◎ *60 W 15th St bet. 6th and 5th Ave, Union Square*
⊕ *kiddingaroundtoys.com*

Kidding Around is a classic toy store with both popular and indie brands in all categories: stuffed toys, kits, games, puzzles, dolls, buildables — you name it, this family-owned store probably has it! I visit frequently for the charming New York City-themed section and to get Maileg mice and Calico Critters for gifting.

Playing Mantis (MANH)
⊚ *32 N Moore St bet. Hudson and Varick St, Tribeca*
⊕ *friendlymantis.com*

Playing Mantis is the city's premiere wooden toy specialist! Visit for timeless, heirloom-quality toys, from all over the world — rockers, puppets, trains, even instruments. Owner Imelda has a knack for souring items that'll spark a kid's curiosity, and align with the values of parents who are particular about the objects they keep in their home.

Pizzazzz Toyz (BK)
⊚ *281 Court St, Cobble Hill*

With two storefronts right next to each other, Pizzazzz is jam-packed with toys, clothing, books, and just about every other kid thing you might need. Check out their selection of NYC-themed things, indie toy brands, and awesome range of science and craft kits. When you need a gift for a birthday party in a pinch, this is the place to go to find something exciting that won't break the bank.

Little Green Brooklyn (BK)
⊚ *447 6th Ave, Park Slope*
⊕ *shoplittlegreen.com*

A one-stop-shop for the whimsical, eco-friendly family, Little Green sells everything from secondhand kids clothes to locally made sidewalk chalk, quality toys by cool new brands, affordable costumes and props, and even party supplies! Things to look for: MAJO IDEAS sticker-based activity books and KIKO+ wooden analog electronics.

Forever Young Kids (QNS)
⊚ *801 Woodward Ave, Ridgewood*
⊕ *shopstayforever.com*

As the kids' counterpart of the popular Ridgewood gift shop Stay Forever, Forever Young Kids is a shop for eclectic kids' things, like non-toxic nail polish, crystal grow kits, as well as aesthetically pleasing games and toys by less mainstream brands. For child-free adults in need of a gift, this spot is great for finding something cool without feeling overwhelmed and confused.

Steph's Creativity Corner

⊚ *7305 Amboy Rd, South Shore*
⊕ *stephscreativitycorner.com*

As Staten Island's only dedicated toy store, Steph's Creativity Corner has all bases covered. Get popular toy brands, classic games, and kid-friendly art supplies here, but what Steph is most known for is her personalized gift sets, which feature funky lettering and stacks of carefully curated curiosities.

> **SINCE 1931!**
>
> The oldest toy store in NYC is **Mary Arnold Toys**, located at 1178 Lexington Ave on the Upper East Side.

> **GREAT GIFTS!**
>
> ### Tenement Museum (MANH)
>
> ⊚ *103 Orchard St, corner of Delancey St, Lower East Side*
> ⊕ *tenement.org*
>
> This important institution is beloved by locals and tourists alike for its enthralling tours about life on the Lower East Side at the turn of the century, but have you been to the shop on the ground floor? It's stocked with some of the New York-iest tchotchkes around town, but hang a left and you'll find a truly terrific selection of city-related kids toys, games, books, and kits. It's my favorite place to buy gifts for the kids in my life when I'm trying to flex my status as the Cool New York Auntie.

Kitchen & Dining

If you're an average home cook, I invite you to stop trying to do your own research on things like Japanese knives and niche coffee makers and just go out to ask someone who actually knows what they're talking about! Put the phone down! Cooking and baking are technical skills, and these shops sell the things you need to succeed with a side of practical advice.

Baking Supplies

NY Cake (MANH)
⊚ *118 W 22nd St bet. 7th and 6th Ave, Chelsea*
⊕ *nycake.com*

Even if you're not a baker, you're sure to walk through NY Cake slack-jawed at the specificity of the items for sale. Over 100 types of edible glitter satisfyingly organized by color, baking pans in every shape and size, retail packaging for pastries, candy melts in every flavor and color that exists, tiny shaped candies and sprinkles, and life-like sugar flowers for cake decorating. It's a pastry chef's paradise, but for those of us who don't know the first thing about baking, there's an on-premises school with a full roster of classes for all skill levels.

Sugar Room (QNS)
⊚ *44-21 Queens Blvd, Sunnyside*
⊕ *sugarroom.com*

Specifically stocked for cake baking, Sugar Room in Sunnyside is the most comprehensive shop in Queens for bakeware and decorating tools. Buckets of colored fondant, structural dowels, intricate silicone molds, and plastic toppers for any type of kids' cake can be found here. Need some help? Sign up for an intro to baking class, or something more specific like gum paste flower-making.

Chopsticks

Yùnhóng Chopsticks Shop (MANH)
◉ *50 Mott St nr. Bayard St, Chinatown*

This classic Chinatown shop is a mainstay on lists of "shops that only sell one thing," and while you might assume it to be a place for novelty, it's actually quite a serious little specialty shop for very elegant chopsticks. Gift boxes line the walls, filled with pairs made of beautiful wood, some with elaborate inlays. Large sets can cost a pretty penny, but you'll also find simple, inexpensive everyday chopsticks and a selection of novelty chopstick rests.

Kitchen Supplies

Zabar's (MANH)
◉ *2245 Broadway nr. W 80th St, Upper West Side*
⊕ *zabars.com*

In 1975, to drum up interest in their kitchen supply area, Zabar's sold 200 Cuisinart food processors in 2 days by slashing the MSRP by a whopping $55. Cuisinart cut them off, Zabar's sued, and the whole thing became a brilliant PR mess. To this day, Zabar's is still the leading retailer for small kitchen appliances in Manhattan with Vitamix blenders, colorful Moccamasters, and yes, Cuisinart food processors occupying a couple of aisles on the upper floor of the shop. They also stock an incredible selection of flatware, specialty tools, and decorative tableware. Don't miss the line of Zabar's-branded products, including cute beeswax wraps printed with illustrations of classic Zabar's products.

Tarzian West (BK)
◉ *194 7th Ave, Park Slope*
⊕ *tarzianwestforhousewares.com*

Do you need something really specific? A small tool by a particular brand that you can't find anywhere else? Ask someone at Tarzian West, and they'll magically make it materialize. This storefront might be small, but it's packed full of handy gadgets, fancy cookware, and nice knives.

A Note On Restaurant Supply Stores:

Have you ever actually gone inside the labyrinth-like, no-frills restaurant supply shops found on the Lower East Side? Don't be intimidated! Sure, these shops mostly serve restaurants, but regular people visit them for great, inexpensive ceramic plates, classic glassware, sheet pans, and utilitarian things that you don't need to be "aesthetic," like Benriner mandoline slicers and packs of plastic-handled paring knives. And if you've ever wanted your very own slushy machine, you can find that, too! Try **Chef Restaurant Supplies** on Bowery, or **Win Restaurant Supplies** on Lafayette.

Whisk (BK)
⊚ *197 Atlantic Ave, Brooklyn Heights*
⊕ *whisknyc.com*

The folks at Whisk have been at it for nearly two decades and have become pros at stocking a kitchen supply store to evoke the friendliness of an actual, real person's kitchen. Every type of necessary item can be found here, alongside decorative linens, specific single-purpose tools and a surprising selection of bitters. Practical things, like replacement parts for coffee makers, Sodastream cartridges, and extra mason jar lids are also regularly available.

Indulge Kitchen Supplies (BK)
⊚ *469 Myrtle Ave, Clinton Hill*
⊕ *indulgekitchensupplies.com*

This friendly, family-operated kitchen shop sells everything you need for cooking and baking, and is known throughout the neighborhood for offering efficient, in-house knife sharpening services. Skip the ecomm store and get your favorite brands of kitchen things here, instead. Instant gratification for the same price, maybe less.

Knife Specialist

Korin (MANH)
◎ *57 Warren St nr. W Broadway, Tribeca*
⊕ *korin.com*

Female founder Saori Kawano opened Korin in 1982 as one of the first specialists in NYC for hand-forged Japanese knives. Known for their harder, thinner, sharper blades, Japanese knives have especially gained popularity in the past decade or so, and the options at Korin cover all of the bases — from $12 fruit knives to $2,000 sushi knives. A standard Korin-brand chef's knife will run you around $200, with left-handed conversion and engraving options. Even if you're not in the market for a knife, pop in for the selection of stunning, but practical, Japanese tableware.

Yanagi Knife Inc. (BK)
◎ *679 54th St, Sunset Park*
⊕ *yanagiknife.com*

On an unassuming street off of 7th Ave lies a very special knife shop. Named simply ("yanagi" is the Japanese word for a long, thin sushi knife), this powerhouse knife shop sells wonderful pieces by a great number of specialist craftspeople. Get hands-on service to find the perfect fit and feel, marvel at the rare masterpieces for sale at prices upwards of $3,000, and learn about the dozen or so knife styles available. The owner is a master knife sharpener, so be sure to bring your new knife back for servicing!

Tableware

Wing on Wo & Co (MANH)
◎ *26 Mott St nr. Pell St, Chinatown*
⊕ *wingonwoand.co*

Founded in 1925, the oldest shop in Chinatown is a quaint shop specializing in imported Chinese porcelain and ceramics, sourced with a creative eye and deep knowledge of tradition and historical context. Colorful, hand-painted rice bowls, tea sets, planters, and plate sets are displayed with care alongside a fabulous little selection of accessories. Mei, the fifth-generation owner, is a force to be reckoned with in an ever-changing Chinatown, as the founder of The W.O.W. Project — an initiative to preserve the cultural integrity of the neighborhood. Visit for extraordinary porcelain, of course, but also to see a perfect example of a legacy shop that's effectively adapting to meet the moment.

Fishs Eddy (MANH)
⊚ *889 Broadway nr. 19th St, Flatiron*
⊕ *fishseddy.com*

Born from a desire to find new homes for American-made plates from old institutions and restaurants, Julie Gaines' famously quirky dish shop is rustic in a way that's surprising for this slick area of Manhattan. The signage and shop vibe exhibits a distinct brand of smart and silly humor that makes time spent here an experience, not just an errand. Pick through stacks of old plates branded for defunct restaurants and member's clubs, or find a perfect set of diner-style mugs. Printed glassware and funny tea towels of their own brand are also available, as are fearlessly biased political items during presidential election cycles.

> **REQUIRED READING**
>
> Check out Julie's 2018 book titled *Minding the Store: a Big Story about a Small Business*, which is illustrated by her son, Ben Lenovitz.

Gem Home (MANH) NEW!
⊚ *181 Mott St bet. Kenmare and Grand St, Nolita*
⊕ *gemhomenyc.com*

Since the opening of Gem, his first restaurant, culinary wunderkind Flynn McGarry has had a razor-sharp eye for objects. His signature style is minimal and cool, with a hint of Shaker and a sprinkle of Italian countryside. As his first foray into retail, this shop and café boasts a small but stunning selection of antique tableware, indie designer treasures, and a line of products bearing the Gem label (specialty salt, snacks, and spice mixes!), alongside gorgeous produce and prepared foods.

Global Table (MANH)

◎ *107 Sullivan St bet. Prince and Spring St, SoHo*
⊕ *globaltable.com*

You'll *only* find tableware at Global Table. No knick knacks or gift-y things — just glass, porcelain, ceramic, and an edited offering of linens and specialty serveware. With a penchant for globally sourced plates, bowls, and glassware, the discerning selection includes mostly handmade things by smaller brands. The stock is diverse and covers a variety of styles — you can even set up a wedding registry here.

Rosemary Home (MANH)

◎ *315 E 9th St bet. 2nd Ave and 1st Ave, East Village*
⊕ *rosemaryhome.com*

While Rosemary Home started as a source for delightfully eccentric vintage trinkets and tableware, it's now equally known for durable, functional candy colored glassware, which owner Rosemary designs and has handmade in Murano, Italy. You can fill a whole kitchen in one fell swoop and totally fool your guests — they'll think you've been collecting for years. From the intricate window displays to the inspiring better-than-registry gift options, this shop is a jewel box of domestic creativity.

Sara Japanese Pottery (MANH)

◎ *950 Lexington Ave bet. E 70th and 69th St, Upper East Side*
⊕ *saranyc.com*

This serene shop houses a fiercely curated collection of artisanal Japanese home goods. Most of what you'll find falls in the tableware category, but don't expect to buy plate sets here. Instead, shop for single glasses that double as works of art, sculptural handmade mugs, and impractical treasures like tiny, tiny, tiny vases from artist Yuta Segawa. Visit for a knockout housewarming gift or small treat to elevate your everyday life.

Something Handmade

NYC is full of talented ceramics artists, and several of them work from storefronts with regular hours for retail shopping! Here are few favorites:

Mellow on the Lower East Side regularly hosts workshops, but is open Thurs-Sun for shopping plates, mugs, cruets, and more in the studio's signature checker, swirl, and sun motifs.

Claireware in Gowanus is a vibrant showroom for artist Claire Weissberg's bright, patterned bowls, plates, and cups, which follow the style of "urban folk pottery."

Helen Levi in Ridgewood has a cult following for her swirly mugs, splattered jugs, and hand-painted plates. Visit her studio on Saturdays for one-offs and samples.

LOCAL

Scully & Scully (MANH)
⊚ *504 Park Ave bet. E 60th and 59th St, Upper East Side*
⊕ *scullyandscully.com*

When I think about what the Upper East Side must've been like in the 1980s, I imagine it was full of shops like Scully & Scully: refined, expensive, and oozing classic luxury. This is where society women do their bridal registries and where traditional homes are furnished. With department store home decor sections diminishing, this is your best bet for things like proper china, crystal glasses, decorative serving dishes, high-end flatware, and lovely giftable trinkets.

Le Fanion (MANH)

⊚ *299 W 4th St nr. Bank St, West Village*
⊕ *lefanion.com*

Antique French country pottery is the extremely niche specialty at Le Fanion. Antique earthenware, etched or painted with little motifs, along with folk art and rustic furniture is brought in from the Provence region to create an exotic world of natural delights in the eccentric little shop.

Big Night (BK) (MANH)

⊚ *154 Franklin St, Greenpoint*
⊚ *236 W 10th St, West Village*
⊕ *bignightbk.com*

We already mentioned Big Night in the Fancy Pantry section (pg. 171), but we'd be remiss to not also highlight the non-fussy tableware that makes up the bulk of the store. The ethos is: buy the fabulous napkins, but don't sweat over ironing them. It's just dinner, and dinner is best enjoyed without the expectation of perfection. Popular brands like Hawkins New York, Dusen Dusen, and Sofie Lou Jacobsen are complemented with vintage pieces and hand-blown decorative glass for a fresh, contemporary selection.

PORTA (BK)

⊚ *360 Atlantic Ave, Boerum Hill*
⊕ *porta-nyc.com*

Everything at PORTA is handmade by small producers in Europe. In fact, most of what's here is sourced so specifically that you've probably never seen it before. Hand-made Portuguese ceramics, hand-stamped striped linens, Venetian carafes that are patterned like ribbon candies, sterling silver sheaths, and caps for popular condiments like Marmite and Tabasco — it's an absolutely singular shop.

Mogutable (MANH) (BK)

◉ *428 E 9th St bet. 1st Ave and Ave A, East Village*
◉ *130 Grand St, Williamsburg*
⊕ *mogutable.com*

Gorgeous little decorative dishes and popular Hasami Porcelain take up most of the space, but look closer and you'll find the teeny, tiny specialty that Mogutable has become known for: food-shaped chopstick rests that are exceptionally detailed, made in Japan, and sold for $10–$14. There are dozens of options, from a whole grilled horse mackerel to a single, minimalist leek or a batard that looks freshly dusted with flour.

INCASA (QNS)

◉ *31-88 37th St, Astoria*
⊕ *incasadecor.com*

Many lovely home things fill this bright storefront, from decorative pillows to Turkish towels and bar tools, but what's most captivating is the selection of thick, colorful Mexican glassware. Drinking glasses swathed with swirls of color and big, bubbly pitchers hang out alongside hand-painted plates and natural wood bowls and cutting boards.

GET CREATIVE!

The Brooklyn Teacup in Park Slope is a charming studio that specializes in turning vintage china into tiered trays for entertaining or displaying tiny treasures. Book a session to have your own pieces transformed, or sift through their extensive collection of plates and cups to find just what you're looking for.

Music

CDs & Records

Ergot Records (MANH)
⊙ *32 E 2nd St bet. Bowery and 2nd Ave, East Village*
⊕ *ergotrecords.blogspot.com*

This unusual record store doesn't discriminate when it comes to genres and instead prioritizes esoteric, hard-to-find and hyper niche music across all of them. Connoisseurs come here for pressings by small, specialized labels in under-the-radar subgenres, but for the curious collector, Ergot Records is also a place you can visit to open your mind to something new.

Limited to One Record Shop (MANH)
⊙ *221 E 10th St bet. 2nd and 1st Ave, East Village*
⊕ *limitedtooneshop.com*

New and limited pressings of indie, alternative, emo, and punk music are the specialty at this subterranean haven for listeners who are always chasing the best of what's new. Come here to revisit your early aughts indie roots (speaking for myself here) or get the lowdown on what's going on in the scene.

Manhattan45 (MANH)
⊙ *220 E 10th St bet. 2nd and 1st Ave, East Village*
⊕ *manhattan45.com*

Accurately self-described as "New York's Electronic Music Specialist," the hand-picked selection at Manhattan45 features disco, house, techno, and electro genres, and has become a destination for DJs and fans of dance music since opening in 2020. Expect new records only, and an expert level of service.

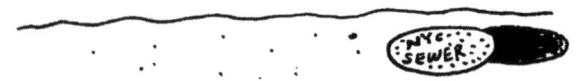

Village Revival Records (MANH)
◎ *197 Bleecker St*
bet. 6th Ave and MacDougal St, Greenwich Village
⊕ *villagerevivalrecordsnyc.com*

Palestinian-born owner Jamal Alnasr is something of a celebrity in the Village. His friendly record store has been packed full of locals hunting for vinyl gems for the past 30 years. Get the classics, find a great deal on something unusual, or pick up the hottest new records from your favorite pop singer here, and be sure to talk to Jamal — he's full of stories and is always willing to help you find what you're looking for. Find all genres, including a particularly good selection of jazz.

Octopus Records (BK)
◎ *204 Irving Ave, Bushwick*
⊕ *octopusrecords.nyc*

"Lurking beneath the surface since 2019," this hilariously self-described online record store opened IRL in 2022. Get electronic music, classic reissues, foreign imports, and an organized selection of niche subgenres at this quirky record store, which also sells a selection of Audio-Technica listening equipment.

Muzik City (BK)
◎ *3135 Fulton St, Cypress Hills*

The legacy of reggae icon and founder of Studio One Records, Clement "Sir Coxsone" Dodd lives on Cypress Hills. Jamaican-born Dodd's label was widely regarded as the "Motown of Jamaica," and in the early 1980s he moved his studio from Jamaica to Cypress Hills, Brooklyn, where he ran a recording studio and record store. His grandson, Ian has recently reopened the store to offer music lovers a place to browse both rare vinyl and newer releases alike. Visit for reggae records with historical significance.

African Record Center (BK)
◎ *1194 Nostrand Ave, Prospect Lefferts Gardens*

There are no photos allowed in this beloved, colorful African music specialty shop. It's a cultural landmark that was opened by the Francis brothers in 1969, who still run the store and share an encyclopedic knowledge of music from all over Africa and the Caribbean. Folks come from all over the world to find rare records with a history lesson on the side.

The Compact Disc Shoppe (BK)
⊚ *2601 Ave U, Sheepshead Bay*

Take a trip back to 1999, when music shops sold mostly CDs and the walls were covered in posters of the latest Top 40 stars. You won't find a more comprehensive selection of compact discs in New York City — a form of media that has officially re-entered the zeitgeist. Ask about transfer services!

Pancake Records (QNS)
⊚ *20-77 Steinway Street, Astoria*
⊕ *pancakerecords.com*

It's a community space, a forum for visual art and live performance, and — most importantly — Astoria's only dedicated record shop. You'll find new releases by local indie artists alongside well-loved classics in these organized stacks. The prices are fair, and there's something for everyone at this small but mighty neighborhood hub for offbeat musos.

EXTRA SPECIAL SPECIALIST

CONTROL (BK)
⊚ *67 West St, Ste 223, Greenpoint*
⊕ *ctrl-mod.com*

The only shop of its kind in all of the five boroughs, CONTROL is a mecca of electronic music, specializing in all things synthesis. Synth modules, both new and used, fill this unsuspecting showroom, alongside fixed and semi-modular synths by big-name brands like Moog, Korg, and Elektron. Whether you want to take the plunge and build your very own synth with modules, or you're looking to get started in electronic music with a brand-new groovebox, this is the place to go.

Casa Amadeo (BX)
◎ *786 Prospect Ave, Longwood*

In 2027, this Puerto Rican landmark will celebrate its 100-year anniversary. Casa Amadeo is the oldest music store in NYC and is even on the National Register of Historic Places for its contributions to Latin American music in America. Owner Miguel Amadeo's destination storefront is full of relics, and while it's very much a place to buy and learn about 20th century Latin music, it's also something of a museum for an important era in the history of the New York City Puerto Rican community.

> **FUN FACT**
>
> The largest density of record stores in NYC spans lower Manhattan, between 14th St and Houston. Make a day of walking from the West Village to Alphabet City on a record hunt! Visit the directory on **thelocavore.com** to see where they're all located.

Guitars

30th Street Guitars (MANH)
◎ *234 W 27th St bet. 8th and 7th Ave, Chelsea*
⊕ *30thstreetguitars.com*

Known especially for top-of-the-line repairs, guitar fiend Matt Brewster is the owner and expert at the helm in this well-stocked guitar shop. Find a tremendous selection of new, vintage, and rare guitars, a strong collection of pedals, and an endless supply of knowledge — a solid one-stop shop for guitar players of all skill levels.

Carmine Street Guitars (MANH)
◎ *42 Carmine St bet. Bedford and Bleecker St, West Village*
⊕ *carminestreetguitars.shop*

Rick Kelly is a guitar master, and this is his sanctuary. His custom-made guitars are world-renowned and crafted from reclaimed wood from iconic New York buildings. The workshop is shared with fellow guitar maker Cindy Hulej, whose instruments are adorned with intricate wood-burned artwork. It's hard to distill the magic of what happens here into a single paragraph, but both Rick and Cindy are featured in the gorgeous 2018 documentary Carmine Street Guitars — a must-watch love letter to New York City and an inspiring tale about craftsmanship and community.

Orphan Guitars (BK)
◉ *493 Court St, Carroll Gardens*
⊕ *orphanguitars.com*

Orphan is a stellar example of what a neighborhood guitar shop can be. It's inclusive, community-oriented, and family-friendly. Beginners and practiced musicians trust that owner Dwight will hook them up with everything they need and nothing they don't. This isn't a shop for gearheads — it's a place for folks who just want a good guitar without spending a fortune.

Main Drag Music (BK)
◉ *50 S 1st St, Williamsburg*
⊕ *maindragmusic.com*

Refreshingly spacious and decidedly modern, Main Drag Music is home to an extensive collection of new, vintage and rare guitars, keyboards, synths, drums, audio equipment, and a packed schedule of nighttime performances on their basement stage. For Brooklyn bands, it's a full-service outfitter, running the gamut from hyper-specific audio accessories to expert repair services.

Instruments

Good Hands Drum Shop (MANH)
◉ *242 W 30th St bet. 8th and 7th Ave, Chelsea*
⊕ *goodhandsdrumshop.com*

Get expert help selecting a new drum kit, consign your old one, rent something for a gig, or seek out repair services at Good Hands Drum Shop. Owner Jess Birch makes shopping for drums approachable by taking out the guesswork and narrowing things down. Drums are large and this is Manhattan real estate, afterall! Trust that only great equipment is for sale here.

Finlay + Gage Musical Instruments (MANH)
◎ 113 Chambers St bet. W Broadway and Church St, Tribeca
⊕ finlayandgage.com

Fretted instruments are the specialty at Finlay + Gage, whose range of cellos, guitars, bass, violas, and violins is unparalleled. Long term rentals are available, and restoration and repairs are done in-house. Keep in mind that it's advisable to make an appointment before stopping by!

Music Inn World Instruments (MANH)
◎ 169 W 4th St nr. Jones St, West Village
⊕ musicinn.nyc

Music Inn possesses a rare, authentically Greenwich Village vibe, with every surface covered in curious objects pertaining to music. There are no limits here — culturally significant instruments, peculiar ones you've never seen before, relics and records fill this small and eclectic space. Visit to try something new, seek something you've only heard about or simply to take a world tour through instruments.

Keur Djembe African Drums (BK)
◎ 568 Union St, Gowanus

Since 1998, shop owner and master drum-maker Ibrahima Diokhane has been making and selling traditional, expertly-crafted djembes — West African string-tuned drums. Seasoned musicians bring their drums here to be re-skinned and tuned, but Ibrahima is notoriously welcoming to those looking to learn.

Johnny Albino Music Center (BK)
◎ 88 Moore St, Williamsburg

This long-standing music specialist sells hundreds of CDs featuring all Latin genres, and a range of instruments you might need to play for yourself. There are standard acoustic guitars, keyboards, and drum kits here, but you can also find more culturally-specific things, like congas, timbales, cabasas, and cowbells.

Astoria Music (QNS)

◎ *34-17 28th Ave, Astoria*
⊕ *astoriamusicstore.com*

For a neighborhood that's so fiercely held onto its Greek heritage, it should come as no surprise that there's a specialist for instruments from the Balkans. Amongst the acoustic guitars and audio cables is an array of Bouzouki — a traditional string instrument that's sort of like a lower-pitched mandolin. The owner is a professional Bouzouki player himself, so you can trust that the imported instruments here are selected with care. Whether you want to learn this regional specialty or something more mainstream, Astoria Music has a program for private lessons.

Beethoven Pianos (QNS)

◎ *36-13 36th Ave, Astoria*
⊕ *beethovenpianos.com*

Until their recent move, this family-owned shop was the very last one on the stretch of 58th St once known as Piano Row. Still, Beethoven Pianos is the oldest piano shop in NYC and boasts over 600 new and used pianos in a full range of types and styles. You should absolutely visit for help selecting your dream model, but the bread-and-butter is their expert tuning and piano moving services.

> **FUN FACT**
>
> Steinway Pianos are manufactured a mere 2 miles from Beethoven Piano's new Astoria location!

Uke Hut (QNS)

◎ *36-01 36th Ave, Long Island City*
⊕ *ukehut-nyc.com*

The ukulele has a rich history as a pint-sized string instrument and an important piece of Hawaiian culture, but I also like to think of it as the most apartment-friendly instrument. Uke Hut is NYC's only dedicated ukulele specialist, offering a particularly joyful shopping experience. Visit to buy your own instrument, but stick around to listen to a live performance, take a lesson, or join in on a jam sesh.

Pets

A conscious effort was made to include shops in this section that sell supplies for every legal type of pet that one might have in NYC, including reptiles, pigeons, and exotic fish. While doing this research, I was surprised to find that the following pets are *illegal* in our five boroughs: iguanas, turtles smaller than 4", tarantulas, ferrets, and weasels. You should probably just stick to a regular dog or cat, but if you want a small rodent or non-venomous snake, here are some ideas for those, too.

Aquarium

My favorite section in the 1972 *New York Magazine* guidebook *The Passionate Shopper* is "Fish as Pets," the intro for which reads, "With the advent of baggies and jet transport, tropical fish have come into their own in this country. According to the industry, tropical fish collecting is America's third most popular hobby — ranking only slightly behind stamp collecting and photography."

The Aquarium section on thelocavore.com shows a shocking density of shops in Brooklyn and Staten Island, where this hobby — while certainly not the third most popular in America — is still alive and well. I myself am no expert in aquatic pets, but I do happen to know two particularly excellent shops where you'll find people who are:

Pacific Aquarium & Plant (MANH)
◉ *46 Delancey St bet. Forsyth and Eldridge St, Lower East Side*
Fish people flock to Pacific Aquarium & Plant from all over the area for the healthy and diverse tropical fish selection, which ranges from recognizable types of clownfish to shocking rarities. You can even get axolotl and other rare morphs here! Ghost catfish, nudibranchs, and thai micro crabs are among the spec-

tacular rotating assortment of unusual creatures here. Also for sale: tanks, supplies, and everything you need to build a nice fish habitat.

Frag Farm (SI)
⊚ *227 Main St, South Shore*
⊕ *fragfarmcoral.com*

While cataloging the quaint Staten Island neighborhood of Tottenville, I was delighted to encounter a shop covered in a mural depicting an underwater habitat and the tagline "Growing Corals is Our Thing." Frag Farm is the brainchild of rare coral specialist Frank Fairechio, who cultivates coral fragments, or "frags" himself, including rare torch and hammer specimens. There's more than just tanks of glowing coral behind this mysterious facade, though — also find a rotating selection of unique tropical fish.

Dog Stuff

Did you know that New York City is home to approximately 600,000 dogs? That's one dog for every fourteen people! Of course, any general pet store will mostly cater to urban canines (see the Pet Supplies section coming up) but here are a couple of specialists:

Wagwear (MANH)
⊚ *48 E 11th St bet. University Pl and Broadway, Greenwich Village*
⊕ *wagwear.com*

Since the 1990s, local brand Wagwear has led the way in modern, utilitarian dog gear. You won't find frivolous outfits here — instead, bring your pooch to get fitted for a warm, colorful coat or a pair of Wagwellies, the shop's signature Crocs-like dog shoes designed for all forms of harsh weather and urban obstacles.

Spoiled Brats (MANH)
⊚ *340 W 49th St bet. 9th and 8th Ave, Hell's Kitchen*
⊕ *bratsnyc.com*

Spoiled Brats is a very good shop catering to mostly dogs (and a little to cats), with a delightfully sassy name. Is that why I initially visited? Maybe. That, and because the front window is stuffed with plush dogs and lit by particularly wild neon signage. Design choices aside, you'll find an unbelievable selection of harnesses, toys, treats, food, and specialty items here. It's a one-stop shop for dog things that's also conveniently close to Central Park.

Who's Your Doggy? (BK)
⊚ *301a Halsey St , Bed-Stuy*
⊚ *803 Halsey St, Bed-Stuy*
⊕ *wydbk.com*

Outfit your best friend in luxe sweaters, stock up on fancy treats, handmade leashes and collars, and a plethora of name brand food — the folks here clearly love dogs and make a point of only stocking the best, most fun, most holistic supplies. It's a very Brooklyn dog shop, indeed.

Gone to the Dogs (BK)
⊚ *103 7th Ave, Park Slope*
⊕ *gonetothedogs.com*

This dog outfitter sells their very own brand of ethically made sweaters, stylish harnesses and leashes, bandanas, and adorable food-shaped felt toys. Play dress-up with your pooch (look for the bowties!), and stock up on toys cute enough you won't mind seeing them all over the floor — all while knowing that everything was produced ethically and with sustainable materials.

Exotics & Birds

Petqua (MANH)
⊚ *2604 Broadway nr. W 98th St, Upper West Side*
⊕ *petqua.com*

Reptiles, rodents, fish, birds, and regular ol' cats and dogs — there's something for all your friends at this well-rounded neighborhood pet store. Downstairs is where you'll find the exotics and fish section, and their famous shop pet: George — a very large, friendly tortoise.

Royal Birds & Supplies (QNS)
◎ *11313 Atlantic Ave, Richmond Hill*

Walking past this Queens bird shop is a treat. A quiet choir of squawks emanates from the entrance, which opens into a haven for exotic birds. Whether you're after a canary, cockatiel, parakeet, or parrot, Royal Birds & Supplies sells well over a dozen different kinds of colorful, beautifully kept birds to enthusiasts who travel here from all over the city. Find all manners of food, shelter, and supplies here, too.

Pet Supplies

Whiskers Holistic Pet Care (MANH) (QNS)
◎ *235 E 9th St, East Village*
◎ *19-25 Ditmars Blvd, Ditmars-Steinway*
⊕ *1800whiskers.com*

It's hard to know sometimes what's actually good for our pets, with all this talk of filler ingredients and clever marketing for new CPG pet brands. Having opened in 1988, Whiskers Holistic Pet Care was ahead of the curve by taking the guesswork out of choosing the right food and supplies. Find natural food brands, non-toxic toys, frozen raw pet food, as well as homeopathic supplements and remedies. Everything stocked in these quirky and colorful pet stores can be trusted as safe and healthy for your four-legged friends.

Trixie's Pet Food Supplies and Accessories (BK)
◎ *575 Flatbush Ave, Prospect Lefferts Gardens*

While cataloging shops in this area of Brooklyn, I was drawn to Trixie's because of the seasonally decorated front window and creative signage, which features a leaping dog with "Trixie's" painted on its side. Inside, I found pet toys and food from small brands I'd never seen before, select supplies for more exotic pets, and that palpable small biz charm I'm always seeking. There's no shortage of great pet stores around the city, but sometimes you just get the feeling that one is particularly invested in the critters that occupy their neighborhood, and Trixie's is one of them.

MR. FRIENDLY (BK)
◎ *228 Clifton Pl, Bed-Stuy*
⊕ *mrfriendly.nyc*

It's not a word typically used to describe a pet store, but MR. FRIENDLY is *cool*. Owners Eddie and Lauren are reimagining the pet shop by infusing good design into the experience of shopping for everyday pet things. Their own line of products includes eco-friendly dog collars and leashes in bright colors that are handmade on-site, while the regular stock items for cats and dogs skews holistic and independent. Be sure to visit their year-round "Curb Creamery" for a fancy ice cream treat for your pup.

Paws Grocer (BK)
◎ *490 Bergen St, Prospect Heights*
⊕ *pawsgrocer.com*

Merchandised like a little grocery store for cats and dogs, Paws Grocer is a shop for the modern pet owner who loves to read ingredient lists. They sell dozens of brands of wet and dry food, with an impressive freezer selection stocked with raw and fresh options. It's nice to know that you can buy anything here — from cleaning products to fun treats — and trust that what you're taking home is truly safe and healthy for everyone.

> **HOT TIP**
>
> Most pet stores offer home delivery! Save the carbon emissions and package waste of shipping and call your local shop instead.

Plants

Florists

There are three places every New Yorker should be shopping for flowers:

1   **The farmers market:** This is always where you're going to find the best prices on seasonal blooms! Visit our Guide to the Greenmarket on pg. __ for more.

2   **The flower district:** The block of 28th St bet. 7th and 6th Ave in Manhattan is packed with wholesale florists catering to the floral trade. Most sell to regular customers, too, and if you ever need a bulk quantity, this is absolutely where you'll find the freshest blooms for the best value. Go in the morning because these shops keep early hours.

3   **The bodega**: Is it the dead of winter? Do you need a quick bouquet on your way to meet someone? The flower stand outside the bodega is always there for you. We should consider ourselves lucky to have access to nice flowers at all times of day.

For everything else, there are old-school florists in just about every neighborhood, but I'm not here to recommend cookie-cutter Teleflora partners. The practice of buying fresh flowers can be fun and accessible! Let's explore some florists doing particularly creative work.

Sunny's Florist (MANH)
◉ 102 2nd Ave nr. E 6th St, East Village
This sweet corner spot has been beloved for its beautiful, affordable arrangements for over 30 years, and while Sunny herself retired in 2023, the stand is now in the care of her niece, Alice.

Swing by for fancy florist bouquets with bodega convenience. $16 mini bouquets are the specialty, but you can also request larger, custom arrangements.

Joy Flower Pot NYC (MANH)
◎ *40 Hester St bet. Ludlow and Essex St, Lower East Side*
⊕ *joyflowerpot.com*

Punchy, maximalist works of floral art are what the stylish denizens of lower Manhattan come to Joy Flower Pot for. Owner Kelly Ngyuen took over in 2020 and has a distinctive sense of style — blending seasonal and exotic blooms in unusual and inspired color palettes. This is the kind of flower shop you can call with a predetermined budget and one-line description, and trust that they'll make you something fabulous.

Park Delicatessen (BK)
◎ *722 Classon Ave, Crown Heights*
⊕ *parkdelibk.com*

Part skate shop and part florist, this pretty storefront is stocked with trendy gift items, ultra-cool decks, and a line of accessories and apparel — owners Michael and Valentine both come from fashion backgrounds. Mostly, though, Park Deli does flowers, with contemporary, organic arrangements for home delivery, big events, and for when you need an above-average bouquet in a pinch.

Flower Aggregate (BK) **NEW!**
◎ *318 Maujer St, East Williamsburg*
⊕ *floweraggregate.com*

Eschewing industry norms, Flower Aggregate is a wholesaler with a focus on pesticide-free, regionally grown flowers. Find seasonal delights in their well-stocked cooler, dramatic foliage, and a selection of tools and vases. Retail customers are welcome to swing by anytime for flowers, DIY buckets or floral design services.

Juliette Flower Shop (BK)
⊙ *170 5th Ave, Park Slope*
⊕ *juliettefloraldesign1.com*

With one foot in the door of traditional floristry, and another in the world of more experimental arrangements, Juliette Flower Shop hits a sweet spot for doing both well. Get tight and orderly roses or overflowing, asymmetrical mixed bouquets for a more creative and modern vibe. Locals also love the expansive selection of dried flowers — available loose or in funky little arrangements.

Ora La Casa De Las Floras (QNS)
⊙ *42-08 43rd Ave, Sunnyside*
⊕ *orabytangni.com*

When our Sunnyside ambassador* first tipped us off about Ora La Casa De Las Floras, we were thrilled to see such a refreshing addition to a neighborhood that hasn't really had a resident contemporary florist. Nicaraguan-born owner Tangni prioritizes using local flowers in her organic, abundant arrangements, but you'll also find a lovely cafe and retail space for Tangni's own skincare products.

*Are you a nosy neighbor? We're always looking for sleuths to recruit as neighborhood ambassadors. Your only job is to check in with us when you notice something close or open in your territory! Email us: general@thelocavore.com.

Florist Supply

Jamali Floral & Garden Supplies (MANH)
⊙ *149 W 28th St bet. 7th and 6th Ave, Chelsea*
⊕ *jamaligarden.com*

Creative decorators come here to shop alongside serious florists because Jamali Floral & Garden Supplies sells so much more than fake flowers (a whole floor of them!) and floral foam. Find glass vases in all shapes, tons of mason jars, rolls of ribbons, well-priced planters, and every type of candle holder. For unexpected decor and creative storage solutions, think of Jamali as your better, urban Hobby Lobby.

Central Floral Supply (MANH)

⊚ *40 W 28th St bet. 6th Ave and Broadway, NoMad*

I first ended up here while on a mission to figure out where to buy rolls of the iconic "Say It With Flowers" paper that's used to wrap bodega flowers. Central Floral Supply is where I finally succeed — with flying colors, too, because they sell it in all 5 available colors, made by a printer in New Jersey. Nelson, the owner, is an old-school guy and deals mostly to trade folks who need baskets in bulk, vases by the dozen and colorful cellophane, but normal people should come here for boxes of locally made, no-frills Patrician taper candles, a rainbow of satin ribbon rolls, and, if you're so inclined, a roll of "Say It With Flowers" paper.

Garden Center

For your fire escape herb garden, rooftop farm or backyard jungle — we do have garden centers in NYC. Call to get 200 lbs of soil delivered to your walk-up, check out plants you probably shouldn't grow indoors but technically can, get supplies for seed bombing, or stock up on heirloom veggies for your community garden plot. Find a wonderful selection of seasonal outdoor plants ranging from potted perennials to fruit trees at the Union Square Greenmarket (see the Greenmarket Guide at the front of this book), especially on Fridays and Saturdays.

*Should you be on the lookout for nutrient rich local compost, check out **BK Rot** on Myrtle Ave in Bushwick. They take orders for their manageably sized bags of compost, which are also sold at retailers across the city (**The Locavore Variety Store** included!). In Manhattan? You can also find great compost via the **Lower East Side Ecology Center**, at farmers markets downtown.*

Urban Garden Center (MANH)

⊚ *1560 Park Ave nr. E 111nd St, East Harlem*
⊕ *urbangardennyc.com*

As the only proper outdoor garden center in Manhattan, Urban Garden Center takes their responsibility very seriously! Find essential tools, mulch, soil, and fertilizer, as well as a healthy selection of plants, small trees, shrubs, and seeds, along with an easy-to-coordinate home delivery service. For indoor plant people, there's also a multitude of house plants.

Indoor Outdoor Gardener (BK)
◎ 8223 5th Ave, Bay Ridge
⊕ hydroponicsnewyorkcity.com

While you'll find your standard garden center offerings here, what Indoor Outdoor Gardener does best is stock hard-to-find equipment for hydroponic growing, irrigation set-up, and indoor grow lights. It's a full-service store for gardening in all forms, and there's nothing else quite like it in the city

Lowlands Nursery (BK)
◎ 25 9th St, Gowanus
⊕ gowanuscanalconservancy.org

It's not a full-service garden center, but the Lowlands Nursery specializes in something you'll be hard-pressed to find elsewhere: native plants! Find shrubs, wildflowers, and grasses like goldenrod, wild bergamot, and New York ironweed — just be sure to pre-order on the website and check the hours for pick-up, because they're limited and subject to change.

Chelsea Garden Center (BK)
◎ 444 Van Brunt St, Red Hook
◎ 87 Havemeyer St, Williamsburg
⊕ chelseagardencenter.com

With two locations in Brooklyn, Chelsea Garden Center is a great resource for backyard plants, tools, and especially for large planters. You'll find enormous urns, wooden planters and beds, as well as pots in all shapes and sizes. For the big stuff that seems ridiculous to buy online, this is a great resource.

Santacroce Greenhouses & Garden Center (SI)
◎ 1313 Richmond Ave, North Shore

Family-owned Santacroce is an island favorite because many of their plants are grown themselves in their own greenhouses, ensuring that they're healthy and ready to thrive in your garden.

Find a nice selection of flowers, fruits, vegetables, and non-flowering plants, as well as seeds imported from Italy.

Houseplants

I'm well aware that three of these four shops are very near each other, but to tell the truth, there aren't actually very many house plant specialists in the city anymore. Several have closed just in 2024 alone, which has us wondering if the 2010s wave of house plant mania just wasn't meant to last. Great farmer's market vendors, florists with a side of house plant, and garden centers will always have an ample supply of greatest hits, but if you're after something specific, check out a specialist:

Dahing Plants (MANH)
◎ *289 Grand St nr. Eldridge St, Lower East Side*
⊕ *dahingplants.com*
This foundational Chinatown/Lower East Side plant shop recently received a bit of a glow-up, but neighbors need not to worry: it's still the best value for the widest range of healthy plants in all of lower Manhattan. Visit to get a traditional Chinese money plant or good luck bamboo for your friend who just opened a business, large houseplants delivered the next day, or simply admire the sheer variety of apartment-friendly plants for sale — to merely call it extensive would be an understatement.

Tend Greenpoint (BK)
◎ *252 Franklin St, Greenpoint*
⊕ *tendgreenpoint.com*
Tend is a small but discerning shop for satisfying your green thumb, with a range of houseplants up front and outdoor varieties out back. Owner Joe has excellent taste and curates a stunning selection of pots by local makers and gardening tools that are both beautiful *and* functional. Nutscene, a beloved British brand of garden twine — rare in the US — can be found here.

Tula House (BK)

⊙ *59 Meserole Ave, Greenpoint*
⊕ *tula.house*

What a place this is! Tula House isn't just the most aesthetically stimulating plant shop in town, it's a full-service business that also offers repotting, plant cleaning, garden design, and even house visits. Come here to shop the diverse range of houseplants, to trade in a healthy plant you no longer want, and to find design inspiration for a brighter, more verdant life.

> **PLANT SWAP!**
>
> Do you have a healthy plant that you no longer vibe with? Bring it to **Tula House** to exchange for store credit so you can pick something more suitable!

Natty Garden (BK)

⊙ *636 Washington Ave, Prospect Heights*
⊙ *383 Marcus Garvey Blvd, Bed-Stuy*
⊕ *nattygarden.com*

With two storefronts in central Brooklyn, Natty Garden is beloved by neighbors for lush, healthy house plants, and everything you need to go with them. Outdoor shrubs, windowsill-friendly herbs, and huge indoor trees — if it's a plant that can grow in NYC, you can find it here. And to those with house plant shame: don't fret! Bring your struggling plants here for re-potting and good advice.

Geometry Garden & Floral Shop (BK)

⊙ *44 Grand St, Williamsburg*
⊕ *geometrygardensshop.com*

This exceedingly chic storefront is decorated in natural tones in order to give all its shine to the plants that occupy it, but don't be fooled — Geometry Gardens sells healthy house plants, large planters, unique vases, and fresh-cut flowers at some of the best prices in North Brooklyn. You'll also find locally sourced seeds, essential garden supplies, and thoughtful gift items.

Specialty Plants

Orchid Man (MANH)
⊙ *762 10th Ave #1 nr. W 52nd St, Hell's Kitchen*
⊕ *orchidmannyc.com*

If you've ever owned an orchid, you know the truth: they're not for a passive plant steward! Orchids require a special type of care to stay alive and bloom as they should, and the folks at Orchid Man won't only sell you something healthy and special, but also teach you everything you need to know to ensure that it thrives in its new habitat.

Dandy Farmer (BK)
⊙ *14 Clermont Ave, Fort Greene*
⊕ *dandyfarmer.com*

While bonsai are known for being miraculously beautiful but extremely fussy plants, Matthew Puntigam has a special way of making anyone feel empowered to adopt their very own tiny work of botanical art. He trained with a bonsai master in Japan before opening his store Dandy Farmer, where you'll find plants you've never seen in miniature form before. They're all potted in signature Dandy Farmer acorn-inspired pots, which are made locally.

Recreation

Shopping for sporting equipment often means seeking something very specific and/or quite large in size. It seems like a ridiculous category of things to buy online, but who can blame us for doing it? We don't even have a sporting goods chain in New York City anymore (RIP Modell's!). What we do have, though, is a community of specialists — even better, if you ask me.

All Sports

Paragon Sports (MANH)
◎ *867 Broadway nr. E 18th St, Union Square*
⊕ *paragonsports.com*

Paragon is a truly exceptional emporium of athletics and is positively unrivaled for the diversity of activities it stocks gear and apparel for. This family-owned three-story institution rotates stock depending on the season. Get tennis racquets serviced and strung year round, ski boots fitted in the winter, a new baseball glove just in time for spring training, and wilderness gear as soon as the winter coats are out. Come here before going online, and if you can't find what you're looking for (unlikely), you'll probably get good advice to help you on your way.

Frank's Sports Shop (BX)
◎ *430 E Tremont Ave, Tremont*
⊕ *frankssports.com*

For over 100 years, Frank's Sports Shop has been supplying the Bronx with quality workwear, utilitarian shoes, and gear for the popular sports: baseball, soccer, basketball, and football, primarily. Paintball gear, life jackets, and survival gear also appeal to outdoors enthusiasts. My favorite part: the window displays are stacked high with methodically placed inventory in a way reminiscent of mid-century variety stores — a feast for the eyes of passersby.

Bike Shops

Tread Bike Shop (MANH)
⊚ *250 Dyckman St bet. Payson and Seaman Ave, Inwood*
⊕ *treadbikeshop.com*

Boasting the title as the largest independent bike shop in NYC, Tread is a trustworthy spot to shop for bikes of all kinds: BMX, road bikes, mountain bikes, beach cruisers, children's bikes, and e-bikes. On any given day, you'll find at least 150 different models in stock at a range of prices. Adult hybrid bikes start at $500. The robust repair center has you covered for any maintenance or repair job, but for those who prefer to tinker, you can find an encyclopedic selection of parts for sale here.

GoGo Gone (MANH)
⊚ *317 Grand St bet. Allen and Orchard St, Lower East Side*
⊕ *gogogone.com*

I am an everyday cyclist of fifteen years, and this is where I go to get my bike serviced — and to replace my lights when they get stolen. The guys at GoGo Gone know their stuff, and will always try to find a workaround before selling you an expensive new part. Come here for road bikes for varying levels of expertise, from occasional commuting to triathlon training, and especially for the efficient and respectful service.

Burrowes Brothers Bicycles (BK)
⊚ *755 Flatbush Ave, Flatbush*
⊕ *burrowesbrothersbikes.com*

Founded by three brothers, all of whom are Category 1 professional cyclists, Burrowes Brothers Bicycles is unlike any other bike shop in New York City, and not for the reason you think. Tucked inside the shop is a secret restaurant called MangoSeed — a popular Caribbean spot that relocated to this quirky locale recently. Before slipping to the back for great jerk chicken, seek advice or repair services from any of the literal pros at Burrowes, and check out the expertly selected range of bikes, for both racing and commuting.

Propel (BK)

◎ *134 Flushing Ave, Fort Greene*
⊕ *propelbikes.com*

Since 2011, the folks at Propel have been working tirelessly to give electric bicycles a good name. For commuting, schlepping, and off-road adventures, Propel has all categories covered, with a distinct brand of approachability. Shoppers need not be intimidated by this brave new world of transportation.

Bike and Spin (QNS)

◎ *46-15 Vernon Blvd, Long Island City*
⊕ *bikeandspin.com*

Bike and Spin is a Queens favorite for its friendly service and curation. You won't find hundreds of bikes here; instead, there is a pared-down selection of proven winners from brands like Specialized, Salsa, and All-City. A nice selection of kids models, attractive helmets, and the latest in accessories and racing gear rounds out this refreshingly edited selection. Start here if you're overwhelmed and just want someone easy going and knowledgeable to tell you what to do.

Boating

Atlantic Service & Equipment (QNS)

◎ *515 B 72nd St, Rockaway Beach*
⊕ *atlanticsvc.biz*

As a city dweller, it's probably unlikely that you own a boat, but if you do, this is a shop for you! Atlantic Service & Equipment is the place to go for parts, accessories, safety gear, and cleaning supplies. The selection is comprehensive, but if you'd rather someone else handle the job, they can do that, too.

Dance

LaDuca Shoes (MANH)

◎ *517 W 45th St bet. 11th and 10th Ave, Hell's Kitchen*
⊕ *laducashoes.com*

Phil LaDuca's jazz and tap shoes are known all over Broadway for comfort, quality, and especially because they come in a range of skin tones — not just one weird light beige. Dancers from all over the world order these Italian-made shoes, but you can try them on IRL at the flagship store in Hell's Kitchen.

On Stage (MANH)
⊚ *49 W 37th St bet. 6th and 5th Ave, Midtown*
⊕ *dancewearnyc.com*

At On Stage, racks upon racks of leotards are hung by color, alongside shelves of organized dance shoes of all kinds — pointe, Irish dance, ballroom, tap, and more. Parents take their kids here to get outfitted for class, recreational adult dancers come for proper footwear, and professionals stock up on garments for practice.

Fishing

New York City is surrounded by water, which is cleaner than you probably think it is, due in no small part to initiatives like the Billion Oyster Project. This region has some of the best fishing in America, and you don't have to go to Montauk to participate. We're living in a New York fishing renaissance!

Urban Angler (MANH)
⊚ *381 5th Ave 2nd Fl bet. W 36th and 35th St, Midtown*
⊕ *urbanangler.com*

Tucked away on the second floor of an unassuming stretch of midtown is a paradise of fly-fishing gear. With everything from fly-tying supplies, top-quality waders, and reels and rods for beginners and experts alike, the experts at Urban Angler have everything you need. Fly fishing is an exercise in understanding hyper-local ecology, but you can find flies for all sorts of environments, from upstate New York to more exotic waters.

Coney Island Hook & Bait Shop (BK)
⊚ *2879 W 24th St, Coney Island*

Behind the muraled facade, proprietor and fisherman Derek presides over an organized mess of fishing gear. He's well equipped to get any fisherpeople set up with a rod, a license and a sidewalk lesson — and be sure to let him wax poetic on the surrounding environment, the increasingly cleanliness of the nearby water and what you'll find swimming in it. Pick up your live bait here before hitting the pier.

Bernie's Bait & Tackle (BK)
◉ *3035 Emmons Ave, Sheepshead Bay*
⊕ *berniesfishing.com*

Serious anglers shop at Bernie's Bait & Tackle, which faces the bay and possesses the most extensive stock of fishing gear of any bait and tackle shop I've encountered in the five boroughs. For consummate fisherpeople, it's a vital resource for top-of-the-line reels, tools, and tackle you might otherwise only find at Bass Pro Shop. The fishing curious are also welcome to explore and ask for help getting set up with something easy to use. Licenses, repairs, and live bait are also for sale.

> **FUN FACT**
>
> The Catskills is widely considered to be the birthplace of American fly fishing, and is a destination for anglers from all over the world!

Golf

Golf is having a moment right now, and the surge in popularity is causing a surprising wave in golf retail as a new generation becomes interested in playing the sport. You might be surprised to hear that there are golf courses located within city limits, from an 18-hole course in the middle of Dyker Heights, Brooklyn, to a sprawling 36-hole complex in Pelham Bay Park in the Bronx.

New York Golf Center (MANH)
◉ *131 W 35th St bet. 7th Ave and Broadway, Garment District*
⊕ *nygolfcenter.com*

Manhattan might be the only borough to not possess a golf course, but it's at least home to the largest shop for golf gear. They've got all the big brands at this 13,000 square foot shop: TaylorMade, Odyssey, Titleist, Callaway, and dozens more. Find an overwhelming selection of ball options, racks full of high end clothes, shoes for men, women and kids, and all the little bits and bobs you'll also need. Though New York Golf Center gives off an old-school vibe, they've done a good job of adapting to the changing demographic of golf by bringing in less traditional styles of course-appropriate apparel, sportier shoes, and even a few novelties. Visit their high tech fitting studio if you're in the market for a new set of clubs, or bring your old ones in for repair. Don't miss the satellite location at Chelsea Piers!

Horseback Riding

Manhattan Saddlery (MANH)
◎ *117 E 24th St bet. Park and Madison Ave, Kips Bay*
⊕ *manhattansaddlery.com*

Manhattan Saddlery in Kips Bay is a beloved resource for equine enthusiasts, who visit for the full range of show garments, saddles, accessories, helmets, and horse care items — truly everything you need for horseback riding. It has been around for over 100 years and has the vibe and merchandise of a luxury shop, but with service that makes you feel like you're being helped by an old friend. You don't have to be a serious rider to shop here — great merch, American-made spur belts, and fabulous gifts for your favorite horse girl add a little flair to this serious specialist.

Martial Arts

Bok Lei Po Trading Inc. (MANH)
◎ *63 Mott St bet. Canal and Bayard St, Chinatown*
⊕ *bokleipo.com*

The last remaining martial arts specialist in Chinatown, Bok Lei Po serves a dedicated community of kung fu enthusiasts, Samurai sword shoppers, and practitioners of other martial arts, like muay thai and karate. Ask for help finding what you're looking for — this little shop may as well be a museum of traditional martial arts, and can feel overwhelming.

> **HOT TIP**
>
> **Bok Lei Po** is also known for being a reliable source for Feiyue shoes, which were designed for kung fu but are also fashionable for everyday wear.

Superare Fight Shop (MANH)
84 Orchard St bet. Broome and Grand St, Lower East Side
superareshop.com

Though the striking, minimalist interior of this shop implies a luxury glorification of the goods that it sells, Superare is actually a very legitimate specialty shop for combat sports gear, including boxing, MMA, jiu-jitsu, and muay thai. Shop this stylish spot for gloves, shoes, and safety gear from brands like Nike and Winning, but especially the in-house Superare brand, which offers gloves, pads, and apparel, with a streetwear flair and customizable options available!

Outdoors

Hatchet Outdoor Supply Co. (BK)
77 Atlantic Ave, Brooklyn Heights
hatchetsupply.com

For the "modern adventurer," Hatchet Outdoor Supply Co. covers the whole gamut of outdoor supplies in their sunny corner storefront on the quiet end of Atlantic Avenue. Come for quality tents, cool binoculars, well-fitted shoes, stylish but functional campsite cooking gear, and all the little bits and bobs you need for safety and comfort — it's all here, and in some of the best-designed versions on the market.

Outlandish (BK)
722 Franklin Ave, Crown Heights
outlandish.nyc

This is Brooklyn's first and only hiking specialty store! Outlandish carries new apparel and gear from top outdoor brands and New York-based companies. The overarching goal here is to encourage people of all backgrounds to reconnect with the outdoors through community events, hiking trips, and by carrying books about nature authored by people of color. Get a great new pair of hiking boots, sign up for a group "hikeish," and maybe make a few new friends in the process.

Racquet Sports

NYC Racquet Sport (MANH)
⊚ *157A W 35th St nr. 7th Ave, Garment District*
⊕ *nycracquetsports.com*

NYC Racquet Sports has all of the bases covered, including table tennis, pickleball, padel, beach tennis, badminton, tennis, squash — a sea of paddles and racquets fill the walls at this sporting specialist. With services like same-day re-stringing and racquet couriers, these folks mean business.

Mason's Tennis (MANH)
⊚ *56 E 53rd St bet. Madison and Park Ave, Midtown*
⊕ *masonstennis.com*

The selection at Mason's Tennis is edited and tasteful — as you might expect from a shop pro who is a 50 year veteran in the industry. Uptown players come here for stylish, preppy apparel and a judicious range of racquets, shoes and accessories, and advice from proprietor Mark Mason. The day I went to get a pair of shoes, two different women ran in to buy last minute whites and left expertly outfitted in mere minutes.

Running

Brooklyn Running Company (BK)
⊚ *480 Bergen St, Park Slope*
⊚ *222 Grand St, Williamsburg*
⊕ *brooklynrunningco.com*

New York City's only running specialty shop is owned by actual runners who have expertise in understanding the minutiae of finding the right footwear. Whether you're a freshly minted recreational runner or an ultra-marathoner, the folks here will know how to help you find the perfect pair. Walk in without a clue, or a specific need, and leave fully outfitted, head to toe. Stocked brands include: Hoka, Mizuno, Brooks, ASICS, Saucony, and more.

Also visit the running department at **Paragon Sports** *in Union Square.*

Snow Sports

Panda Ski and Sport (BK)
⊚ *9213 5th Ave, Bay Ridge*
⊕ *pandasportdirect.com*

This charming family-owned sporting goods shop specializes in seasonal equipment: skiing and snowboarding in the winter, golf and inline skating in the summer. When the winter season hits, enthusiasts from all over the city flock here for new gear, to get their boards and skis serviced, and for boot fittings (also available year round). As if to prove a point that this is really a one-stop shop for snow sports, you can even purchase and have a car rack installed at Panda!

Soccer

Euromex Soccer (MANH)
⊚ *246 E 116th St nr. 2nd Ave, East Harlem*
⊕ *euromexsports.com*

Planted in the heart of Spanish Harlem, Euromex Soccer caters to the thriving local community of soccer players and enthusiasts. Find racks full of jerseys for players from all over the world, balls of all kinds, and a spectacular selection of cleats to choose from. It's family-owned, occupies two stories and exudes a palpable sense of community. Bring your kid on a special trip here to get set up for their first year in the youth league — they'll remember it forever.

Skating

Upper West Skates (MANH)
◎ *2768 Broadway bet. W 107th and 106th St, Upper West Side*
⊕ *upperwestskates.com*
It's no accident that UWS is located in close proximity to Alan Kessler Skate Park in Riverside Park. New York native Chris Vidal thought it was a travesty to not have a skate shop near such a popular park, so he took matters into his own hands. Chris fosters an environment that's so family-friendly and community oriented, you'd never guess that his shop has only been around since 2022. Come here for parts, a ready-to-ride complete, or for a new pair of sneakers and some safety gear.

Uncle Funkys Boards (MANH)
◎ *128 Charles St, Basement nr. Greenwich St, West Village*
⊕ *unclefunkysboards.com*
This subterranean skate shop exudes an earnest charm that can only be earned with time. There's a friendly old dog hanging out, cozy lighting, ephemera and stickers covering surfaces, boards slotted onto the wall in a satisfying order, and a friendly guy chatting up a neighbor. Uncle Funkys Boards is a picture-perfect skate shop with nearly 20 years of accumulated charm and expertise. Longboards are the specialty here, but you'll also find a terrifically technicolor range of skateboards, too.

Tenant (BK)
◎ *1096 Dekalb Ave, Bed-Stuy*
⊕ *tenantny.com*
Underground, local, and super indie brands make up the bulk of what's for sale at Tenant. Their creative point of view is straight out of 1997 and tinted with a very current hypebeast edge that's authentic, not obnoxious. Boards aside, the clothing and accessories selection at Tenant is particularly inspired. Come here for something out of the ordinary.

Five Stride Roller Skates (BK)

176 Bushwick Ave, East Williamsburg
fivestride.com

On a quiet stretch of Bushwick Ave in East Williamsburg is the only remaining roller skate specialist in NYC! Five Stride Skate Shop has been supplying the city with a wide selection of wheels for outdoor and rink use since 2010. Skates are made up of three parts: the boot, the plate and the wheels, with additional options like a toe stop. At Five Stride, you can find full package sets that are ready to wear starting at around $160, or piece together your own perfect pair from all of the components on offer. You're in great hands here, and should most certainly return for a tune-up or to stock up on stylish safety equipment.

Surf

Phase Surf (QNS)

189 Beach 96th St, Rockaway Beach
phasesurf.com

Not just a surf shop! Locals come here for cold-foam iced lattes, great breakfast burritos, and a side of community. You'll also find hand-shaped boards and a small but curated selection of surf gear and supplies. If you're just in for the day, swing by Phase to get hooked up with a board for rent!

Boarders (QNS)

1-92 Beach 92nd St, Rockaway Beach
boarderssurfshop.com

With a year-round shop and several seasonal outposts along the beach, Boarders is owned by a Rockaway-native, father-and-son duo with a serious passion for surfing. Shop here for everything from wetsuits and board gear to Made in NYC bikinis and actually water-resistant sunscreen. For beginner surfers, this is a great place to start — they even offer surf lessons!

Everything Else

Esoteric and Mystical

Enchantments (MANH)
◎ 165 Ave B bet. E 11th and 10th St, Alphabet City
⊕ enchantments.nyc

In my social circle, Enchantments is referred to simply as "the Witch Shop." The main attraction here is their candle carving services — you can order custom-carved 7-day candles* for casting spells and manifesting, or buy candle blanks to make your own. Books on all things magic, tarot cards, oil blends, and supplies for rituals and spells fill the bulk of the store.

A 7-day candle is a type of colored wax candle in a tall jar, designed to burn continuously for 7-days (more or less). They're used in all sorts of religious and spiritual practices depending on your culture — varying from honoring the dead, praying for someone, or manifesting.

Aum Shanti Bookshop (MANH)
◎ 230 E 14th St bet. 3rd and 2nd Ave, East Village
⊕ aumshantibookshop.com

The center table is the main attraction for many at Aum Shanti, with hundreds of types of crystals organized by chakra color. Books for sale cover topics like Eastern religion, herbal medicine, yoga, meditation, and all things metaphysical. What I like about Aum Shanti in particular is that, due to its small size, it's not overwhelming for those who know nothing about this stuff. Like any great specialist, they strike the delicate balance of being accessible for beginners, while being extensive and niche enough for longtime practitioners. A rotating cast of great tarot readers work here, too!

Ruby's House of Crystals (BK)
⊚ *119 Columbia St, Brooklyn Heights*
⊕ *rubyshouseofcrystals.com*

Rock nerds and crystal believers unite at this haven of geology. This cozy storefront is artfully merchandised with beautiful bowls laden with your average crystal shop fare, along with rare specimens of rocks and crystals that are ethically sourced from all over the world. This is the crystal shop you visit when you can't find the type you're looking for, or if you're in the market for a larger, decorative piece.

Botánica San Miguel (MANH)
⊚ *2079 Amsterdam Ave nr. W 163rd St, Washington Heights*

A botánica is a type of shop that sells spiritual products catering more towards the esoteric. Prayer candles, herbs and oils, statues and amulets — they're typically found in historically Hispanic and African neighborhoods and serve an important purpose for the practice of Dominican santeria, Hoodoo, Catholic rituals, and maybe a little mysticism.

Botánica San Miguel in Washington Heights is a primo example of a neighborhood botánica. Owner Gisette has a knack for reading people and knowing what they need. Neighbors come in simply to buy a new bottle of Florida Water, and to ask for her advice. Tell Gisette about a prayer you need answered, a problem you're trying to solve, or the relationship you're trying to heal, and she'll tell you what to do (and which candles to burn) with a sincerity that feels familiar and trustworthy.

Most of the candles sold here are made locally by Crusader Candle Company in Gowanus, Brooklyn!

Motorcycles

Indian Larry (BK)
◎ *70 N 15th St, Greenpoint*
⊕ *indianlarry.com*
With the focus of honoring the legacy of motorcycle icon Indian Larry, this standout bike shop sells specialty parts that are designed and made in-house, as are the incredible custom-built bikes, which are true works of art, made in the traditional style of American motorcycle design. In fact, the history and tradition of motorcycle culture is so strong here, that Indian Larry is something of a pilgrimage site for bikers from all over the world.

Motogrrl (BK)
◎ *42 Dobbin St, Greenpoint*
⊕ *motorgrrl.com*
Woman-owned and operated Motogrrl is a garage for parking, repairing, and rebuilding motorbikes of all kinds. Join this inclusive community of enthusiasts with a membership for garage access, or come by to shop great parts and a selection of refurbished secondhand bikes.

Luggage

Altman Luggage (MANH)
◎ *135 Orchard St*
bet. Rivington and Delancey St, Lower East Side
⊕ *altmanluggage.com*
In a sea of identical, generic black suitcases (you know the ones), Altman Luggage shines as a place where curious, refined globetrotters shop for something more specific. For 100 years, this Orchard Street shop has been adapting to the changing tastes of travelers by stocking traditional brands like American Tourister and Travelpro, alongside more niche ones like better-than-Rimowa aluminum specialist Aleon. Also find smaller bags and backpacks from Manhattan Portage and Kipling, as well as great garment bags and suitcase organizing systems.

Pertutti (MANH)

⊚ *49 Greenwich Ave bet. Perry and Charles St, West Village*
⊕ *pertutti.com*

When your wheel falls off and it seems ridiculous to ship a giant suitcase to your apartment (because it is), this is where you go. What's nice about Pertutti is the range of options, with everything from $60 duffel bags to Tumi suitcases over $1,000 — this place is for everyone. Don't expect to find any of the slick brands you see on TikTok, because this shop specializes in the OG standbys like Samsonite, Bric's, and Briggs & Riley.

Party Supplies

Village Party Store (MANH)

⊚ *13 E 8th St bet. 5th Ave and University Pl, Greenwich Village*
⊕ *villagepartystore.com*

I love this kind of shop: one that sells everything and nothing at the same time. As expected, there's always a reliable spectrum of paper plates, matching cups, napkins, and an ample assortment of gift bags here, but where Village Party Supply Store shines is in costume accessories and themed decor. Sort through mountains of playful decor and wearables for Halloween or Christmas, but be sure to visit during the seasons in between for the extra weird stuff. Last time I visited, I delighted in an exceptional array of food-themed decor.

Balloon Saloon (MANH)

⊚ *133 West Broadway nr. Duane St, Tribeca*
⊕ *balloonsaloon.com*

Chances are, you've seen the Balloon Saloon van driving around town — wrapped in a rainbow balloon print and likely full of decorative mylar balloons, ones filled with specially chosen confetti or printed with nostalgic marbled patterns. No one has a larger selection of out-of-the-ordinary balloons than this shop. Put in your balloon order at the back counter and shop for silly prank toys, nostalgic games, party favors, and decor from boutique brands like Meri Meri.

Fiesta Pop Supplies (BK)

⊚ *4422 4th Ave, Sunset Park*
⊕ *fiestapopsupplies.com*

Last year, I was sent on a wild goose chase to figure out where to buy authentic Mexican piñatas, and after running around three boroughs, this Sunset Park specialist fulfilled my mission. Fiesta Pop sells proper piñatas in traditional Mexican shapes, and a whole zoo of cute animals, numbers, sports balls, and various refreshingly non-branded characters. Expect to pay around $50, with the add-on option of having it filled with candy on-site.

Party Glitters (QNS)

⊚ *35-31 Junction Blvd, Jackson Heights*
⊚ *80-11 Roosevelt Ave, Jackson Heights*
⊕ *partyglittersonline.com*

Party Glitters is a small family-owned local party supply empire, with three locations in Brooklyn and Queens. If there's a party supply store that can compete with Party City, this is it! They have a comparable selection of disposables, decorations, treat bag knick-knacks, and an impressive aisle of cake-making supplies. Especially for kids birthday parties, Party Glitters has you covered on all fronts — including balloons and piñatas.

Trophies & Engraving

Trophy World (BK)

⊚ *46 Hoyt St, Downtown Brooklyn*
⊕ *trophyworld.com*

I don't know about you, but although I haven't had a proper trophy since childhood, I frequently daydream about ones I'd have made for adult life. While walking New York City, I've been endlessly amused by the trophy shops I've encountered — more than I'd have guessed, and with so much to offer. Trophy World is one of them — a place to get your engraved medals, trophies, object-specific statuettes, and plaques, with no minimums and personalized service. Additionally, you can get custom promotional merch here: mugs, highlighters, coolers, pens — pretty much anything you'd find on a generic corporate website but with small biz service.

Did We Miss Something?

We want to hear from you!

Get in touch to let us know if there's an exceptional shop we should consider adding in future editions of this book! We'll be back in 2026 with an expanded and revised version, including new features and even more specific subcategories.

Email us at **general@thelocavore.com** with any suggestions or inquiries,
DM us **@thelocavorenyc**,
or send a letter to our office:

The Locavore Guide
1 Union Square W, 810
New York, NY 10003

Index

#

3 Aunties Thai Market, 187
3 Guys from Brooklyn, 177
3rd Ave Dollar and More, 143
4th Street Food Co-op, 176
10ft Single By Stella Dallas, 130
21 Tara, 234
30th Street Guitars, 277
180 the Store, 91

A

AAA Avocados, 175
Abbode, 92
Abracadabra, 88
A&E Bowery Lighting, 236
Aedes Perfumery, 248
Aeon Bookstore, 78
African Record Center, 275
Agata & Valentina Gluten-Free, 166
Aigner Chocolates, 199
Albee Baby, 258
Albert Lam Bespoke, 185
Alizé Clothing NY, 95
Aljo Dyes, 54
All City Legends, 63
All-in-One Suppliers, 62
Alphabet City Beer Co., 151
Al's Men Shop, 213
Altman Luggage, 134, 307
Amarcord Vintage, 129
Amsale, 120
Anaïs, 70
Anime Castle, 72
an.mé, 259
Annie's Blue Ribbon General Store, 230
Apotheke, 249
Aqua Best, 162
Archie's Press, 239
Argosy Books, 77
Argyle Yarn Shop, 60
Arthur Ave Retail Market, 193
Art of Play, 148
Art Retail Therapy (A.R.T.), 50
Assembly Line, 244
Assembly New York, 90
Astoria Music, 280
Astor Wines & Spirits, 153
A Sustainable Village, 167
Atlantic Halal Meat, 161
Atlantic Service & Equipment, 296
Audio46 Headphones, 138
Aum Shanti Bookshop, 305
Azaleas, 107

B

Balady Market, 195
Balloon Saloon, 308
Bangkok Grocery Center, 184
Batsheva, 110
BeadKraft, 51
Beads of Paradise, 51
BEAM, 244
BEDSTUYFLY, 94
Beethoven Pianos, 280
Belgian Shoes, 201
Bellocq Tea Atelier, 160
Ben's Market, 173
Benz's Food Products, 164
Bernard James, 217
Bernie's Bait & Tackle, 298
Bernie's Glass & Mirror, 83
Berriez, 129
Big Bag, 209
Big Cheers, 190
Big Night, 171, 272
Bike and Spin, 296
Bin Bin Sake, 157
Bios Apothecary, 227, 249
B&J Fabrics, 55
Black Cat Wines, 154
Blacker & Kooby Vanessa, 133
Black Spring Books, 77
Bleecker Trading, 149
Bleeker Digital Solutions, 141
Bluestockings, 74
Boarders, 304
Bode, 105
Bok Lei Po Trading Inc., 299
BonBon, 197
Bondy Appliances, 139
Bonnie Slotnick Cookbooks, 73
Book Club Bar, 69
Books Are Magic, 71
Books of Wonder, 71
Borgatti's Ravioli and Egg Noodles, 192
Botánica San Miguel, 306
Bronx Native, 95
Brooke's Appliances, 139
Brooklyn Craft Company, 52

Brooklyn Film Camera, 142
Brooklyn General Store, 59
Brooklyn Herborium, 256
Brooklyn Made Store, 223
Brooklyn Queens Furniture & Things, 246
Brooklyn Running Company, 301
Brooklyn Terminal Market, 177
Brooklyn Video Games, 150
Bungee Space, 90
Burnt Books, 78
Burrowes Brothers Bicycles, 295
Búzios, 195
By Liv Handmade, 130

C

Cafe con Libros, 75
Café Forgot, 117
Calabria Pork Store, 193
Canal Plastics Center, 61
Canal Rubber Supply Co., 85
Carlos de la Puente Antiques, 236
Carmel Grocery, 158
Carmine Street Guitars, 277
Carpet Culture, 241
Carriage Suite, 258
Casa Amadeo, 277
Casa Magazines, 76
Caserta Eye, 211
Casey Rubber Stamps, 61
Cato's Army & Navy, 96
Cellini Uomo, 207
Central Floral Supply, 289
Cerini Coffee & Gifts, 158, 193
Charles P. Rogers Bedmakers, 238
C'H'C'M, 99
Chef Restaurant Supplies, 267
Chelsea Garden Center, 290
Chess Forum, 148
Chinatown Lumber, 84
City Hats, 212
City Opera Thrift Shop, 246
City Papery, 133
Claireware, 271
Classic Sofa, 245
Cleo's Yarn Shop, 59
Cobbler Bushwick Co., 206
C.O. Bigelow, 253
Coclico, 205
Colbo, 98, 105
Collina Strada, 105, 110
Collyer's Mansion, 245
Colony, 236
Colorant, 91
Coming Soon, 105, 232
Community Wine and Spirits, 153
Coney Island Hook & Bait Shop, 297
Coney Island USA Gift Shop, 228
Confectionery!, 198
Consignment Brooklyn, 123
CONTROL, 276
Cook's Arts and Crafts Shoppe, 53
Corkscrew Wines, 154
Corridor, 103
Cosenza's Fish Market, 192
Creel & Gow, 233
Crown Machine Services, 142
Crust Baker, 165
Cueva, 99
Cure Thrift, 124

D

Da-Bar Too Shoes, 203
Dahing Plants, 291
Dana Foley, 110
Dandy Farmer, 293
Daniella Shevel, 205
dAN's Parents' House, 145
Dashop Corp., 144
Dashwood Books, 69
Dave's, 95
Daytona Trimming, 66
D. Coluccio & Sons, 191
dear friend books, 70
Deluxe Meat Market, 160
Dépanneur Wines, 154
Desert Island Comics, 71
Desert Vintage, 105, 127
Desi Attire NY, 121
Dimes Market, 171
Don't Blink Magic Shop, 146
Dover Street Market, 220
Down & Quilt Shop, 237
Downright, 238
Downtown Yarns, 58
Dream Fishing Tackle, 243
Duals Natural, 183
Dukan Syko, 186
Duman Home, 237
Duo NYC, 126

E

Earth & Me, 167
East Coast Trimming, 65
Eastern District, 152
East Village Hats, 212
East Village Organic, 174
East Village Postal, 131
Eckhaus Latta, 90
Economy Candy, 196
Eddie's Place African Market, 189
Edith Machinist, 128
Edy's Grocer, 196
Elegance NYC, 215
Elm Wellness, 257
ELPÍDA NYC, 243
Elsi Intimate, 108
Emilia George, 115
Emily's Pork Store, 162

Enchantments, 305
Ends Meat, 161, 226
Enfleurage, 248
Epstein's Paint Center, 84
Ergot Records, 274
E. Rossi & Company, 222
Esenshel, 212
Esposito Meat Market, 161
Esquire Menswear, 107
Essex Card Shop, 136
Eugene J Candy, 197
Euromex Soccer, 302
Eva Joan, 94
Everyone Comics & Collectibles, 72
Everything But the Baby, 258
Every Thing Goes Book Cafe, 79
Every Thing Goes Furniture & Clothing, 247
EWA Trading, 184
Exotic Fragrances, 249
Exposure Therapy, 141

F

FABSCRAP, 58
Fabulous Fanny's, 210
Fantasy Explosion, 126
F.E. Castleberry, 102
Fe Noel Little Caribbean, 114
Fiesta Pop Supplies, 309
fig., 100
Fine & Dandy Shop, 214
Fine & Raw Chocolate, 198
Finlay + Gage Musical Instruments, 279
Fishs Eddy, 269
Five Stride Roller Skates, 304
Flatbush Central Caribbean Market, 188
Flower Aggregate, 287
Flower Power Herbs & Roots, 250
Fong On, 179
Forces of Nature, 174
Fordham Fish Market, 163
Forêt Wines, 156
Forever Young Kids, 263
Formaggio Essex, 168
Foster Sundry, 171
Fountain Pen Hospital, 134
Frag Farm, 282
Francis Waplinger, 227
Frankel's, 96
Frank Hardware, 87
Frank's Sports Shop, 294
French Wink, 189
Friends NYC, 229
Front General Store, 128
Fugazi, 105
Furnish Green, 246
FYL NYC, 94

G

Gabrielle Carlson, 116
Gamestoria, 149
Garber Hardware, 85
Gem Home, 269
General Wear Inc., 93
Geometry Garden & Floral Shop, 292
Geshmake Fish, 163
Gift Man, 228
Global Table, 270
GoGo Gone, 295
Gone to the Dogs, 283
Good Hands Drum Shop, 278
Goods for the Study, 132
Gotham Thrift Shop, 125
Gothic Cabinet Craft, 245
Gothic Renaissance, 88
grace land new york, 130
Graham Wine Co., 157
Gramercy Typewriter Company, 137
Grandma's Place, 262
Grand Tea & Imports, 184
Grape Collective, 153
Greene Hill Food Co-op, 176
Greenwich Letterpress, 135
Greenwich Locksmiths, 84
Greenwich St. Jewelers, 220
Grimm Artisanal Ales, 152
Gringer & Sons, 140
Grown and Sewn, 102
Guerra Paint & Pigmen, 55

H

Halloween Adventure Shop, 88
Happy Isles Salon, 120
Haricot Vert's Dreamworld, 218
Harlem Haberdashery, 101
Harlequin Vintage, 242
Hatchet Outdoor Supply Co., 300
Heatonist, 179
Heirloom, 241
Helen Levi, 271
Hellenic Aesthetic, 119
Henry Harde's Wines & Liquors, 154
Her Winter Flowers, 133
Holiday Beverage, 152
Hong Kong Supermarket, 182
Horseman Antiques, 242
Horseradish Market, 175
Horton's Market!, 173
Household by Nickey Kehoe, 232
House of Kellogg, 129
Hudson & Charles, 161
Hung Chong Imports, 185
Hyer Goods, 210

I

iGirl, 217

INCASA, 273
Indian Larry, 307
Indoor Outdoor Gardener, 290
Indulge Kitchen Supplies, 267
Ink & Toner, 136
In Living Stereo, 138
Iris Lingerie, 109
Irving Green, 221

J

Jamali Floral & Garden Supplies, 288
James Veloria, 126
Jane's Exchange, 259
Janoff's Stationery, 50, 134
J. Baczynsky Meat Market, 189
Jensen-Lewis, 244
J. Mueser, 106
John Derian Company, 231
Johnny Albino Music Center, 279
JoMart Chocolate, 199
Joy Flower Pot NYC, 287
Judaica Creations, 165
Judi Rosen, 113
Juliette Flower Shop, 288
Just Shades, 236

K

Kallmeyer, 112
Kalustyan's, 180
Kartik Research, 99, 105
Kathe's Jewelry, 219
KC Arts, 51
Keaton Quilts, 56
Kermanshah, 241
Kettle & Cord, 165
Keur Djembe African Drums, 279
Kidding Around, 262
Kidstown, 261
Kidult Brick, 144
Kimera, 115

Kingston Bake Shop, 164
Kitchen Arts & Letters, 73
KK Discount, 185
Knickerbocker, 101
Korin, 268
K&P Games Express Inc, 150
Kremer Pigments, 54
Kyichu Tibetan Handicrafts, 223

L

LaDuca Shoes, 296
Lana's Loft, 116
Lanka Grocery, 187
Laura Lombardi, 218
Lauren Trimming, 64
Lee Anderson Couture, 120
Lee's Sneakers, 208
Le Fanion, 272
Leffot, 207
Left Bank Books, 77
Left Field, 96
Leif Home + Woman, 119
Lein Studio, 121
Leroy's Place, 224
Liberty Panel and Home Center, 86
LifeThyme, 174
Lily's Vegan Pantry, 166, 185
Limited to One Record Shop, 274
Linder Sport, 102
Little Green Brooklyn, 263
Liz's Book Bar, 70
Lockwood, 229
Loom & Stars, 56
Loop of the Loom, 59
Love Adorned, 216
Lowlands Nursery, 290
Lubavitch Matzah Bakery, 165
Lucas Electronics, 139
Lucky Wang, 260

M

Magazine Cafe, 76
Magazzino, 155
Maguire Shoes, 205
Main Drag Music, 278
Maison Jar, 168
Makié, 259
Manhattan45, 274
Manhattan Saddlery, 299
Manhattan Wardrobe Supply, 97
Mani Market Place, 190
Marché Rue Dix, 254
Maryam Nassir Zadeh, 112
Mason's Tennis, 301
Mast Books, 68
Material Good, 220
McNulty's Tea & Coffee Co., 160
Measure Twice, 135
Mediterranean Foods, 194
Mellow, 271
Memories of New York, 225
Mendel Goldberg Fabrics, 57
Mercado Central, 191
Merlette, 114
Mermaid's Garden, 163
Metropolis, 125
Metropolitan Fish Market, 163
Mexico In My Pocket, 222
M. Fine Lumber, 85
Michael's Luxury Consignment, 123
Michele Varian, 234
Miista, 204
Miju Sewing Corp., 63
Millo, 256
Millport Dairy, 169
Mil Mundos Books, 75
Minus Moonshine, 159
Misha & Puff, 260
M. Kessler Hardware, 82
M&M Vacuums, 142
Mociun, 217

Modify, 124
MogMog Japanese Market, 187
Mogutable, 273
Monger's Palate, 170
Montgomery Stationery, 136
Mood Fabrics, 56
MooShoes, 209
Morph., 123
Motogrrl, 307
MozzLab, 169
MR. FRIENDLY, 285
Mr. Throwback, 125
M&S Schmalberg, 64
MTV Super Sound, 139
Mumu Bath, 256
Muse Shop, 216
Museum of Nostalgia, 145
Mushtari Hardware, 86
Music Inn World Instruments, 279
Music Planet Games & Records, 150
Muzik City, 275
Myrtle Wombat, 183

Naomi Nomi, 111
Natty Garden, 292
Nature's Prescriptions, 255
Nazz Forge and Adventurers Supply, 226
Nepenthes New York, 98
Neto's Market, 177
New Era Factory Outlet, 106
New Hi-Tech Corp, 138
New Kam Man, 184
Newtown HQ, 229
New York Golf Center, 298
Niconeco Zakkaya, 131
Night Owl Video, 147
Noni Styles, 121
Nose Best, 249
NOT, 111
November 19, 233

NuFrame, 235
Nuthouse Hardware, 87
NY Cake, 265
NYC Racquet Sport, 301

Ocean Star Wine & Spirits, 157
Octopus Records, 275
Olde Good Things, 82
Old The Best, 128
Only Hearts, 108
On Stage, 297
Ora La Casa De Las Floras, 288
Orchard Corset, 108
Orchard Grocer, 166
Orchid Man, 293
Organicer, 239
Oroboro, 117
Oro Latino Jewelry Inc., 219
Orphan Guitars, 278
Osakana, 162
Outlandish, 300
Outline, 118
Outta Pocket, 64
Owl Tree, 261

Pacific Aquarium & Plant, 281
Pacific Trimming, 65
Page Sargisson, 216
Pancake Records, 276
Panda Ski and Sport, 302
Parachute Brooklyn, 261
Paragon Sports, 294
Park Delicatessen, 287
Park Slope Food Coop, 176
Parkview Sports Center, 93
Party Glitters, 309
Pashmina Fashions, 122
Pasteur Pharmacy, 253
Paul Discount Shoes, 206

Paws Grocer, 285
Pearl River Mart, 222
Pêche, 105
Pertutti, 308
Peter Hermann Leather Goods, 210
Petqua, 283
Phase Surf, 304
Philip Williams Posters, 240
Phil's Stationery, 136
photodom., 141
Physical Graffitea, 159
Picture Room, 240
Pillow-Cat Books, 79
Pizzazzz Toyz, 263
Playground, 74
Playing Mantis, 263
Please, 251
Plug-ins, 140
Plum Paperie, 134
Plus BKLYN, 130
Poetry Of Material Things, 218
Pompette Wine, 155
Pop Up Grocer, 171
Porta, 272
Porto Rico Coffee Importers, 157
Posteritati, 240
Precycle, 168
Preferred Pharmacy, 255
Pretty Well Beauty, 252
Printed Matter, 68
Propel, 296
Purim Megastore, 89
Purple Passion, 251

Quimby's Bookstore, 81

R

Rachel Comey, 114
Radicle Wine, 155
Randazzo's Seafood, 192
Raskin's Fish Market, 164
Redline Hobbies, 146
Renewfinds, 243

Richmond Appliance, 140
RIDER Gifts, 224
Rita's Needlepoint, 60
RJJ Deli, 200
Robinson Brooklyn, 107
Roni-Sue's Chocolate Shop, 198
Rosemary Home, 270
Rosie Assoulin, 111
Rothman's, 103
Royal Birds & Supplies, 284
Royal Collectibles, 72
Royal Sports & Entertainment, 149
Ruby's House of Crystals, 306
Rudy's Hobby & Art, 146
Rue Saint Paul, 118
Runnin' Wild Kids, 202

S

Sacred Vibes Apothecary, 250
Sahadi's, 196, 226
Sakaya, 156
Salter House, 233
San Art Framing & Supply, 235
Sandy Liang, 105, 112
Santacroce Greenhouses & Garden Center, 290
Sara Japanese Pottery, 270
Save-a-Thon, 52
Scent Bar NYC, 248
Schaller & Weber, 190
Schott, 91
Schweitzer Linen, 237
Screaming Mimi's, 89
Scribbles, 53
Scully & Scully, 271
Secret Riso Club, 69
Seed and Oil by Suryaside, 168
SEED Brklyn, 99
Seigo Neckwear, 214
Selima Optique, 211
Senti Senti, 252
Sermoneta Gloves, 213
Shag, 252
Shoe Market, 204
Shulman Paper, 137
SHW, 215
Sil Thread, 66
Silver Age Comics, 72
Silver Lining Opticians, 211
Simon's Hardware and Bath, 83
Sincerely, Tommy, 117
Sister's Uptown Bookstore, 74
SKKM West Indian Market, 188
Slope Home, 234
Small Mommi African Market, 188
Soho Art Materials, 50
Solestice, 208
SOS Chefs, 178
Soula Shoes, 203
Soybean Chan Flower Shop, 182
Spandex House, 56
Spice Professors, 179
Spina Bride, 120
Spirited Away, 158
Spoiled Brats, 283
Stand Alone Cheese, 170
Steinlauf & Stoller, 65
Stéle, 249
Steph's Creativity Corner, 264
Steppe, 243
Stereo Exchange, 139
Steven Alan, 100
Still Here, 113
Stitches, 93
St. Mark's Comics, 227
Stock Vintage, 127
Strand Books, 76
Sugar Room, 265
Sullivan Street Tea & Spice Company, 178
Sunny's Florist, 286
Sunrise Mart, 226
Sunset Sewing Machine Supplies, 63
Superare Fight Shop, 300
Susan Alexandra, 218
Sutton Clock Shop, 231
Suzanne Couture Millinery, 213
Sweet Pickle Books, 78

T

Table Wine, 155
Tailored Industry, 227
Takamichi Beauty Room, 253
Take Me With You, 223
Talas, 53
Talea Beer, 152
Tamara Malas, 113
Tangerine, 119
Tannens, 137
Tannen's Magic, 147
Tarin Thomas, 216
Taro's Origami Studio Shop, 227
Tarzian West, 266
Tashkent Supermarket, 186
Tavola Italian Market, 194
Teitel Brothers Market, 192
Tenant, 303
Tend Greenpoint, 291
Tenement Museum, 264
The Analog Stationer, 132
Theater Circle, 225
The Big Reuse, 247
The Boozery, 164
The Brooklyn Circus, 102
The Brooklyn Teacup, 273
The Brownstone Woman, 116
The Cast, 101
The Compact Disc Shoppe, 276
The Compleat Sculptor, 62
The Compleat Strategist, 147
The Drama Book Shop, 80

The Fajas Store, 109
The Fragrance Shop, 249
The Greene Grape, 173
The House of Glatt, 165
The Lit. Bar, 75
The Locavore Variety Store, 262
The Makers Guild, 227
The Meadow, 178
The Mysterious Bookshop, 80
The Old Print Shop, 239
The Pickle Guys, 172
The Pleasure Chest, 251
The Rack Shack, 109
The Red Caboose, 145
The Ripped Bodice, 80
The Sock Man, 215
The Wild, 259
The WonderMart, 224
Thirst Wine Merchants, 156
Thompson Alchemists, 254
Tiny Arts Supply, 51
Tiny Doll House, 54
Tip Top Kids Shoes, 202
Tip Top Shoes, 203
Tip Top Super Fine Fabrics, 58
T.O. Dey Shoes, 206
Tokyo Joe, 123
Tools for Working Wood, 86
Top Hat, 230
Top Hops Beer Shop, 151
Topos Too, 70
Top Tomato, 173
Tortilleria La Malinche, 195
Toy Tokyo, 144
Trash & Vaudeville, 90
Tread Bike Shop, 295
Treasures of NYC, 128
Tribes of Morocco, 221
Trim Fabrics, 66
Trixie's Pet Food Supplies and Accessories, 284
Trophy World, 309
Troubled Sleep, 78

Tsar Caviar, 162
T-Shirt City, 92
Tula House, 292
TUMBAO, 105, 117
Twenty Sided Store, 148

U

Uke Hut, 280
Uncle Edik's Pickles, 164
Uncle Funkys Boards, 303
Unimax Supply Co., 257
Unisecon, 105
Unnameable Books, 79
Upper West Skates, 303
Upstate Stock, 225
Urban Angler, 297
Urban Garden Center, 289

V

Valentino Food Market, 177
Vanilla Gourmet Specialty Food, 191
Veka Bridal, 121
Ven. Space, 100
VERS :: Clothing for People, 92
Veterans Caning, 247
Via Della Scrofa, 189
Videogamesnewyork, 150
Village Party Store, 308
Village Revival Records, 275
Village Works, 80
Vinny's Men Store, 103
Vintage Thrift Shop, 124

W

Wagwear, 282
Watson Ellis, 106
Weinstein's Hardware and Houseware, 165
West NYC, 208
West Village Knit & Needle, 60

Whisk, 267
Whiskers Holistic Pet Care, 284
Who's Your Doggy?, 283
Williams Candy, 197
Wing on Wo & Co, 268
Wing & Weft Gloves, 214
Win Restaurant Supplies, 267
W.M. Robins, 106
WOODstack Treehouse, 260
Wythe, 105

Y

Yamadaya, 183
Yanagi Knife Inc., 268
Yesterday's News, 242
Yoseka Stationery, 132
Yu & Me Books, 74
Yun Hai Shop, 186
Yúnhóng Chopsticks Shop, 266

Z

Zabar's, 172, 266
Zaidi's NYC, 228
Zapateria Mexico, 204
Zarin Fabrics, 57
Zero + Maria Cornejo, 113
Ziello, 235
Zitomer Pharmacy, 254
Zoe's Beauty, 256
Zola's Original Herbal Remedies, 250

By Location

Alphabet City

Alphabet City Beer Co., 151
Book Club Bar, 69
Enchantments, 305
Essex Card Shop, 136
Jane's Exchange, 259
Mast Books, 68
SOS Chefs, 178

Chelsea

30th Street Guitars, 277
BeadKraft, 51
City Opera Thrift Shop, 246
Community Wine and Spirits, 153
Dave's, 95
French Wink, 189
Furnish Green, 246
Garber Hardware, 85
Good Hands Drum Shop, 278
Gramercy Typewriter Company, 137
Heatonist, 179
Jamali Floral & Garden Supplies, 288
Keaton Quilts, 56
Kremer Pigments, 54
Manhattan Wardrobe Supply, 97
NY Cake, 265
Printed Matter, 68
Purple Passion, 251
Shulman Paper, 137
Spina Bride, 120
Steven Alan, 100
The Compleat Sculptor, 62
Watson Ellis, 106

Chinatown

Albert Lam Bespoke, 185
Bangkok Grocery Center, 184
Batsheva, 110
Bok Lei Po Trading Inc., 299
Dashop Corp., 144
Deluxe Meat Market, 160
Eckhaus Latta, 90
EWA Trading, 184
Fong On, 179
Hong Kong Supermarket, 182
Hung Chong Imports, 185
James Veloria, 126
KK Discount, 185
Lily's Vegan Pantry, 166, 185
M. Kessler Hardware, 82
New Kam Man, 184
Oro Latino Jewelry Inc., 219
Senti Senti, 252
T-Shirt City, 92
Wing on Wo & Co, 268
Yu & Me Books, 74
Yùnhóng Chopsticks Shop, 266

East Harlem

Carriage Suite, 258
Euromex Soccer, 302
Exotic Fragrances, 249
Save-a-Thon, 52
Urban Garden Center, 289

East Village

4th Street Food Co-op, 176
an.mé, 259
Archie's Press, 239
Aum Shanti Bookshop, 305
Azaleas, 107
Bonnie Slotnick Cookbooks, 73
Casey Rubber Stamps, 61
Confectionery!, 198
Cure Thrift, 124
Downtown Yarns, 58
Duals Natural, 183
Duo NYC, 126
East Village Hats, 212
East Village Organic, 174
East Village Postal, 131
Ergot Records, 274
Esenshel, 212
Fabulous Fanny's, 210
Flower Power Herbs & Roots, 250
Gothic Renaissance, 88
Gringer & Sons, 140
Halloween Adventure Shop, 88
iGirl, 217
Irving Green, 221
J. Baczynsky Meat Market, 189
John Derian Company, 231
Kathe's Jewelry, 219
Limited to One Record Shop, 274
Manhattan45, 274
Mr. Throwback, 125
Niconeco Zakkaya, 131
Osakana, 162
Physical Graffitea, 159
Pillow-Cat Books, 79
Porto Rico Coffee Importers, 157
Rosemary Home, 270
Sakaya, 156
Salter House, 233
SHW, 215
Stock Vintage, 127
Sunny's Florist, 286

The Fragrance Shop, 249
The Sock Man, 215
Tokyo Joe, 123
Toy Tokyo, 144
Trash & Vaudeville, 90
Tribes of Morocco, 221
Via Della Scrofa, 189
Videogamesnewyork, 150
Village Works, 80
Whiskers Holistic Pet Care, 284

Financial District

Pretty Well Beauty, 252

Flatiron

Abracadabra, 88
City Papery, 133
Fishs Eddy, 269
Loom & Stars, 56
Memories of New York, 225
Rothman's, 103
The Old Print Shop, 239

Garment District

B&J Fabrics, 55
Daytona Trimming, 66
East Coast Trimming, 65
Lauren Trimming, 64
M&S Schmalberg, 64
Miju Sewing Corp., 63
Mood Fabrics, 56
New York Golf Center, 298
NYC Racquet Sport, 301
Pacific Trimming, 65
Sil Thread, 66
Spandex House, 56
Steinlauf & Stoller, 65
The Drama Book Shop, 80
Wing & Weft Gloves, 214

Gramercy

3rd Ave Dollar and More, 143

Takamichi Beauty Room, 253
Vintage Thrift Shop, 124

Greenwich Village

A Sustainable Village, 167
C.O. Bigelow, 253
Chess Forum, 148
Goods for the Study, 132
Household by Nickey Kehoe, 232
Kermanshah, 241
LifeThyme, 174
Metropolis, 125
Strand Books, 76
Sullivan Street Tea & Spice Company, 178
Tashkent Supermarket, 186
The Locavore Variety Store, 262
Village Party Store, 308
Village Revival Records, 275
Wagwear, 282

Harlem

All City Legends, 63
Grandma's Place, 262
Harlem Haberdashery, 101
Modify, 124
Mushtari Hardware, 86
Pompette Wine, 155
Solestice, 208
The Brownstone Woman, 116

Hell's Kitchen

All-in-One Suppliers, 62
Don't Blink Magic Shop, 146
Epstein's Paint Center, 84
Esposito Meat Market, 161
Fine & Dandy Shop, 214
LaDuca Shoes, 296
Nepenthes New York, 98
Orchid Man, 293

Spoiled Brats, 283

Inwood

Tread Bike Shop, 295

Kips Bay

Dover Street Market, 220
Kalustyan's, 180
Manhattan Saddlery, 299
Nuthouse Hardware, 87
Simon's Hardware and Bath, 83

Little Italy

E. Rossi & Company, 222

Lower East Side

A&E Bowery Lighting, 236
AAA Avocados, 175
Aedes Perfumery, 248
Aeon Bookstore, 78
Altman Luggage, 134, 307
Aqua Best, 162
Assembly New York, 90
Big Cheers, 190
Bluestockings, 74
BonBon, 197
Bondy Appliances, 139
Bungee Space, 90
Café Forgot, 117
Cellini Uomo, 207
Chinatown Lumber, 84
Colbo, 98, 105
Collina Strada, 105, 110
Coming Soon, 105, 232
Dahing Plants, 291
Dana Foley, 110
Desert Vintage, 105, 127
Dimes Market, 171
Economy Candy, 196
Edith Machinist, 128
Formaggio Essex, 168
Fugazi, 105
GoGo Gone, 295
Grand Tea & Imports, 159, 184

Joy Flower Pot NYC, 287
Kallmeyer, 112
Kartik Research, 99, 105
Laura Lombardi, 218
Magazzino, 155
Maryam Nassir Zadeh, 112
Mellow, 271
Mendel Goldberg Fabrics, 57
Miista, 204
MooShoes, 209
New Era Factory Outlet, 106
New Hi-Tech Corp, 138
November 19, 223
Orchard Corset, 108
Orchard Grocer, 166
Pacific Aquarium & Plant, 281
Pêche, 105
Roni-Sue's Chocolate Shop, 198
Sandy Liang, 105, 112
Superare Fight Shop, 300
Susan Alexandra, 218
Sweet Pickle Books, 78
Tamara Malas, 113
Tenement Museum, 264
The Cast, 101
The Pickle Guys, 172
Top Hat, 230
Top Hops Beer Shop, 151
Tumbao, 117
Unisecon, 105
Wythe, 105
Zaidi's NYC, 228
Zarin Fabrics, 57

Meatpacking

Caserta Eye, 211

Midtown

Amsale, 120
Argosy Books, 77
Audio46 Headphones, 138
Belgian Shoes, 201
Búzios, 195
Classic Sofa, 245
Elegance NYC, 215
Jensen-Lewis, 244
Just Shades, 236
Magazine Cafe, 76
Mason's Tennis, 301
Pasteur Pharmacy, 253
Phil's Stationery, 136
Sermoneta Gloves, 213
Tannen's Magic, 148
The Red Caboose, 145
Urban Angler, 297

Morningside Heights

Janoff's Stationery, 50, 134

Murray Hill

On Stage, 297

NoHo

Astor Wines & Spirits, 153
C'H'C'M, 99
Chef Restaurant Supplies, 267
Dashwood Books, 69
In Living Stereo, 138
Selima Optique, 211
Win Restaurant Supplies, 267
Zero + Maria Cornejo, 113

Nolita

Abbode, 92
Bleeker Digital Solutions, 141
Carpet Culture, 241
City Hats, 212
Coclico, 205
Colorant, 91
Corridor, 103
Gem Home, 269
Goods for the Study, 132
Judi Rosen, 113
Left Field, 96
Love Adorned, 216
Maguire Shoes, 205
Only Hearts, 108
Oroboro, 117
Scent Bar NYC, 248
Schott, 91
Spirited Away, 158
Stéle, 249
Still Here, 113
The Meadow, 178

Nomad

Central Floral Supply, 289
The Compleat Strategist, 147

SoHo

Canal Plastics Center, 61
Canal Rubber Supply Co., 85
Global Table, 270
Happy Isles Salon, 120
Knickerbocker, 101
Lein Studio, 121
Makié, 259
Material Good, 220
Pearl River Mart, 222
Peter Hermann Leather Goods, 210
Posteritati, 240
Rachel Comey, 114
Selima Optique, 211
Silver Lining Opticians, 211
Soho Art Materials, 50
The Brooklyn Circus, 102
Thompson Alchemists, 254
Treasures of NYC, 128
Unimax Supply Co., 257

Theater District

T.O. Dey Shoes, 206
Theater Circle, 225

Tribeca

180 the Store, 91
Aljo Dyes, 54
Balloon Saloon, 308
Bode, 105
Colony, 236
Emilia George, 115
F.E. Castelberry, 102
Finlay + Gage Musical

Instruments, 279
Fountain Pen Hospital, 134
Greenwich St. Jewelers, 220
Korin, 268
Merlette, 114
Philip Williams Posters, 240
Playing Mantis, 263
The Mysterious Bookshop, 80

Union Square

Beads of Paradise, 51
Books of Wonder, 71
Charles P. Rogers Bedmakers, 238
Kidding Around, 262
Paragon Sports, 294
Stereo Exchange, 139

Upper East Side

Agata & Valentina Gluten-Free, 166
Blacker & Kooby Vanessa, 133
BonBon, 197
Carlos de la Puente Antiques, 236
Creel & Gow, 233
Gabrielle Carlson, 116
Kallmeyer, 112
Kitchen Arts & Letters, 73
Lee Anderson Couture, 120
Loop of the Loom, 59
Michael's Luxury Consignment, 123
Pasteur Pharmacy, 253
Rita's Needlepoint, 60
Sara Japanese Pottery, 270
Schaller & Weber, 190
Schweitzer Linen, 237
Scully & Scully, 271
Seigo Neckwear, 214
Selima Optique, 211
Still Here, 113
Sutton Clock Shop, 231
Suzanne Couture Millinery, 213
The Pleasure Chest, 251
Tiny Doll House, 54
Zitomer Pharmacy, 254

Upper West Side

Albee Baby, 258
Big Bag, 209
Bleecker Trading, 149
Crown Machine Services, 142
Down & Quilt Shop, 237
Goods for the Study, 132
Gothic Cabinet Craft, 245
Grape Collective, 153
Hudson & Charles, 161
Mani Market Place, 190
Millport Dairy, 169
NOT, 111
Olde Good Things, 82
Only Hearts, 108
Petqua, 283
Poetry Of Material Things, 218
Schweitzer Linen, 237
Strand Books, 76
Tip Top Kids Shoes, 202
Tip Top Shoes, 203
Upper West Skates, 303
West NYC, 208
Zabar's, 172, 266

Washington Heights

Botánica San Miguel, 306
Elsi Intimate, 108
Neto's Market, 177
Sister's Uptown Bookstore, 74
Tākout, 208

West Village

an.mé, 259
Big Night, 171, 272
Bleecker Trading, 149
BonBon, 197
Carmine Street Guitars, 277
Casa Magazines, 76
Corridor, 104
Cueva, 99
Daniella Shevel, 205
Elm Wellness, 257
Enfleurage, 248
Eva Joan, 94
Garber Hardware, 85
Greenwich Letterpress, 135
Greenwich Locksmiths, 84
Hudson & Charles, 161
Hyer Goods, 210
J. Mueser, 106
Le Fanion, 272
Leffot, 207
Left Bank Books, 77
Linder Sport, 102
Lucky Wang, 260
McNulty's Tea & Coffee Co., 160
Muse Shop, 216
Music Inn World Instruments, 279
NuFrame, 235
Old The Best, 128
Pertutti, 308
Pop Up Grocer, 171
Porto Rico Coffee Importers, 157
Screaming Mimi's, 89
Tarin Thomas, 216
The Pleasure Chest, 251
Uncle Funkys Boards, 303
West Village Knit & Needle, 60
Yamadaya, 183

Bay Ridge

Balady Market, 195
Henry Harde's Wines & Liquors, 154
Indoor Outdoor Gardener, 290
Panda Ski and Sport, 302

BK

Bed-Stuy

Al's Men Shop, 213
BEDSTUYFLY, 94
Bernie's Glass & Mirror, 83
Berriez, 129
dear friend books, 70
Exposure Therapy, 141
Greene Hill Food Co-op, 176
Kidstown, 261
MR. FRIENDLY, 285
Myrtle Wombat, 183
Natty Garden, 292
Outta Pocket, 64
Playground, 74
SEED Brklyn, 99
Sincerely, Tommy, 117
Who's Your Doggy?, 283

Bensonhurst

Brooklyn Video Games, 150
D. Coluccio & Sons, 191
Ocean Star Wine & Spirits, 157

Boerum Hill

21 Tara, 234
Anaïs, 70
Assembly Line, 244
Books Are Magic, 71
Consignment Brooklyn, 123
Horseman Antiques, 242
House of Kellogg, 129
Iris Lingerie, 109
Michele Varian, 234
Misha & Puff, 260
Outline, 118
Page Sargisson, 216
Porta, 272
Soula Shoes, 203
Take Me With You, 223
The Brooklyn Circus, 102
Veka Bridal, 121
Veterans Caning, 247

Borough Park

Montgomery Stationery, 136
Organicer, 239
Plug-ins, 140
Scribbles, 53

Brighton Beach

Tashkent Supermarket, 186
Tsar Caviar, 162
Vanilla Gourmet Specialty Food, 191

Brooklyn Heights

Art of Play, 148
Books Are Magic, 71
Collyer's Mansion, 245
Grown and Sewn, 102
Hatchet Outdoor Supply Co., 300
Picture Room, 240
Ruby's House of Crystals, 306
Sahadi's, 196, 226
Salter House, 233
Whisk, 267

Brownsville

WOODstack Treehouse, 260

Bushwick

Book Club Bar, 69
Brooklyn Queens Furniture & Things, 246
Cleo's Yarn Shop, 59
Cobbler Bushwick Co., 206
Eugene J Candy, 197
Foster Sundry, 171
Harlequin Vintage, 242
Horseradish Market, 175
Mil Mundos Books, 75
Octopus Records, 275
photodom., 141
Preferred Pharmacy, 255
Secret Riso Club, 69
VERS :: Clothing for People, 92

Canarsie

Brooklyn Terminal Market, 177

Carroll Gardens

Atlantic Halal Meat, 161
Liz's Book Bar, 70
Mercado Central, 191
Mexico in my Pocket, 222
MozzLab, 169
Orphan Guitars, 278
Owl Tree, 261
Rue Saint Paul, 118
Runnin' Wild Kids, 202
Ven. Space, 100
Yesterday's News, 242

Clinton Hill

21 Tara, 234
Corkscrew Wines, 154
Indulge Kitchen Supplies, 267
Radicle Wine, 155

Cobble Hill

Duman Home, 237
Measure Twice, 135
Not in V2 index but has a listing
Pizzazzz Toyz, 263
Rachel Comey, 114
Tavola Italian Market, 194

Columbia Heights

Brooklyn General Store, 59
Brooklyn Herborium, 256

Coney Island

Coney Island Hook & Bait Shop, 297
Coney Island USA Gift Shop, 228

FYL NYC, 94
Williams Candy, 197

Crown Heights

Benz's Food Products, 164
Cafe con Libros, 75
Duals Natural, 185
Everything But the Baby, 258
Judaica Creations, 165
Kettle & Cord, 165
Kingston Bake Shop, 164
Lubavitch Matzah Bakery, 165
Marché Rue Dix, 254
Outlandish, 300
Park Delicatessen, 287
Raskin's Fish Market, 164
The Boozery, 164
The House of Glatt, 165
Vinny's Men Store, 103
Weinstein's Hardware and Houseware, 165
Ziello, 235
Zola's Original Herbal Remedies, 250

Cypress Hills

Liberty Panel and Home Center, 86
Muzik City, 275

Downtown Brooklyn

Brooklyn Made Store, 223
Trophy World, 309

Dumbo

Front General Store, 128
Loop of the Loom, 59
Mumu Bath, 256
Naomi Nomi, 111

Dyker Heights

3 Guys from Brooklyn, 177

East Flatbush

Paul Discount Shoes, 206

East New York

Lee's Sneakers, 208
Small Mommi African Market, 188

East Williamsburg

Brooklyn Film Camera, 142
Fine & Raw Chocolate, 198
Five Stride Roller Skates, 304
Flower Aggregate, 287
Friends NYC, 229
Grimm Artisanal Ales, 152
M. Fine Lumber, 85
Nose Best, 249
Soho Art Materials, 50
Talas, 53
The Rack Shack, 109

Flatbush

Burrowes Brothers Bicycles, 295
Flatbush Central Caribbean Market, 188
Sacred Vibes Apothecary, 250
Trim Fabrics, 66

Fort Greene

Corridor, 105
Dandy Farmer, 293
Propel, 296
The Greene Grape, 173
Thirst Wine Merchants, 156

Gowanus

Black Cat Wines, 154
Claireware, 271
Keur Djembe African Drums, 279
Kimera, 115
Lowlands Nursery, 290
Mercado Central, 191
San Art Framing & Supply, 235
The Big Reuse, 247

Gravesend

Kidult Brick, 144
Millo, 256

Greenpoint

Bellocq Tea Atelier, 160
Bernard James, 217
Big Night, 171, 272
Bin Bin Sake, 157
Bios Apothecary, 227, 249
Brooklyn Craft Company, 52
Burnt Books, 78
Cato's Army & Navy, 96
CONTROL, 276
Cueva, 100
Dream Fishing Tackle, 243
Eastern District, 152
Edy's Grocer, 196
Fantasy Explosion, 126
General Wear Inc., 93
Indian Larry, 307
Lockwood, 229
Lucas Electronics, 139
Maison Jar, 168
Minus Moonshine, 159
Monger's Palate, 170
Motogrrl, 307
MTV Super Sound, 139
Music Planet Games & Records, 150
Parachute Brooklyn, 261
Plus BKLYN, 130
Renewfinds, 243
RJJ Deli, 200
Tenant, 303
Tend Greenpoint, 291
The WonderMart, 224
Tip Top Super Fine Fabrics, 58
Tula House, 292
Yoseka Stationery, 132

Zoe's Beauty, 256

Greenwood Heights

Bios Apothecary, 227, 249
Brooklyn Made Store, 223
ELPÍDA NYC, 243
Francis Waplinger, 227
Nazz Forge and Adventurers Supply, 226
Tools for Working Wood, 86

Marine Park

Save-a-Thon, 52

Midwood

JoMart Chocolate, 199
Morph., 123
Purim Megastore, 89

Mt. Eden

Kidstown, 261

Park Slope

Annie's Blue Ribbon General Store, 230
Brooke's Appliances, 139
Brooklyn Running Company, 301
Dukan Syko, 186
Eastern District, 152
fig., 100
Gift Man, 228
Gone to the Dogs, 283
Juliette Flower Shop, 288
Leroy's Place, 224
Little Green Brooklyn, 263
Owl Tree, 261
Park Slope Food Coop, 176
Please, 251
RIDER Gifts, 224
Slope Home, 234
Tarzian West, 266
The Brooklyn Teacup, 273

The Ripped Bodice, 80
Troubled Sleep, 78

Prospect Heights

Mermaid's Garden, 163
Minus Moonshine, 159
Natty Garden, 292
Paws Grocer, 285
Precycle, 168
The Analog Stationer, 132
Unnameable Books, 79

Prospect Lefferts Garden

African Record Center, 275
Crust Baker, 165
Fe Noel Little Caribbean, 114
Frank Hardware, 87
Gothic Cabinet Craft, 245
Noni Styles, 121
Trixie's Pet Food Supplies and Accessories, 284
W.M. Robins, 106

Red Hook

Apotheke, 249
Chelsea Garden Center, 290

Sheepshead Bay

Bernie's Bait & Tackle, 298
Forces of Nature, 174
Ink & Toner, 136
The Compact Disc Shoppe, 276

Sunset Park

Downright, 238
Ends Meat, 161, 226
FABSCRAP, 58

Fiesta Pop Supplies, 309
Frankel's, 96
Sahadi's, 196, 226
St. Mark's Comics, 227
Sunrise Mart, 226
Sunset Sewing Machine Supplies, 63
Tailored Industry, 227
Taro's Origami Studio Shop, 227
The Makers Guild, 227
Tortilleria La Malinche, 195
Yanagi Knife Inc., 268
Zapateria Mexico, 204

Williamsburg

10ft Single By Stella Dallas, 130
Amarcord Vintage, 129
BEAM, 244
Black Spring Books, 77
BonBon, 197
Brooklyn Running Company, 301
By Liv Handmade, 130
Chelsea Garden Center, 290
Corridor, 106
Dépanneur Wines, 154
Desert Island Comics, 71
Duals Natural, 184
Eastern District, 152
Emily's Pork Store, 162
Geometry Gardens, 292
Graham Wine Co., 157
Haricot Vert's Dreamworld, 218
Heatonist, 179
Heirloom, 241
Her Winter Flowers, 133
Johnny Albino Music Center, 279
Leif Home + Woman, 119
Lockwood, 229
Maguire Shoes, 205
Main Drag Music, 278
Metropolitan Fish Market, 163
Mociun, 217
Mogutable, 273

INDEX | 325

Night Owl Video, 147
Robinson Brooklyn, 107
Senti Senti, 252
Shag, 252
Shoe Market, 204
Stéle, 249
Talea Beer, 152
Tangerine, 119
The Wild, 259
Twenty Sided Store, 148
Upstate Stock, 225
Yun Hai Shop, 186

Windsor Terrace

Argyle Yarn Shop, 60
Brooklyn Herborium, 256
Steppe, 243

QNS

Astoria

Astoria Music, 280
Beethoven Pianos, 280
Earth & Me, 167
Esquire Menswear, 107
Gamestoria, 149
Hellenic Aesthetic, 119
Horton's Market!, 173
INCASA, 273
Lockwood, 229
Mediterranean Foods, 194
Mediterranean Foods, 194
Museum of Nostalgia, 145
Newtown HQ, 229
Pancake Records, 276
Rudy's Hobby & Art, 146

Ditmars-Steinway

Silver Age Comics, 72
Whiskers Holistic Pet Care, 284

Elmhurst

The Fajas Store, 109

Far Rockaway

Alizé Clothing NY, 95
SKKM West Indian Market, 188

Flushing

Anime Castle, 72
Soybean Chan Flower Shop, 182
Uncle Edik's Pickles, 164

Forest Hills

Aigner Chocolates, 199
Carmel Grocery, 158
Royal Collectibles, 72
Royal Sports & Entertainment, 149

Glendale

Cook's Arts and Crafts Shoppe, 53
Spice Professors, 179

Jackson Heights

Art Retail Therapy (A.R.T.), 50
Party Glitters, 309
Pashmina Fashions, 122
Stand Alone Cheese, 170
Table Wine, 155
Zapateria Mexico, 204

Jamaica

Zola's Original Herbal Remedies, 250

Long Island City

Bike and Spin, 296
Everyone Comics & Collectibles, 72
MogMog Japanese Market, 187
Nature's Prescriptions, 255
Uke Hut, 280

Maspeth

Da-Bar Too Shoes, 203
Gothic Cabinet Craft, 245
Guerra Paint & Pigmen, 55

Richmond Hill

Royal Birds & Supplies, 284

Ridgewood

Forêt Wines, 156
Forever Young Kids, 263
Gotham Thrift Shop, 125
grace land new york, 130
Helen Levi, 271
Left Field, 96
Tiny Arts Supply, 51
Topos Too, 70
Valentino Food Market, 177

Rockaway Beach

Atlantic Service & Equipment, 296
Boarders, 304
Lana's Loft, 116
Phase Surf, 304

Sunnyside

Kyichu Tibetan Handicrafts, 223
Ora La Casa De Las Floras, 288
Seed and Oil by Suryaside, 168
Sugar Room, 265

Whitestone

Stitches, 93

Woodside

3 Aunties Thai Market, 187

Belmont

Arthur Ave Retail Market, 193
Borgatti's Ravioli and Egg Noodles, 192
Calabria Pork Store, 193
Cerini Coffee & Gifts, 158, 193
Cosenza's Fish Market, 192
Randazzo's Seafood, 192
Teitel Brothers Market, 192

City Island

dAN's Parents' House, 145

Concourse

Eddie's Place African Market, 189

Concourse Village

Kidstown, 261

Fordham Heights

Fordham Fish Market, 163
Tākout, 208

Kingsbridge

Parkview Sports Center, 93

Longwood

Casa Amadeo, 277
K&P Games Express Inc, 150
Kidstown, 261

Mott Haven

Bronx Native, 95
Classic Sofa, 245

Tannens, 137
The Lit. Bar, 75

Norwood

Redline Hobbies, 146

Riverdale

Geshmake Fish, 163

Spuyten-Duyvil

Ben's Market, 173

Tremont

Frank's Sports Shop, 294

University Heights

Save-a-Thon, 52

East Shore

Plum Paperie, 134
Top Tomato, 173

North Shore

Every Thing Goes Book Cafe, 79
Every Thing Goes Furniture & Clothing, 247
Lanka Grocery, 187
Santacroce Greenhouses & Garden Center, 290

South Shore

Frag Farm, 282
Holiday Beverage, 152
Richmond Appliance, 140
Steph's Creativity Corner, 264
Top Tomato, 173

INDEX | 327

ART of PLAY

GAMES
PUZZLES TOYS
HOME GOODS
BOOKS

Present this tearaway card for a complimentary cup of Japanese Cold Brew Coffee.

69 ATLANTIC AVE, BROOKLYN HEIGHTS

spirits! **BLACK CAT WINES** natural wines!

15% off for our neighbors!

★ BLACKCATWINESBK.COM ★

BROOKLYN HERBORIUM

LOCATIONS

275 Columbia Street
Brooklyn, NY 11231
(347) 689-4102

1301 Prospect Avenue
Brooklyn, NY 11218
(917) 909-0569

FREE MINERAL MIST (2OZ) OF YOUR CHOICE

With the booking of any facial treatment!
One Per Customer – Must have paper coupon

Find the listing for **Art of Play** on pg. 148
in the Entertainment section of this book.

This coupon is valid for one use only and must be
cut out and presented in person, in its physical form.

EXPIRES ON OCTOBER 31ST 2026.
LIMIT: ONE PER CUSTOMER.

Find the listing for **Black Cat Wines** on pg. 154
in the Food & Beverage section of this book.

This coupon is valid for one use only and must be
cut out and presented in person, in its physical form.

EXPIRES ON OCTOBER 31ST 2026.
LIMIT: ONE PER CUSTOMER.

Find the listing for **Brooklyn Herborium** on
pg. 256 in the Health & Beauty section of this book.

This coupon is valid for one use only and must be
cut out and presented in person, in its physical form.

EXPIRES ON OCTOBER 31ST 2026.
LIMIT: ONE PER CUSTOMER.

MUST PRESENT PHYSICAL COUPON · VALID IN STORE ONLY · THROUGH OCTOBER 31, 2026

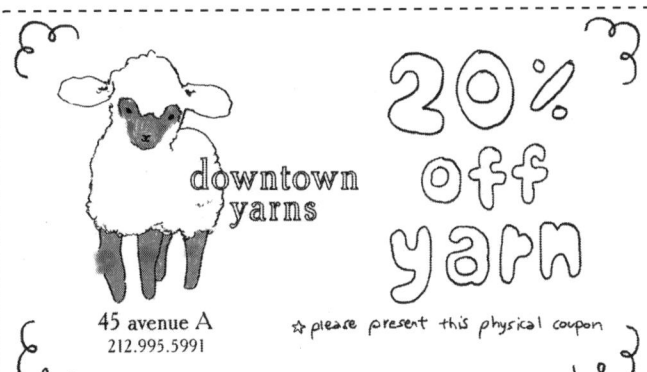

Find the listing for **Cocolico** on pg. 205
in the Footwear & Accessories section of this book.

This coupon is valid for one use only and must be
cut out and presented in person, in its physical form.

```
EXPIRES ON OCTOBER 31ST 2026.
   LIMIT: ONE PER CUSTOMER.
```

Find the listing for **Coming Soon** on pg. 105, 232
in the Home section of this book.

This coupon is valid for one use only and must be
cut out and presented in person, in its physical form.

```
EXPIRES ON OCTOBER 31ST 2026.
   LIMIT: ONE PER CUSTOMER.
```

Find the listing for **Downtown Yarns** on pg. 58
in the Arts & Crafts section of this book.

This coupon is valid for one use only and must be
cut out and presented in person, in its physical form.

```
EXPIRES ON OCTOBER 31ST 2026.
   LIMIT: ONE PER CUSTOMER.
```

**We appreciate you!
Please enjoy**

15% off

**your next purchase
at Edy's Grocer** ♥

136 Meserole Ave. Brooklyn, NY 11222
(Discount valid one time, in-store only)

Cut flowers from regional farms!

Flower Aggregate

318 Maujer St.
East Williamsburg

20%

For first-time retail customers

Furnish Green

Vintage furniture & home decor. Any style. Any function.

16% OFF
WITH PRESENTATION OF THIS COUPON

132 1/2 West 24th Street, New York, NY 10011 | furnishgreen.com | 917.583.9051 | furnishgreen@gmail.com

Find the listing for **Edy's Grocer** on pg. 196
in the Food & Beverage section of this book.

This coupon is valid for one use only and must be
cut out and presented in person, in its physical form.

```
EXPIRES ON OCTOBER 31ST 2026.
    LIMIT: ONE PER CUSTOMER.
```

Find the listing for **Flower Aggregate** on pg. 287
in the Plants section of this book.

This coupon is valid for one use only and must be
cut out and presented in person, in its physical form.

```
EXPIRES ON OCTOBER 31ST 2026.
    LIMIT: ONE PER CUSTOMER.
```

Find the listing for **Furnish Green** on pg. 246
in the Home section of this book.

This coupon is valid for one use only and must be
cut out and presented in person, in its physical form.

```
EXPIRES ON OCTOBER 31ST 2026.
    LIMIT: ONE PER CUSTOMER.
```

Find the listing for **Grand tea & Imports** on pg. 159, 184 in the Food & Beverage section of this book.

This coupon is valid for one use only and must be cut out and presented in person, in its physical form.

```
EXPIRES ON OCTOBER 31ST 2026.
   LIMIT: ONE PER CUSTOMER.
```

Find the listing for **Hellenic Aesthetic** on pg. 193 in the Footwear & Accessories section of this book.

This coupon is valid for one use only and must be cut out and presented in person, in its physical form.

```
EXPIRES ON OCTOBER 31ST 2026.
   LIMIT: ONE PER CUSTOMER.
```

Find the listing for **Her Winter Flowers** on pg. 133 in the Desk section of this book.

This coupon is valid for one use only and must be cut out and presented in person, in its physical form.

```
EXPIRES ON OCTOBER 31ST 2026.
   LIMIT: ONE PER CUSTOMER.
```

HOUSEOFKELLOGG
15% OFF

First time customers only. Must present physical coupon.
House of Kellogg 65 Bond Street, Brooklyn 11217
Valid through October 30, 2026.

ENJOY **10%** OFF AT *Knickerbocker*
357 CANAL ST, SOHO

Workshirts **10% OFF** CHINOS

CODE: COUPON10
EXPIRES 10/01/25

LEFTFIELDNYC.COM

Find the listing for **House of Kellogg** on pg. 129
in the Clothing section of this book.

This coupon is valid for one use only and must be
cut out and presented in person, in its physical form.

EXPIRES ON OCTOBER 31ST 2026.
LIMIT: ONE PER CUSTOMER.

Find the listing for **Knickerbocker** on pg. 101
in the Clothing section of this book.

This coupon is valid for one use only and must be
cut out and presented in person, in its physical form.

EXPIRES ON OCTOBER 31ST 2026.
LIMIT: ONE PER CUSTOMER.

Find the listing for **Left Field** on pg. 96
in the Clothing section of this book.

This coupon is valid for one use only and must be
cut out and presented in person, in its physical form.

EXPIRES ON OCTOBER 31ST 2026.
LIMIT: ONE PER CUSTOMER.

Find the listing for **Leroy's Place** on pg. 224
in the Gifting section of this book.

This coupon is valid for one use only and must be
cut out and presented in person, in its physical form.

```
EXPIRES ON OCTOBER 31ST 2026.
   LIMIT: ONE PER CUSTOMER.
```

Find the listing for **Mexico in my Pocket**
on pg. 222 in the Gifting section of this book.

This coupon is valid for one use only and must be
cut out and presented in person, in its physical form.

```
EXPIRES ON OCTOBER 31ST 2026.
   LIMIT: ONE PER CUSTOMER.
```

Find the listing for **Mr. Friendly** on pg. 285
in the Pets section of this book.

This coupon is valid for one use only and must be
cut out and presented in person, in its physical form.

```
EXPIRES ON OCTOBER 31ST 2026.
   LIMIT: ONE PER CUSTOMER.
```

15% OFF

For online purchases use code: PRMLOCAVORE15.

Excludes gift cards. Cannot be combined with other discounts. Excludes Pearl River Mart Foods.

452 Broadway, Soho
74 9th Ave, Chelsea Market

PEARL RIVER
EST. **MART** 1971
珠江

$5 OFF
on in-store purchases of $50 or more

please
AN EDUCATED PLEASURE SHOP

635 5th Avenue
Brooklyn, NY 11215
pleasenyc.com

Must present physical coupon • Valid through October 31, 2026

PWB PRETTY WELL BEAUTY

10% off full price items

185 Greenwich St
Tribeca

excludes bundles, gift cards, and select brands

Find the listing for **Pearl River Mart** on pg. 222
in the Gifting section of this book.

This coupon is valid for one use only and must be
cut out and presented in person, in its physical form.

EXPIRES ON OCTOBER 31ST 2026.
LIMIT: ONE PER CUSTOMER.

Find the listing for **Please** on pg. 251
in the Health & Beauty section of this book.

This coupon is valid for one use only and must be
cut out and presented in person, in its physical form.

EXPIRES ON OCTOBER 31ST 2026.
LIMIT: ONE PER CUSTOMER.

Find the listing for **Pretty Well Beauty** on pg. 252
in the Health & Beauty section of this book.

This coupon is valid for one use only and must be
cut out and presented in person, in its physical form.

EXPIRES ON OCTOBER 31ST 2026.
LIMIT: ONE PER CUSTOMER.

10% off
In-store only, doesn't apply to sale items.

**Located at 211 W 20th St
Chelsea, Manhattan**

M-W Noon-7pm, Th-Sa Noon-8pm, Sun 1-7pm

MUST PRESENT PHYSICAL COUPON. VALID THROUGH OCTOBER 31 2025

---

536 Metropolitan Ave
Williamsburg, Brooklyn

20% Off

any sale item

RADICLE WINE

293 GREENE AVE
CLINTON HILL, BROOKLYN

15% OFF YOUR ORDER

Find the listing for **Purple Passion** on pg. 251
in the Health & Beauty section of this book.

This coupon is valid for one use only and must be
cut out and presented in person, in its physical form.

```
EXPIRES ON OCTOBER 31ST 2026.
    LIMIT: ONE PER CUSTOMER.
```

Find the listing for **Quimby's Bookstore** on pg. 81
in the Bookshelf section of this book.

This coupon is valid for one use only and must be
cut out and presented in person, in its physical form.

```
EXPIRES ON OCTOBER 31ST 2026.
    LIMIT: ONE PER CUSTOMER.
```

Find the listing for **Radicle Wine** on pg. 155
in the Food & Beverage section of this book.

This coupon is valid for one use only and must be
cut out and presented in person, in its physical form.

```
EXPIRES ON OCTOBER 31ST 2026.
    LIMIT: ONE PER CUSTOMER.
```

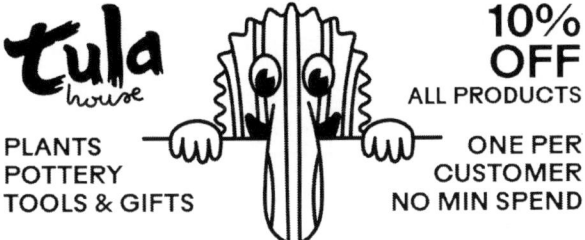

Find the listing for **RIDER Gifts** on pg. 224
in the Gifting section of this book.

This coupon is valid for one use only and must be
cut out and presented in person, in its physical form.

EXPIRES ON OCTOBER 31ST 2026.
LIMIT: ONE PER CUSTOMER.

Find the listing for **Shag** on pg. 252
in the Health & Beauty section of this book.

This coupon is valid for one use only and must be
cut out and presented in person, in its physical form.

EXPIRES ON OCTOBER 31ST 2026.
LIMIT: ONE PER CUSTOMER.

Find the listing for **Tula House** on pg. 292
in the Plants section of this book.

This coupon is valid for one use only and must be
cut out and presented in person, in its physical form.

EXPIRES ON OCTOBER 31ST 2026.
LIMIT: ONE PER CUSTOMER.

THE W NDERMART

Locally Made Goods & Gifts

141 India St, Brooklyn, NY 11222
Hours: Wednesday-Sunday, 12-7pm

www.thewondermart.shop

Shop Small & Save Big!

Spend $75
Get 10% Off

Spend $150
Get 15% Off

Spend $250
Get 20% Off

Valid in store only. One discount per customer.
Present to sales associate before paying to redeem.

Yun Hai Shop
雲海嚴選柑仔店
a *Taiwanese General Store*

free bag of
dried fruit
with purchase
of $50 or more

170 Montrose Ave
Brooklyn, NY 11206

yunhai.shop
@yunhaishop

The Locavore
VARIETY
STORE

Mystery Sticker — FREE

???

Located at:
434 6th Avenue
Greenwich Village
Manhattan

WITH ANY PURCHASE

Find the listing for **The WonderMart** on pg. 224
in the Gifting section of this book.

This coupon is valid for one use only and must be
cut out and presented in person, in its physical form.

EXPIRES ON OCTOBER 31ST 2026.
LIMIT: ONE PER CUSTOMER.

Find the listing for **Yun Hai Shop** on pg. 186
in the Food & Beverage section of this book.

This coupon is valid for one use only and must be
cut out and presented in person, in its physical form.

EXPIRES ON OCTOBER 31ST 2026.
LIMIT: ONE PER CUSTOMER.

The Locavore Variety Store is powered by The
Locavore Guide, the makers of this very book!
It's a weird and wonderful little general store for
products mademostly within 100 miles of New York
City, by independently-owned brands located at
434 6th Ave in the Village.

This coupon is valid for one use only and must be
cut out and presented in person, in its physical form.

EXPIRES ON OCTOBER 31ST 2026.
LIMIT: ONE PER CUSTOMER.